Camba and Kolla

COBIJA

PANDO

BENI

LA PAZ

TRINIDAD

LA PAZ   COCHABAMBA

COCHABAMBA

SANTA CRUZ

ORURO

SANTA CRUZ

ORURO

SUCRE

POTOSÍ

POTOSÍ

CHUQUISACA

TARIJA

TARIJA

Bolivia

Camba and Kolla

Migration and Development in Santa Cruz, Bolivia

Allyn MacLean Stearman

University Presses of Florida
University of Central Florida Press
Orlando

UNIVERSITY PRESSES OF FLORIDA is the central agency for scholarly publishing of the State of Florida's university system, producing books selected for publication by the faculty editorial committees of Florida's nine public universities: Florida A&M University (Tallahassee), Florida Atlantic University (Boca Raton), Florida International University (Miami), Florida State University (Tallahassee), University of Central Florida (Orlando), University of Florida (Gainesville), University of North Florida (Jacksonville), University of South Florida (Tampa), University of West Florida (Pensacola).

ORDERS for books published by all member presses should be addressed to University Presses of Florida, 15 NW 15th Street, Gainesville, FL 32603

Library of Congress Cataloging in Publication Data

Stearman, Allyn MacLean, 1943–
  Camba and Kolla.

  Bibliography: p.
  Includes index.
  1. Migration, Internal—Bolivia—Santa Cruz (Dept.)
2. Rural-urban migration—Bolivia—Santa Cruz (Dept.)—
Case studies. I. Title.
HB2022.S26S743 1985   307'.2   84–26978
ISBN 0–8130–0802–6 (alk. paper)

I dedicate this book to the memory of
Bill Carter
teacher, colleague, and friend

His great love and understanding of Bolivia and
its people shall always be an inspiration in my
own work.

Contents

Maps and Figures

Introduction

There is nothing like a first experience in a foreign culture. Every sight and smell, every new face is met with the anticipation of yet another adventure. For many anthropologists, it is the promise of this novelty that piques their curiosity as trained observers. But there is also something to be said for returning to the familiar time after time. While perhaps not as exhilarating as the first encounter, going back to a place over the years provides texture and depth to the craft of doing fieldwork. Going back to Lowland Bolivia is now like that for me. It is comforting to know that each time I return, enough will have remained the same to mitigate culture shock. Yet there are changes, new threads in the fabric, new folds and wrinkles. This is my novelty, the challenge that can come only from contrast—from knowing that what is now is somehow different from what was then.

I also take pleasure in contemplating the roles I have played in the lowlands for the past two decades. They were, of course, in no way planned; but these experiences afforded me insights into life in the *oriente* that could never have come from a single exposure or from only one vantage point. In 1964 I came to the Department of Santa Cruz as a Peace Corps volunteer assigned to work in colonization and community development. In this era, Bolivia, as well as other South American nations, was in the throes of attempting to develop its portion of the Amazon Basin. I lived and worked in a small peasant village, and over four years I watched it evolve from an isolated community into one being inexorably pulled into the social and economic mainstream of Bolivia.

After four years in the Peace Corps, I returned to the United States to begin studies in anthropology, the one discipline that could help me place my Bolivian experience in some conceptual framework. There was never any question that I would return to eastern Bolivia for my dissertation research. A fellowship from the Social Science Research Council enabled me to spend 1975 in the lowlands for this purpose. Since then, I have returned to Bolivia as a consultant for AID and as the recipient of two faculty summer research awards from the Division of Sponsored Research, University of Central Florida. Because this volume is a compilation of my work spanning almost twenty years, some of the material presented has been published elsewhere. I wish to note in particular the journals *Human Organization, América Indígena, El Dorado*, and several book chapters in edited works.

Over the years I have received encouragement, advice, and support from so many individuals that I begin the acknowledgement of this assistance with trepidation lest I inadvertently omit someone. If this should occur, I can only beg their forebearance.

There are many people in Bolivia to whom I owe a great debt, especially to Adela Campos and Nelfy León, who cared for my children and home, giving me the freedom to conduct fieldwork in 1975. To Father Ray Cowell, a longtime friend who has repeatedly offered me his home and hospitality, a special thank you. I am also grateful for the help of the villagers of San Carlos, especially Germán and María Estremadoiro and Margarita León, who gave me shelter and the advice of lowlanders with a lifetime of experience. I have also received assistance from the Bolivian academic and public sectors; José Mirtenbaum, Daniel Candia, Guido Ardaya, Ulrich Reye, Antonio Cisneros, Beatriz Rossels, and Fr. Tito Solari are only a few of the individuals who offered me their expertise. Acknowledgment should also be made to the many migrants and their families who freely gave me their time.

I am also grateful to Bill Carter, who, over many years, guided my research and offered suggestions for improvement or new direction for study. The manuscript was read and criticized by several colleagues, including Bill Carter, Ida Cook, Ray Crist, Brian Du Toit, and Waltrud Morales, who all offered helpful suggestions. Thanks also go to Sheila Call, who typed the original draft, and to Betsy Swayne and her staff, who assisted in the preparation of the press version. I, of course, take final responsibility for the text.

Last, I would like to acknowledge the contributions of my family. My daughter spent her first year with me while I was in Bolivia working on my dissertation. My son has been back again to spend an additional summer with his friend and age mate, David Campos, while I was engaged in research. My husband, Mike, has had the greatest patience of all, meeting the demands of his career in planning and city management while husbanding family, dogs, cats, rabbits, bees, garden, and all the other accoutrements of the years of our marriage. Without his help and understanding, I would never be able to take leave of these responsibilities or would simply have very little to come home to.

1

Migration Patterns

Population movement, or migration, is as old as the history of humankind. The earliest groups of people were nomadic followers of game and plant foods which varied by season and locality. Although this epoch in our cultural evolution lasted longer than any other and remains the way of life for many of the earth's inhabitants, it has been forgotten or ignored by those who support the idea that sedentism is in some way a more "natural" form of human existence. Out of this belief has been spawned the myth of the so-called static society, which "implies by harking back to some pre-existing rural utopia, that the natural condition of man is sedentary, that movement away from the natal place is a deviant activity associated with disorganization and a threat to the established harmony of Gemeinshaft relationships which are implied by a life lived within a fixed social framework" (Jackson 1968:3).

Migration from one's birthplace and population movement itself is portrayed frequently as a pathological response to an untenable life situation, which, in many instances, has been the case. Well-known migrants in recent history were the tens of thousands of persons forced from their homes by natural and social disasters. The potato famine sent boatloads of Irish countrymen to North America. Both world wars displaced countless individuals. The "Violencia" era in modern Colombia provoked a large-scale migration to the country's urban centers to escape the bloody consequences of a political feud.

In 1970, the Peruvian earthquake, perhaps the worst natural recorded disaster in the Western hemisphere, left nearly half a million persons homeless. Many from the mountain hinterlands of north-central Peru flooded into towns and cities to obtain food and shelter, and many are there still.

Many migrants leave their homes not as refugees but as individuals with strategies for maximizing their goals. They view temporary or permanent relocation as a means of expanding their access to available resources. Some continue to move throughout their productive years for this purpose. We know that hunting and gathering people and nomadic pastoralists use migration as an adaptive mechanism for exploiting resources. So too do today's corporate executives who expect to relocate periodically as positions of increasing responsibility become available. A comment that it is interesting how middle-class Americans "move" while the less affluent, particularly those in the Third World, "migrate" reflects the common negative attitudes toward migration. While population movement is usually viewed as a normally occurring social process in industrialized societies, it acquires other characteristics in other areas.

In the case studied here—that of highland Bolivians moving to the lowland regions of Santa Cruz—the myth of the static society is challenged further. Bolivian migrants frequently exhibit a life-style that includes moving within the highlands, to the lowlands, and perhaps back again to their places of origin. Some of this migration is seasonal in nature, but much is based on particular strategies, especially that of expanding economic resources, and was not perceived in negative terms. In this respect, "migration, like other forms of occupational and social mobility, has become a functional imperative. . . . It facilitates the allocation of human resources in a way which is not only more productive economically but also enables the individual to optimize his own material and social satisfactions by widening a range of opportunity and choice open to him" (Richmond 1968:245).

Strategies and Decision-Making

Whether rural or urban poor, the migrant frequently has been portrayed in the tradition of Oscar Lewis's Puerto Rican and Mexican families, caught up in the stream of a "culture of poverty" which inexorably sweeps them through life (Lewis 1965). The impression is left that migrants have little, if any, power of self-determination. Lewis's research notwithstanding, other case studies, including this one, reveal that most migratory activities involve the interplay of definite strategies, which are employed by migrants making rational decisions based on available information. Prospective migrants are presented with several alternatives for action, and some choice must be exercised to determine the most advantageous in terms of individual priorities and needs. This choice is influenced to a large degree by the background and personal attributes of the migrants. A study of pairs of Peruvian brothers, one who had migrated from Huaylas and one who had not, showed that factors such as educational skills, independence, marital status, and age not only determined the likelihood of migration but also affected the selection of a destination (Bradfield 1973).

Similarly, highland Bolivians who migrate to the lowlands have to choose among numerous destinations. I found that the migrant's personal attributes and the nature of the place of origin (whether urban or rural) had a major influence on the particular strategy employed. In the new environment, additional strategies come into play as new income or settlement opportunities arise. Migration to the Santa Cruz lowlands, for example, may be based on an original set of operational plans; but once the initial move has occurred, opportunities for subsequent migrations to diversify or expand available resources become incorporated into these plans. A similar situation has been reported in Lima, Peru, among the migrants arriving from the Peruvian mountain regions. They frequently take up residence in the crowded inner city, where they find assistance in obtaining jobs and shelter through kinship networks and contacts made through regional associations. Since living in central Lima is expensive and uncomfortable, migrants frequently join a group of individuals with similar problems; the group then stages an "invasion" of public or private land on the outskirts of the city. Thus are new homesites obtained at relatively little cost and living situations improved significantly (Turner 1970). The Peruvian *serrano* (highlander) probably left his or her place of origin intending to migrate to the capital city of Lima and gave little thought to other possibilities that might be presented. A subsequent move from the central slum of Rimac represents a modification of the original strategy and evolves out of a new set of circumstances that affect the decision-making process. Thus migration strategies tend to be highly flexible mechanisms for adapting to a changing physical and social environment.

The decision whether to migrate is often couched in terms of push or pull factors that act on the migrant. Conditions such as economic decline, lack of job opportunities, diminishing resources, poor or nonexistent educational facilities, and isolation may contribute to "push" the migrant from the place of origin. The point of destination has certain attractions, or "pull," such as adequate employment, better farmland, or the activity and excitement of a large urban center. While entirely valid and useful, the concepts of push and pull nevertheless are somewhat simplistic in their approach to motivations for migration. Everett Lee (1968) has added to these basic concepts other influences on the decision to migrate: factors associated with the area of origin and with the area of destination, intervening obstacles, and personal factors.

Kinship ties and social obligations as well as familiarity with the physical surroundings are factors "pulling" one to remain in the place of origin; economic stagnation and a sense of relative deprivation would be classified as "push" factors. At the destination, a lack of adequate housing is a negative point; employment opportunities and educational advantages are positive factors. Some elements have a null effect, such as a childless migrant faced with the presence or absence of schools in either the place of origin or the destination.

Obstacles between the points of origin and destination are distance, road conditions, and transportation availability and costs, which all influence the decision to migrate, and, to a certain extent, the migration strategies employed. Personal factors include migrant attributes, such as those studied by Stillman Bradfield (1973) in Huaylas to determine the nature and characteristics of the individual who does decide to leave the natal place.

For analyzing migration flows into Santa Cruz, Lee's model seems to have particular relevance. For the Bolivian highlander, the lowlands present both positive incentives for relocation and negative aspects that inhibit it. Likewise, Bolivia's entire highland area is experiencing grave economic problems that act negatively on continued residence in small rural communities as well as in urban areas. At the same time, the Bolivian interior is the center of highland tradition and culture and contains all that is cherished by the mountain inhabitant—a strong incentive to remain. The intervening obstacles of distance, roads, and transportation have also influenced the regional flows of migrants and highlander settlement patterns in the lowlands. Personal factors, such as the nature of the place of origin, education, and job skills acquired there, and the perception of self, all contribute to the employment of particular strategies in movement from one locality to another.

Single-factor explanations of migratory behavior, especially those related to economics, are commonly reported as primary incentives for relocation. While perceived deprivation and economic instability at the place of departure and expected opportunities at the destination frequently play a major role in decision-making, other factors have been shown to act in concert with those of economic origin. Social and psychological components, often somewhat more difficult to identify, also enter into motivational behavior. Stoltman and Ball, in a study of rural-urban migration in Mexico, have stated that

> The decision to migrate from one location to another certainly represents a complex of variable impulses in an inferential probability framework. Migration is predicated upon the analysis of data available to an individual in projecting or predicting his relative well-being (economically, socially, psychologically, etc.) in a new place. (1971:55)

Stoltman and Ball might have expanded their framework to include those perceptions affecting individuals in their evaluation of the point of departure as well. In his study of Argentine migrants, Richard Wilkie has generalized motivational problems to include both push and pull factors and stresses the necessary inclusion of other than economic incentives in analyzing migration motivation:

> The economic component, while important, was found to be less controlling as a factor in the migration process than many social scientists have normally recognized. The economic factor *helps condition the need to migrate*, but whether the final decision to migrate is made or not reverts in most cases to the psychological, social, spatial and environmental perceptions and attitudes within the family unit. (1968:109, emphasis supplied)

Finally, J. Beaujeu-Garnier, commenting on the emphasis on economic motivations in the decision to migrate, notes, "It seems, however, difficult to accept such a categorical assertion, for psychological factors play a considerable and often vital part, and in any case, even in a decision urged by precise economic facts, one finds also some other aspects, of which the subject was perhaps barely conscious, but which played its part in the final moment of choice" (1966:212).

A Typology of Migration Patterns

The process of migration may be analyzed in terms of its range of possible dimensions based on factors such as degree of temporality, direction of flow, time sequence, influence of other migrants, and resource exploitations. Thus a typology of migration patterns would include *single-phase* migration, *temporary or seasonal* migration, *step* migration, *sequential* migration, *chain* migration, and *multiple-resource* migration.

In each case, the nature of the place of origin and the place of destination will be articulated with the migration pattern. The categories "rural" and "urban" in their four combinations are commonly used to describe origin and destination. A single-phase migration, for example, might entail a rural-urban move, an urban-rural move, a rural-rural move, or an urban-urban move. It is also important to note that any migration pattern is not mutually exclusive. Seasonal migration could include step and chain migration strategies as well. This case might be exemplified by the migrant unit (i.e., an individual, family, or group) that leaves the place of origin on a seasonal basis but each season chooses points of destination that are progressively closer to either the rural or the urban end of the settlement continuum. Other individuals might be encouraged by the migrant unit to make the trip as well, thereby contributing to the process of chain migration.

Scott Whiteford and Richard N. Adams (1973) have described such a pattern among Bolivian migrants working in Argentina. Several seasonal migrations are made from Bolivia each year by the migrant unit, usually in conjunction with a progression toward more urban involvement. At some point the decision is made to remain in Argentina, family members may be sent for, and the process begins of working toward stable urban Argentine residence.

> In most cases, the rural-urban proletariat experience is transitory, abandoning work in the *zafra* [sugarcane harvest] and either joining the urban proletariat or becoming a self-employed urbanite. This decision is usually not made until the migrant and his family feel they are established in the urban environment. (p. 11)

Although temporary migration has been included in the typology of migration patterns, the category "permanent migration," although encountered from time to time in the literature, has not. Permanent migration is a contradiction in terms since migration implies movement, not stability. Permanent residence may occur as the result or purpose of migration but cannot properly be considered as pertaining to the actual migration process.

Single-phase migration.—Single-phase migration is the movement of the migratory unit from the place of origin to the place of destination in a single operation. Many contemporary as well as historical migration studies encompass this type of movement. The most prevalent today, of course, is the worldwide phenomenon of rural-urban migration.

John C. Caldwell (1969), in a report on rural-urban migration in Ghana, concentrated on single-phase migration from rural hamlets to the country's urban centers. His analysis included information gathered from a survey of rural persons intending to migrate as well as from a similar sample of the more commonly studied de facto urban migrants. In Peru, William Mangin (1973) reported that three-quarters of the population of a Lima migrant neighborhood selected for study had followed the pattern of moving directly from the place of origin to the coastal city.

The occurrence of urban-rural, single-phase migration has been cited much less frequently than its rural-urban counterpart. One such case, however, has been described by Morton D. Winsberg (1968, 1969). As the result of increasing anti-Semitic activities in eastern Europe, Jewish organizations and philanthropists arranged for the purchase of farmland in a sparsely settled area of Argentina to serve as a refuge for European Jews fleeing religious and political persecution. Several agricultural colonies were established, including the one studied by Winsberg, Entre Ríos. The majority of the European Jews who arrived in Entre Ríos came directly from urban ghetto situations. Because the colonies existed in a marginal environment, out-migration to the Argentine cities was common. According to Winsberg, "most colonists never developed a strong attachment to rural life, and many retained urban skills acquired in Europe. In addition, most had more affluent relatives or friends in the cities who were willing to help them establish themselves if they chose to move there" (1968:427). It is interesting that the urbanite often seems to find adjustment to the rural milieu incompatible with a previous lifestyle, while the rural-urban migrant is seeking to alter old patterns to conform to the urban way of life. It might be hypothesized, then, that "reverse" adaption generally is more difficult and less desirable for the urban dweller than it is for the rural inhabitant. This supposition would also seem to be in keeping with the proposition that "migrants seek situations that permit participation in higher degrees of organization as circumstances permit" (Whiteford and Adams 1973:1).

Temporary or seasonal migration.— Temporary or seasonal migration is the movement by the migratory unit from the place of origin to the destination with the intent that residence will be transitory. Young individuals commonly migrate with the idea that relocation is only for a trial period. Because they often have little to risk, migration is viewed more as an adventure than as a definitive commitment. If success in the form of employment and shelter is achieved, the temporary migration strategy may evolve into one that includes permanent residence as a possible alternative. Other types of temporary migration may occur as the result of duty in the armed services, visiting, or fulfilling educational needs.

If temporary migration is tied to a specific time sequence or cycle, it is said to be seasonal. The greatest incidence of seasonal migration occurs in conjunction with crop harvests that require large amounts of short-term labor. In this case, the migrant's movements are ruled by the demands of an external schedule. In discussing migration patterns in Guatemala, Bryan Roberts states:

> Though Indians are likely to migrate to supplement their subsistence agriculture, their migration is likely to be short-term and circulatory, involving return to their home village. This is, in fact, one outstanding trait of Guatemala's internal migrations. Indian migrations are usually for a period of three to four months when workers leave for the coffee or other cash-crop harvests on the coast and return to cultivate their land for the rest of the year. (1973:61)

Seasonal migration also may depend on certain seasonal obligations at the place of origin. For example, fallow or slack periods on a family farm are a good time to migrate to another rural area or even to an urban center in search of temporary wage labor. In some areas, seasonal wage labor and farm responsibilities do not conflict—the fallow period at home coincides with the harvest season in another locality. Much of the seasonal migration occurring in eastern Bolivia operates in this manner. The commercial crops of sugarcane and cotton are harvested in the lowlands during the winter dry season when fields lie fallow in the highlands.

Step migration.—Step migration is the progressive movement by the migratory unit toward a specified settlement situation and is frequently associated with rural-urban movement. In rural-urban step migration, the migrant often seeks intermediate "steps" along the rural-urban continuum which afford a gradual adaptation to the urban environment. From the rural homestead, the migratory unit may progress to a nearby town or provincial capital, then to a large metropolitan area. Rural-urban step migration has been described by many researchers (Ghersi and Dobyns 1963; Pool 1968; Whiteford 1972; Orellana 1973).

Step migration nevertheless may also involve movement from the urban end of the continuum to the rural, as in pioneering, or from an already rural place to one that is perceived as even more remote. Perhaps the best-known examples of rural-rural step migration involve the opening of frontier lands or colonies. Roads into new agricultural areas often encourage step migration or the progressive movement by rural migrants into wilderness areas through the acquisition of land in stages along the route. Settlement of certain frontier areas of Bolivia (Cusack 1967; Henkel 1971), Venezuela and Colombia (Crist and Nissly 1973), and Brazil (Margolis 1973) was accomplished in this manner.

Step migration may also involve economic progression in terms of monetary gain and greater prestige. As mentioned, many U.S. families become locked into a two-year moving cycle in which the male spouse, often engaged in corporate enterprise, is transferred from one place to another in order to climb the corporate ladder. Members of the military also may be involved in such migration, where the steps from one duty station to another may bring advancement in rank along with income increments. In many societies today, upward mobility may require spatial mobility as well.

Sequential migration.—In sequential migration, the migratory unit moves from one locality to another but not in a geographic, economic, or status step progression. Among industrialized nations, horizontal mobility of the working classes is contributing to the formation of a migrant group which Anthony Richmond terms the "transilient type": "They are part of a highly mobile and skilled labor force ready to move from one urban industrial center to another, wherever their particular education and occupational skills are in demand, irrespective of political or cultural boundaries" (1968:244).

The phenomenon of migrating from city to city or from one rural hamlet to another is also encountered in nonindustrialized nations.

In the Bolivian case, interurban migration is a common occurrence and may be attributed in great part to economic pressures and employment instability. Reported cases of interrural migration, however, are relatively rare. Stephen Brush (1974) alludes to the existence of this process among the Andean rural villages, haciendas, and indigenous communities. He ascribes interrural migration in two Andean areas to regional economic differences. As will be seen, sequential movement from one rural situation to another is prevalent in lowland Bolivia and may be viewed as a direct consequence of the demands of shifting agriculture.

   Chain migration.—In chain migration, the migratory unit or other communication networks or both become direct or indirect instruments in influencing the migration of additional individuals. Unless it is the result of some natural or social catastrophe that creates a population of sudden evacuees, migration normally builds gradually to a crescendo. Although one may speak abstractly of population flows and waves, a major factor influencing these rates and volumes of migration is the individual. Someone must make an initial move. If this person (or persons) attains relative success in the new surroundings, a beachhead has been established and the way is cleared for additional migration.

   Chain migration may result from firsthand contact with the migrants themselves, either when migrants return to the place of origin or when family and friends visit the migrants' place of destination. It may also result from secondhand information about the migrants' exploits and attainments that reaches the point of origin through informal communication networks. More formal networks can play an important role in chain migration. Radio, newspapers, and television are often inadvertent seducers of rural dwellers who are exposed almost daily to commercial propaganda extolling the virtues of innumerable goods and services available in the city and thus are made aware of the popularized benefits of urban life. In Peru, Doughty reports,

   There are many small town [radio] stations but most of these can scarcely be heard a few blocks from their transmitters. Instead, several very powerful stations in Lima serve the country at large. The national government runs its own strong station and, recently, has moved to acquire considerable control over all other stations. It is, nevertheless, difficult to estimate just what the impact of radio is, especially in rural areas, but we assume it is significant in whetting the appetites of people for things they do not have. In this sense, the radio is an urban tool, an instrument in provoking the potential migrant. (1972:38)

Multiple-resource migration.—In multiple-resource migration the migrant unit establishes colonies, or archipelagos, in two or more areas for the purpose of simultaneously exploiting different environmental or economic niches. To my knowledge, this final category of migration has not appeared in the literature except in my own work which was reported in an earlier article (Stearman 1978). John Murra (1972) discusses a precedent to multiple-resource migration in his study of vertical archipelagos in the Andes. He does not, however, relate his findings to migration patterns per se, but rather to the concept of zonal ecological adaptive strategies. (A lengthier account of the phenomenon of multiple-resource migration may be found in a later chapter.) In Santa Cruz, many rural migrants are engaging in multiple moves but are not abandoning previous settlement sites. Instead, properties are acquired and maintained by members of the migrant unit for the purpose of exploiting several economic niches simultaneously. This pattern offers greater economic diversity and, therefore, security of capital resources.

The Rural-Urban Continuum

Most literature dealing with migration has tended to concentrate on a single aspect of population flow from one point on the rural-urban continuum to another, on particular migrant characteristics, or on migration trends as they affect a certain urban or rural locality. Moreover, there has typically been a division between rural and urban migration studies. An entire field of literature deals specifically with problems of migration and urbanization. A different collection must be consulted with regard to rural migration, particularly colonization. In addition, most researchers have supported this urban or rural orientation by making use of data from a single study site such as Lima (Mangin 1970), Rio de Janeiro (Bonilla 1961), the Chapare colonization project of Bolivia (Henkel 1971), or the Jewish agricultural scttlcmcnts at Entre Ríos, Argentina (Winsberg 1968, 1969).

Although these forays into the field of migration have contributed substantially to a general understanding of population movement, for the most part they present a limited view of the migratory processes developing within a wider context. Even more important, they may leave an impression that migrations to a designated locality or from one settlement situation to another (i.e., rural-urban) are the only significant incidences of migration occurring in a given territory or nation-state. This problem is greatly magnified in areas where a classic primate city is attracting substantial numbers of rural-urban migrants. In Peru, Stephen Brush set out to attack the voluminous research preoccupied with rural-urban migration to Lima by investigating the phenomenon of inter-Andean rural migration: "The extent of this migration . . . belies two former images: (1) that the relationships between the various social units of the Andean region are generally confined to economic (trade) and institutional (political-administrative) levels; and (2) *that the only significant migration which concerned the Andean area was emigration to the coast*" (1974:1, emphasis supplied).

While Brush's study opens for consideration another aspect of migration, it is based on a single locality, Huaylas, Peru. The question remains: what patterns and strategies of migration are evident in both the rural and urban sectors of a region which has become an arena for internal migration and how do these rural and urban elements interact in the total migration process? Another problem that must be addressed is the tendency to deal with migration only in terms of the rural and urban extremes when in reality there may be several points between. Once again, because single locations are so frequently studied, they are presented either as urban or rural primarily because the context is so limited. Thus a town that is the place of origin of migrants being studied in a primate city is considered "rural" because of a single contrast. To the colonist living on the frontier, however, moving to that same town would be viewed as an "urban" migration. For this reason it is important to look at migration from a broader perspective if the process is to be better understood.

A Typology of Migration Destinations: Santa Cruz

The Department of Santa Cruz in lowland Bolivia offers an ideal opportunity to explore many of these important questions. It is the recipient of increasing numbers of highland migrants and of foreign immigrants to a lesser degree; it is also experiencing internal migration of local inhabitants. Most significantly, Santa Cruz offers varying degrees of urban and rural points of destination where the migrant may be studied.

My Peace Corps experience in Santa Cruz, which spanned almost four years of continuous lowland involvement, from 1964 to 1968, was of inestimable value when I returned to the area in 1975 for the purpose of conducting research. With a prior understanding of the region in addition to what had become a nearly native command of the local dialect of Spanish, I was able to assess rapidly the problem at hand and begin fieldwork. George Foster, Thayer Scudder, Elizabeth Colson, and Robert B. Kemper in their study *Long Term Field Research in Social Anthropology* comment on this phenomenon:

> Psychologically, the seasoned worker probably also has an advantage. Return to the field is associated with a sense of anticipation that is hard to equal. Not only is it a pleasure to renew acquaintances, to see the genuine pleasure of those who welcome the anthropologist back, and to catch up on local gossip and developments, but psychologically reentry is easier than shifting to a totally different society. Not only is "culture shock" minimized, but often the anthropologist is fully engaged in research within a few hours of arrival (Foster et al. 1979:331).

Because of familiarity with the field situation, I was acutely aware of changes that had occurred during my absence. I have no doubt that had I arrived in Santa Cruz entirely as a novice to the area my research would have taken a much narrower perspective. Admittedly, I returned to Bolivia to study colonization because during the early 1960s, or the time of my first visit, most highland-lowland migration was occurring in that sector. Upon my return it was evident that highlanders had diffused throughout the Santa Cruz region, an event that likely would have escaped my notice had it not been for this prior experience. I, like many others, would have chosen a site for study and would have concentrated on the particulars of that case. Instead, I selected to look at the dynamics of migration on a regional scale.

What became immediately apparent was that certain types of migrants were selecting certain types of destinations. As the result of an initial survey of the region, therefore, I developed, in addition to the typology of migration patterns previously described, a typology of settlement destinations. These destinations followed a rural-urban continuum but had other dimensions important in the migration process as well: primate city, secondary service center, agribusiness centers, semisubsistence horticulture centers, and pioneer fringe zone.

In the most urban case, the primate city, there was only one possibility to be considered for study—the lowland capital, the city of

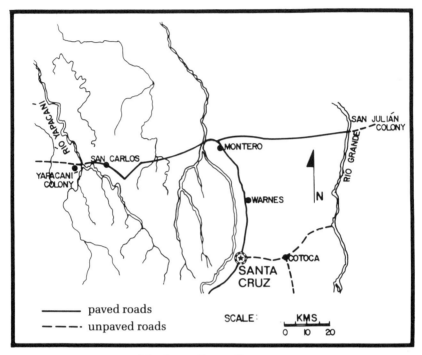

Northern Santa Cruz area

Santa Cruz. In addition to being the departmental capital, it is also the largest lowland city in Bolivia. Because of its isolation from highland population centers, its importance to the region far outstrips its actual size relative to other cities such as La Paz. The other study sites were selected from among several possibilities. The decision on the places finally chosen was based on their regional significance or my prior familiarity with them. On the far end of the continuum, and also the greatest distance from the city of Santa Cruz, was the pioneer fringe zone exemplified by the Yapacaní and San Julián colonies, the most ambitious settlement projects in the Santa Cruz region. The remaining three study sites were Montero, a secondary service center, Warnes, a town tied economically and socially to commercial agriculture, and San Carlos, a village tied to semisubsistence horticulture and cattle ranching.

Each site was studied separately and provided a link in the chain of information out of which eventually emerged a well-defined model of population movement into, out of, and within the department. The order in which each locality was investigated followed a spatial progression outward from the city of Santa Cruz. Since there is only one road north into the area of highest migrant concentration, this route to some extent determined the order in which the sites were studied. Except in two instances, the relative spatial disposition of each locality coincided with appropriate points along an urban-rural continuum. An ordering by this latter criterion would be Santa Cruz, Montero, Warnes, San Carlos, Yapacaní/San Julián. By following the road, the actual sequence is Santa Cruz, Warnes, Montero, San Carlos, Yapacaní/San Julián, the order in which the 1975 study was conducted.

In 1978 and 1980 I again had opportunities to study migration trends in the lowlands. The 1978 research trip involved my participation as a member of a multidisciplinary evaluation team contracted by AID to look at the progress of the San Julián colony. While my interests were centered on this one project, I also took advantage of being in the area to visit my other study sites, if only briefly. In 1980 I returned to update some of my data and was fortunate in learning of a project sponsored by the Dirección Departamental de Estadística to carry out some ethnographic work among migrants. A year earlier, the DDE had conducted a survey of 3,587 migrant households selected randomly from the 1976 census tracts. Unfortunately, because of budget limitations, the resulting data had not been analyzed. A rural sociologist, José Mirtenbaum, had agreed to do part of the analysis but only after some in-depth interviewing had been completed to complement the survey questionnaire. At this point I arrived in Bolivia and was invited to assist with the formulation of an interview guide, the training of university students as interviewers, and the interviewing process itself. As a consequence of having sent my 1975 research results to several agencies in Bolivia, both the 1979 and 1980 follow-up studies essentially retraced my work, one of many advantages in making research available to the host country. While the data from the three study periods were not always comparable, they contributed to an overall understanding of migration in the Santa Cruz region as it has developed since 1964.

2

The Lowland Territories and the Department of Santa Cruz: History and Economic Development

Bolivia has always been considered an Andean nation, both in terms of its geographical location and its cultural and historical involvement with other peoples along the western fringe of South America. So much has transpired in the highlands that it seems almost ironic that two-thirds of the country's national domain actually lies in the Amazon Basin. This lowland region, known as the *oriente*, or east, remained virtually unknown to the rest of the nation and to the world until well into the twentieth century. Except for a small mestizo population and scattered groups of aborigines, the eastern reaches were reserved for adventurers, political exiles, and criminals. For many, the oriente meant uninhabitable jungles filled with fierce animals, insect- and disease-ridden swamps, and unknown territories with savages hiding behind every tree. Such works as Julian Duguid's *Infierno Verde* (*Green Hell*) were held up as examples of the terror and danger that awaited anyone foolish or unfortunate enough to travel into Bolivia's Amazon region. But those who knew the area were also appreciative of its great natural wealth. The land was productive, there were almost limitless expanses of grasslands for cattle, and the forests held unimagined riches in hardwoods. Later, petroleum would be discovered, adding to the promise of the eastern wilderness.

Explorers' journals and missionary reports produced a vague awareness of the potential of the lowlands that had always been part of Bolivian folklore, but it was not until the Social Revolution of 1952 that the Bolivian government seriously began to consider the eastern region as anything other than a dumping ground for undesirables.

The new revolutionary government inherited many problems that had plagued its predecessors and created some new ones as well. The Agrarian Reform gave the peasants control of the land they had tilled in usufruct for generations, but many individuals remained without adequate farm property to meet even basic subsistence needs. The mine-centered economy of the nation had made millionaires of a few and had enslaved thousands, but nationalization proved only to increase operating costs through featherbedding and to lower production (Zondag 1968). At the same time, Bolivia was wrestling with long-lived insurrection and unrest on the part of its eastern inhabitants, and the achievement of national integration became yet another problem to be resolved. In 1954, a paved highway was pushed through from the highland city of Cochabamba to the capital of the largest lowland department, Santa Cruz. The opening of the road was a first step in realizing the goals of the revolutionary government to increase agricultural production, exploit lowland oil deposits, create new opportunities for the highland peasant, and, it was hoped, unite for the first time the highland and lowland dominions of the Bolivian nation.

Since its construction, the 500-kilometer long Santa Cruz–Cochabamba highway has never been repaved, a problem that is endemic throughout Bolivia. Road crews fight an ongoing battle to patch holes and repair washouts, but constant heavy transport and the processes of erosion have all but removed the asphalt from most of the road. The route to the lowlands begins in the city of Cochabamba, which rests in a teacup valley at an elevation of 2,000 meters. From there it winds up through the mountains, clings perilously to the cliff walls overhanging a rocky riverbed, and finally reaches the 3,000-meter-high cloud forest known popularly as "Siberia." Vehicles slow to a crawl as they feel their way along the narrow track lined with towering tree ferns and a tangle of tropical vegetation. It is an eerie, ethereal land, and most travelers are glad to leave the swirls of mist to start the descent to the lowlands.

The edge of the highway is dotted with the small, white, wooden crosses of those travelers who failed to negotiate a curve, lost their brakes, or made the trip while tired or drunk. Every so often a ragged scar appears in the rocky wall beside the road where a recent slide came crashing down to cut off traffic until a bulldozer could be brought in to clear the way. The descent is abrupt, a series of hairpin curves and switchbacks. Driving it is a relentless chore, but for those who just ride, the scenery is spectacular. Small farms appear wherever there is any hope of clearing away enough rock to free the scant topsoil for cultivation. Scattered along the river are gristmills, always with women washing clothes in nearby pools. Throughout it all there are the mountains, the ever-present mountains, the easternmost slopes of the Andes. Until they reach the lowland plain, they are great slabs of rough-hewn rock, new mountains in terms of geological time, which have yet to be torn down by erosion.

The mountains end suddenly at about 400 meters elevation, and the road spills out onto the plains. The final 50 kilometers are a long, undulating ribbon crossing farmlands and cattle ranches until the highway reaches its destination, the lowland capital, the city of Santa Cruz de la Sierra. Now the distinctive countryside of the oriente is evident. Peasant homes are no longer adobe bricks roofed with straw but are mud and wattle with palm thatch. Everything is verdant and lush, in sharp contrast to the arid and barren *altiplano* or even the Cochabamba Valley with its patchwork quilt of green where water is available.

Cleared fields and pasturelands near the city of Santa Cruz are interrupted by the many varieties of palm that in earlier times were the mainstay of the lowland inhabitants. The tall, stately *chonta* not only provides excellent wood for building and decoration (the airport in the nation's capital, La Paz, is adorned with this lowland hardwood), but it also produces a nutritious fruit which, when boiled, has a flavor and consistency not unlike potatoes. The massive *motacú*, perhaps the most sacred of lowland palms, is used to roof the peasant houses, or *pauhuichis*; its tender center shoot, the *cogollo*, is woven into baskets, hats, and sleeping mats. The heart of the motacú is extracted with an axe and boiled to make palm-heart salad, a feast-day food. On Palm Sunday it is the motacú frond that is brought to church by villagers and city dwellers alike to be blessed by the parish priest. Another palm, the thorny *totaí*, is pictured on the coat of arms of the Department of Santa Cruz. It, too, has an edible and tasty fruit, but for the children of the countryside the totaí has additional importance. The *totaíces*, as the fruits are called, are perfectly spherical in shape and are about the size of large marbles. Young boys keep their pockets full to have a ready supply of ammunition for their slingshots.

The Department of Santa Cruz is marked by a diverse landscape. To the south the desert of the Gran Chaco dominates the region. Population is predictably sparse here and tends to be clustered along the 540-kilometer railroad linking the city of Santa Cruz with Argentina. The northern reaches of the department merge into the grassy floodplain of the Beni and are broken only by large stands of tropical forest. To the east lies the Brazilian Shield, a hilly country of plains and forest, also sparsely populated. It is the wide alluvial plain, captured in the basin formed by the Andean block to the west and the Brazilian Shield to the east, that has offered the greatest opportunity for successful settlement. The city of Santa Cruz was located, or rather relocated, in this area and it is where 70 percent of the department's 710,000 inhabitants reside (Bolivia 1976). The terrain varies from flat plains to gently rolling subtropical forest to dense jungle. It is a beautiful land characterized by clear blue skies and great mounds of white clouds. Wide, meandering rivers crisscross the region, moving slowly northward, converging into larger and more powerful streams until they reach the Amazon and are carried out to sea. At dusk, large flocks of parrots shriek noisily across the sky in search of a place of safety to pass the night. The great packs of wild pigs, the agouti, the peccary, the tapir, and the jaguar are all but gone now, hunted out of existence for their meat and hides. Those animals that escaped retreated farther into the wilderness, but they too are being hunted to extinction.

As one moves north from the city of Santa Cruz the landscape changes from sandy, dry grasslands to large cultivated expanses of cotton and sugarcane. Farther north the terrain becomes more heavily forested, and rice and banana fields begin to dominate the countryside. There is a paved road from the city north, extending 60 kilometers to the smaller city of Montero, where it then divides, one branch heading west to the Yapacaní River and the other east to the Río Grande. Within this triangle are located most of the department's inhabitants, its major commercial centers, and the most productive agricultural lands.

The climate is generally warm and humid with a well-defined dry season beginning about May and terminating in September. The heaviest rains fall in December, January, and February, so crops are usually planted in October and November with the hope that the rainy season will arrive on schedule and be adequate to assure a good harvest. Only the cold winter winds interrupt the warm days and mild nights. Several times a year, normally in June, July, and August, the cold Antarctic southerlies, or *surazos*, blow unhampered through the Argentine pampas. They cross the Santa Cruz plain and finally reach the Andes, where they stall and are dissipated. Once the prevailing winds shift from north to south the temperature can drop 20 degrees in a matter of hours. In 1975, temperatures of $-4°C$ were recorded on three consecutive nights during the midwinter month of July, killing coffee and banana trees throughout much of the region. The people of Santa Cruz are ill prepared in their clothing and housing for these abrupt climatic shifts. They must weather the surazo as best they can, sitting huddled in blankets by the cookfire or by a makeshift heater of live coals in an old lard can. The cold winds take their yearly toll from among the very young, the very old, and the infirm.

The inhabitants of the Santa Cruz region are known as Cambas, a term believed to have originated from the Guarani word meaning "friend." It was first applied to the peasant class and was synonymous with the peon who was tied to a large agricultural establishment, or *finca*, by debt. As time went by, Camba became an all-inclusive term for lowland society, both peasant and aristocratic. It also became a means by which lowlanders could demonstrate their cultural as well as geographical distance from highlanders, whom they referred to as Kollas (from the Quechua word *Kollasuyo*, the Bolivian sector of the Inca Empire). All of these uses continue to the present day, although the first, that of a class distinction among lowlanders, has declined in popularity in recent years.

The Camba for the most part is mestizo, and even those families professing "pure Castilian heritage" would be hard pressed to prove this claim. It is a well-known fact that not many European women accompanied the Spanish conquest so that mestization proceeded at a rapid pace. In Santa Cruz, the taking of wives and concubines from among the native populations was even more pronounced because of its extreme isolation and rusticity. If a Spanish woman were hesitant about crossing the Atlantic to make her home in Buenos Aires or even Lima, she certainly was not going to consider living in a place like Santa Cruz. At the same time, many Cambas exhibit phenotypic characteristics that would indicate some African influence, giving credence to the numerous tales that Santa Cruz became a refuge for black slaves escaping Brazilian plantations. Thus the Camba tends to be a potpourri of highland Indian (Quechua and Aymara), lowland Indian (Guaraní, Guarayo, Chiquitano, and many more), European (primarily from southern Spain), and perhaps African heritage.

Camba society has existed since the Iberian conquest and traces its origins to the first Spanish conquistadores who rode east from the

Andes and west from the Argentine. From this point, unfortunately, Cruceñan history becomes a muddle of oral tradition and scant documentation. Camba historians attribute the loss of most records to the ravages of time and climate and to the destructive uses to which they were put. Montero Hoyos tells us that "During the times when troops were sent [to Santa Cruz] from the interior of Bolivia, they were quartered in the Colegio Nacional, which gave these generally illiterate soldiers access to the using of the archives as toilet paper; for this reason Santa Cruz does not preserve anything of historic tradition, because it was in that church (El Sagrario) and in the Colegio where the archives were kept" (quoted in Jisunú 1974:13, my translation). Another historian explains how the cannon from the War of Independence, which was kept in the Prefectura and fired every September 24 to commemorate the Cruceñan bid for freedom from Spain, was wadded with colonial documents (also related in Jisunú 1974:13). Because of inadequate sources of documentation, the piecing together of Camba history since the conquest has occasioned no small amount of controversy among national historians. The most heated debate centers on the degree of impact the highlands may have had in the birth and development of lowland society.

The well-known Bolivian historian Enrique Finot, who is himself a lowlander, has been accused of overemphasizing the importance of Andean geopolitical influence during the period of Spanish colonization in the lowlands. In his *Historia de la Conquista del Oriente Boliviano* he remarks:

> A curious account taken from the *Archivos de Indias* and which constitutes the sole document known which refers to the inhabitants of the Grigotá [Santa Cruz] plains during the period of the conquest or immediately prior to it, sheds a great deal of light on the fact that, upon arrival of the first Spaniards, the territory was found to be under the domination of the Incas of Peru. This is one more reason to recognize the totally Altoperuvian origins of the city of Santa Cruz de la Sierra. (Finot 1939:67, my translation)

More recent studies (Sanabria Fernández 1973) indicate that the Incas were never successful in their efforts to subjugate the lowland aborigines and were therefore required to build a series of fortresses to keep them from invading highland settlements. But whatever the particular historical interpretation may be, one salient point emerges

from this dispute. Lowland Bolivians will disavow whenever possible any substantive Andean influence in the formation of their
culture and tradition. The separatist philosophy of the Camba began
and was cultivated during colonial times and continues to present
day. In any event, the first Spaniards to arrive in the area were from
the Argentine, not from the Peruvian highlands. From that moment
on, what is now the Department of Santa Cruz was caught in a crossfire of conflicting interests and petty quarrels. The most current treatment of colonial Santa Cruz, that written by Sanabria Fernández
(1973), is recognized by lowlanders and highlanders alike as perhaps
the best and most accurate documentation presently available. In the
following brief summation of lowland conquest and settlement, then,
it is the Sanabrian interpretation that is used.

In 1549, Captain Domingo Martínez de Irala set out from Asunción,
Paraguay, in quest of the legendary "Mountain of Silver" reputed to
lie in the mountains to the west. He halted his march at the Guapay
River (now the Río Grande), where he was informed by the aborigine
residents that other Spaniards had already claimed the highland dominions formerly ruled by the Incas. Irala was bitterly disappointed
to find that his dreams of conquest and riches would never be realized, but he decided to try to salvage what he could from the expedition. Rather than return empty-handed to Asunción, Irala sent an envoy to the *Audiencia Real* in Lima to lay claim to the territories he
had discovered east of the Peruvian viceroyalty.

The envoy was Captain Ñuflo de Chávez, well known in the La
Plata region for his audacity in battle and his leadership qualities.
After weeks of travel through the Andes, Chávez arrived in Lima only
to be told curtly by the authorities that Irala and his followers were to
cease their explorations westward or be held in royal disobedience.
With this news Irala had no choice but to retreat to Asunción, where
he began planning his return to the area to establish a permanent
colony and thereby secure his claim. These aspirations of empire
were permanently ended on October 3, 1556, when Domingo Martínez de Irala died suddenly, never again to cross the plains of Grigotá. Ñuflo de Chávez had no intention, however, of permitting the
death of Irala to crush the La Plata effort to colonize the lowland
plains. By February 1558, Ñuflo had gathered together an army of
150 Spaniards and more than 2,000 Guaraní Indians to begin the
march to the Río Guapay. Bloody battles with hostile Indians along
the route, treachery, and mutiny reduced the expedition to no more
than 50 Spaniards and only a few hundred Guaraní. The ragged group

finally reached the Río Guapay on August 1, 1559, where the first permanent settlement was established. Ñuflo christened the site Nueva Asunción in honor of the distant post in Paraguay where his journey had begun.

Only days after the founding of Nueva Asunción, another contingent of Spaniards rode into the small camp on the banks of the river. The band was led by Captain Andrés Manso, who had left Peru with permission from the Audiencia to colonize the lands now occupied by Chávez. Ñuflo dared not risk the wrath of the powerful viceroyalty in Lima, so, rather than use force to keep what he felt was rightfully his, he tried guile. Manso was persuaded to remain in the lowlands to govern both groups of colonists in Nueva Asunción while Chávez, along with Manso's emissary, took the land dispute to Lima to be decided by higher authority. Acting on his own behalf, Ñuflo de Chávez was in a much stronger bargaining position than his adversary, who was only a spokesman for the absent Manso. On February 15, 1560, Viceroy Andrés Hurtado de Mendoza, Marqués de Cañete, created the province of Moxos, which he granted to his son, García Hurtado de Mendoza. In the absence of the latter, Ñuflo de Chávez was appointed lieutenant general of the entire region. Manso was summoned to Lima but defied his recall, choosing instead to settle near Nueva Asunción where he was killed by a group of hostile Chiriguano Indians.

For his return to the lowlands, Ñuflo was given weapons, supplies, Spanish soldiers, and highland Indians to assist in the colonization of the Moxos territory. Throughout the march to the east, the local aborigines encountered along the way were brought peacefully or by arms under the yoke of Spanish rule. One such group were the Chiquitanos, who at the time of conquest were in control of the lowland plains. Ñuflo befriended the Chiquitanos, and they in turn helped him locate the site that was to be the headquarters of the Moxos colonies. The area chosen was at the base of the Brazilian Shield beside a clear stream known as the Sutos. In a formal ceremony on February 26, 1561, the settlement was inaugurated. Ñuflo named the newly founded town Santa Cruz de la Sierra after the Spanish village in Extremadura where he had been born forty-four years earlier. Having firmly established his claim in the lowlands, Chávez rode east to Asunción where he gathered his wife, children, and numerous settlers, both Indian and European, to return to Santa Cruz. With the impetus of additional colonists, the town began to grow and prosper. In 1568, however, the fierce Itatines invaded from the north, and

Ñuflo de Chávez was killed in the skirmish. The populace voted Diego de Mendoza to succeed Chávez. Mendoza began his stewardship by putting down the Itatín revolt and reestablishing peace in the region.

But once again adversity in the form of highland interference was to plague the Santa Cruz colony. Upon the rise to power of Francisco de Toledo as viceroy of Peru, Diego de Mendoza was deposed as governor of Moxos. The position was to be occupied by one of Toledo's men, Juan Pérez de Zúrita. Shortly after his arrival in Santa Cruz, Zúrita was routed from the town by Mendoza's followers and was sent packing back to Toledo. Incensed by the rebellious Cambas, Toledo himself led an expedition into the lowlands to punish the offending settlement. The viceroy's troops were no sooner onto the lowland plain when they were attacked by the Chiriguanos and forced into a hasty retreat in which Toledo barely escaped alive. He prudently decided at that point to let Santa Cruz manage its own affairs. During the next two years Santa Cruz was torn in bitter civil strife between the supporters of Mendoza and those faithful to the viceroyalty in Lima. Finally, Toledo sent word of amnesty for all and extended an invitation to Mendoza to visit the highlands. Upon his arrival in Potosí, Mendoza was taken prisoner on order from the viceroy and was beheaded a few days later.

For the next several years, the Audiencia of Charcas, under whose jurisdiction Santa Cruz fell, tried to persuade the viceroyalty of Peru to establish another lowland city closer to the highlands where it could be governed more expeditiously. The inhabitants of Santa Cruz would then be moved to the new location and the old settlement abandoned. In October 1580, Lorenzo Suárez de Figueroa was charged with the task of founding this new lowland capital. Combat with the Guaraní Indians led to an abortive attempt to build a fort on the plains between the Piray and Guapay rivers. A second settlement, San Lorenzo el Real, was finally secured on the west bank of the Guapay, and here a governing body for the region was established. The inhabitants of Santa Cruz protested loudly at the usurpation of their ruling powers over the region and made good their protest by refusing to move into San Lorenzo. The new capital soon met with disaster when the Guapay River flooded, carrying away most of the settlement. San Lorenzo was then moved to the site of the old fort, the Guaranís having been dispersed.

The inhabitants of Santa Cruz continued their former existence, but their rebellious attitude remained a source of aggravation for the

Audiencia of Charcas. In 1604 an envoy sent by the Charcas authorities arrived in Santa Cruz with the order that the city was to be moved. The residents acceded to the decree, but they refused to cohabit with the San Lorenzo community. Instead, the Cruceñans located five leagues away, where they remained for seventeen years. At the end of this period, the governor of San Lorenzo, Nuño de la Cueva, working with the Jesuits, began to seek means to unite the two settlements. It finally was agreed that Santa Cruz would be moved to San Lorenzo, but it would not give up its autonomy or its sovereign rights to govern its citizens. Gradually the Cruceñans began to take over the city, and in a matter of a few years even the name San Lorenzo was cast aside in favor of Santa Cruz de la Sierra. Charcas may have succeeded in moving the city closer to the highlands, but it was incapable of reshaping its independent, intractable inhabitants.

The postcolonial history of Santa Cruz is long and complex, but throughout its course two themes recur: isolation and local autonomy. When the new viceroyalty of La Plata was created in 1778, Santa Cruz as part of Upper Peru passed from control of the Audiencia of Charcas to that of Buenos Aires. The shift in government had little effect on the remote lowland province. It was just as difficult to maintain adequate communication with Santa Cruz from Buenos Aires as it had been from the highlands. Thus the region continued to conduct its affairs as a semiautonomous state.

The first moves toward emancipation from Spain went virtually unnoticed by the Cambas. It was not until two patriots, Eustaquio Moldes and Juan Manuel Lemoine, rode down from Cochabamba with word of the insurrection that Santa Cruz became involved in the War of Independence (Urquidi 1944:117). There was little doubt that the city would support the rebel forces rather than side with the royalist cause. On September 24, 1810, Santa Cruz formed a *junta revolucionaria* and seceded from Upper Peru. The Santa Cruz region was not to be the scene of any major battles during the fifteen-year war, but the Cambas contributed to the harassment of royalist forces by the effective guerrilla warfare they waged. Led by Argentine Colonel Ignacio Warnes in 1814, the Cruceñan guerrillas ambushed the royalist army led by General Blanco and claimed a victory over nine hundred enemy troops, an event still celebrated every May 25.

Venezuelan General Antonio José de Sucre, emissary of Simón Bolívar, arrived in La Paz on February 9, 1825, to promulgate the Independence Decree for the provinces of Upper Peru. The Santa Cruz representative was still in Buenos Aires awaiting the convocation of the Assembly of the United Provinces of Río de la Plata. It must have come as some surprise when he learned that Santa Cruz had been annexed to the recently formed highland nation of Bolivia rather than to one of the La Plata republics as had been anticipated (Finot 1954:184–95). Thus Santa Cruz was not fully represented when the Assembly of the Provinces of Upper Peru gathered, but the business of nation-building was carried on despite this oversight. By the time Antonio Vincente Seoane had been dispatched from Santa Cruz and arrived in the highlands, the formal Independence Decree had been prepared and signed by the other delegates. Seoane entered the city of Chuquisaca (Sucre) on August 6, 1825, and, on that same day, affixed what was to be the final signature to the document. Thus the independent nation of Bolivia officially came into being.

Once the war ended, Santa Cruz settled back into the anonymity of isolation it had previously enjoyed. Presidents came and went in the highlands, but the lowlands remained virtually oblivious to the political turmoil seething beyond its boundaries. In the countryside, the Camba peasant, or *campesino*, continued his insular existence much as he had since the first years of settlement. The French explorer Alcide d'Orbigny visited the Santa Cruz plains shortly after Independence: "The campesino of Santa Cruz is the happiest of men. He does not know, nor does he care to know, anything of other regions. For him, the world is a radius of a few familiar places, held in by the mountains which he sees as a vast curtain across the horizon" (d'Orbigny 1835–37:536).

This slow-paced existence continued until the latter third of the nineteenth century when the rubber boom hit the entire Amazon region, and for the first time in its history the city of Santa Cruz de la Sierra embarked on a period of true economic prosperity. Hordes of rubber tappers, the *siringueros*, flooded north into the Beni and Pando, attracted by the high wages offered by the rubber barons of Santa Cruz. The pound sterling became the standard currency in the lowlands, and even today many Cambas retain these coins among old family treasures. Those who remained behind had a ready market for all the rice, manioc, beef jerky, and other staples that could be produced in surplus to feed the tappers. Still, the siringuero's existence was one of tremendous hardship. Many went hungry; they suffered from chronic illness and were brutalized by their employers. Others died, from malaria, flooding, or at the hands of Indians. Fawcett (1924) reported that the laborers on the Madeira River had a working life of only five years. When men could no longer be recruited for the jungles, they were taken as slaves.

Both the great surge in the lowland economy and the countless atrocities committed to ensure its continuation ended in 1910 when Southeast Asia flooded the market with great quantities of cheap rubber. Bolivia no longer could compete in the world market, and Santa Cruz returned to the somnolence of its past. Fortunes were quickly depleted and prosperity drained away.

The beginning of the twentieth century witnessed renewed interest by the highland government in the lowlands to the east. Several unsuccessful attempts were made at integrating Santa Cruz into the national sphere. In 1909 a telegraph line was strung between Cochabamba and Santa Cruz in an effort to increase communication with the isolated province. All major political offices in the lowland were given to highlanders appointed by the La Paz government. These measures served only to heighten the rebellious attitudes of the Camba. Secessionist revolts occurred in 1920 and 1924, both quickly put down by federal forces, but the seed of fear had been planted.

Since the early 1920s, when the Standard Oil Company had secured concessions for exploration in the Gran Chaco desert, Bolivia and Paraguay had been disputing the undemarcated boundary zone in this region. Moves on both sides to gain control of the potentially oil-rich land resulted in several border skirmishes, and in 1932 war broke out between the two contenders. The La Paz government, fearing that Santa Cruz would side with the Paraguayans with whom they had much stronger cultural ties, took immediate steps to prevent the department from any renewed attempt to secede. All political posts were again given to highlanders, military command was denied to Cruceñans, and the Cambas were forbidden to form their own regiments (Heath 1959:30–31). Rather than uniting lowlanders and highlanders in a common cause, the war served only to entrench more deeply the old regional hatreds. One Chaco veteran recalled the war:

It was an incredibly horrible time! War is always ugly, I guess, but this was like Hell. The worst part of it was that we had not one enemy but three—we had constantly to fight thirst and the Kollas, as well as the Paraguayans. There were many who went mad with thirst and killed themselves or were killed. And there were also many who were killed by the Bolivians—the Kollas had only to say that a Camba was a spy to have him shot. This way they amused themselves when the war was slow, and as many of our buddies were killed by Kollas as by the enemy on the other side. Of course, we were able to kill a few of them too, but it was dangerous. (quoted in Heath 1959:31)

The treaty of 1938 ended the war but brought defeat to Bolivia. The major portion of the disputed desert area was awarded to Paraguay, and Bolivia was left counting its dead. The Cambas were grateful to return to their farmlands, away from the savagery of war and their despised compatriots, the Kollas. The highlanders were just as eager to leave the lowland wastes and be reunited with their families. Once again the national government was thrown into a frenzy of political turmoil by a series of coups which kept the highland politicians preoccupied with their own affairs. Santa Cruz slipped from national attention and settled back into the isolation of earlier years.

In 1952 the MNR (Movimiento Nacionalista Revolucionaria) party led by Victor Paz Estenssoro came to power. The Cruceñan factions of the party, centered primarily in the city of Santa Cruz, were appointed to major political posts and began to seek a wider following in the lowland countryside. Sweeping reforms instituted by the new government radically altered the old social order throughout the entire nation. Perhaps the greatest impact was the Agrarian Reform Law enacted in 1953, which effectively put an end to the traditional land tenure system.

The highland campesino had been tied in perpetual serfdom to an agricultural establishment, the *hacienda*. In return for the privilege of cultivating a small parcel of the poorest soil, he was required to give his landlord three to five days of labor weekly. Contrary to the views of writers such as José Romero Loza, who states that the Camba campesino "was never subjected either historically, economically, or socially to servile and free labor" (Romero Loza 1974:296), the lowland version of the hacienda, the finca, was operating in a similar manner. Because of differences in settlement patterns, it is true that entire villages were never transferred like chattel from the hands of the Incas to those of the Spaniards and their descendants as occurred in the highlands. Nevertheless, the Camba landlord depended on free or inexpensive labor to sustain his agricultural enterprise just as did his highland counterpart. The Camba peon was tied to his landlord not by a long tradition of servitude but by debt. Wages were always kept low enough to ensure that no farm family could possibly live off its earnings. In order to meet their basic needs, Camba peons were forced to buy supplies on credit from the *finquero*. The debt was passed from generation to generation and, just as in the highlands, ensured a stable work force.

The lowlands presented one major difference, however. There never existed there a true shortage of arable land such as prevailed in the mountains. Anyone with a spirit for adventure and the fortitude to withstand hardship and solitude could escape into the wilderness and carve out a homestead. He may not have been able to market his produce, but he would be safe from the demands of the finquero and relatively free from hunger. Many of the more courageous Cambas did just that, opening up new territories to the north and east. Others were content to remain on the finca, which robbed them of dignity and self-determination but at the same time provided some security. On the finca the Camba peons had access to a few comforts such as kerosene for their lamps, sugar, salt, tobacco, and the ever-important cane alcohol, all purchased on credit and assuring greater indebtedness and more years of toil. Some of the *patrones* took their paternalistic role seriously, providing medical attention for their laborers and schools for the children. Others were ruthless and cruel to those who worked their lands. The *huasca* (leather whip) was always ready and seldom spared. Runaway peons were hunted down with dogs and men on horseback and were severely punished if caught.

The days of the great landlords came to an abrupt end in Bolivia when the Agrarian Reform laws were enacted in 1953. In the mountains, the land previously held by wealthy upper-class Bolivians, often in absenteeism, was confiscated by the government and redistributed to the impoverished serfs. Landowners in such places as the Cochabamba Valley, where the population is extremely dense, were totally divested of their holdings. Because of the pressure in the highlands for arable land, patrons were left with a small part of their original estates. In many instances, land was taken forcibly by groups of campesino unions, the *sindicatos*, which were unwilling to await the due process of law. Large tracts of land were also expropriated in the less densely populated Santa Cruz region, but here properties were of an enormous size compared to those in the interior and the demand for land by the lowland campesinos could be met easily. While the patrons in Santa Cruz were also divested of large portions of their original holdings, in most cases they retained adequate amounts to continue extensive farming. What broke the lowland finquero was not so much the loss of land but the loss of the labor necessary to work it, for hand-in-hand with the Agrarian Reform went a decree to abolish all forms of debt peonage and a cancellation of all outstanding accounts held against the finca workers. Even the promise of higher wages was insufficient enticement for the peons who could secure their own farms nearby for little more than the cost of title registration. Those finqueros with available capital began to mechanize their operations or turned to cattle ranching and ultimately were spared the financial ruin experienced by many others. Most, however, were forced by economic necessity to sell off their remaining land and move to the cities where they sought other forms of income. The property in turn was purchased by individual farmers and by agribusiness enterprises which foresaw the coming economic expansion in the lowlands.

After more than five years under the revolutionary government, Bolivia began to evaluate the results of many of its programs for change. Efforts were made to assess the effect of the Agrarian Reform on agricultural production throughout the nation. Some observers, such as the United Nations Economic Commission for Latin America (1958), reported a 15 percent drop in production as a result of land reform and forecast grave economic problems. Ronald J. Clark (1968) countered the ECLA report by pointing out that production had not necessarily fallen off but simply may have been rechanneled. Due to the reform, he argued, campesinos were now able to keep more of their produce for personal consumption instead of handing it over to the hacienda. Hence less of the nation's agricultural products were reaching urban centers where they could be counted. Clark added that the revolution had also destroyed the old marketing system, formerly in the hands of the landowners, and that it would take time for the campesino to establish a new marketing network.

Even so, as Zondag noted in his study of the postrevolution Bolivian economy, the peasant was given land to work but little monetary or technical assistance to permit him to rise much above a subsistence level. In such localities as Cochabamba, becoming a landholder meant little in terms of economic betterment. More than 8,000 families in the Cochabamba Valley received less than 1.5 hectares of arable land (Zondag 1968:186). By 1964 the economy began to recover, but social pressures in the highlands continued to increase as well. For the children of many families there would be no land, or at least not enough for them to eke out a living. The cities offered only temporary relief, since Bolivia had no industrial base to support large urban populations. By the early 1960s the government was beginning to look toward Santa Cruz and its abundant farmland as a possible solution to its economic problems.

Prior to the enactment of the Agrarian Reform laws, the three largest mines in Bolivia, those owned by Patiño, Hoschchild, and Aramayo, were nationalized and brought under the control of COMIBOL (Corporación Minera de Bolivia), an agency of the central government. According to Zondag (1968:109), "From an economic point of view, the impact of the 1952 revolution on the . . . mining industry has been a disaster." As the result of political patronage, COMIBOL was required to take on greater numbers of additional employees. The labor rolls jumped from 24,000 mine employees in 1951 to 36,558 in 1958, but at the same time production slumped from 34,600 metric tons of tin ore mined in 1949 to COMIBOL's figure for 1961 of only 15,000 metric tons (Zondag 1968:120). Low market prices, poor administration, depletion of ore deposits, and featherbedding all contributed to the decline of the mining sector. The labor situation became acute. Mining unions represented a formidable obstacle to attempts to streamline mining operations and efforts to increase mechanization in the mines. At one point it became more profitable to pay miners to remain at home than put them on the job using up expensive materials such as explosives to quarry what was mostly worthless rock.

In 1961 the crisis of COMIBOL reached its peak. The mines had been operating in the red for almost ten years without any indication that conditions would improve. Losses for the period 1952–57 are not known, but between 1958 and 1961 the deficit totaled approximately $52.2 million (U.S) (Romero 1974:303). The rise to power of Fidel Castro in 1959 coupled with the rumored offers by the USSR to bail out COMIBOL spurred Western governments to a hastily proposed loan of $37,750,000 (U.S.). The Plan Triangular, as it was known, would supply technical as well as financial assistance to the failing industry. There were conditions to the loan, however, requiring COMIBOL to make major alterations in its administrative practices. By 1964, COMIBOL, aided by the rising price of tin on the world market, was at last operating at a profit. But solvency was short lived: production costs rose at a much greater rate than the market could absorb, and in 1966 COMIBOL was once again in debt—$41 million. This deficit was transferred to the Presupesto Nacional (national budget), which in turn was covered by U.S. financial assistance to Bolivia.

Another $20 million over the original loan was allocated under the plan, but the mining industry failed to respond. As Romero stated somewhat cryptically, "The agency remains as an untouchable monument to inefficiency" (1974:308).

During the three years the Plan Triangular was in operation, COMIBOL was required by provisions of the loan agreement to cut back on mine personnel. Miners were laid off amidst the hue and cry of the union leaders, but even they were incapable of wielding enough coercive power to maintain previous employment levels. The industry was sick, and there was no cure in sight. One major problem faced by the Bolivian revolutionary government was that of relocating the ex-miners. Many simply drifted into the cities or back into the countryside in search of some alternative source of income. Others justifiably argued that the government should make some provision for them. Aid was sought from several international agencies, including the Interamerican Development Bank (IDB), to fund colonization projects in the lowlands. It was hoped that these programs would not only offer a solution to the problem of unemployed miners but at the same time would serve as an escape valve for the pressures created by land-hungry campesinos. In reality, colonization accomplished neither of these goals, but it contributed to the first trickle of highland migrants into the lowlands that in succeeding years was to become a major flow.

Though there has been heated debate over whether the 1952 revolution was of any significant economic advantage to the highlands (that it represented definite achievements in the social sphere has not been denied), it proved to be the necessary impetus to shake Santa Cruz from its years of lethargy and plunge it into the modern capitalistic system. Cornelius Zondag opens his chapter on the lowlands of Santa Cruz with this statement:

> Even the most severe critics of the Movimiento Nacionalista Revolucionaria admit one thing: the developmental efforts of the MNR discovered a new, tropical Bolivia. Admitting that the idea of developing the plains was not new, it was now up to the nationalist revolutionary government to make this dream a reality. (1968:193, my translation)

The Cochabamba–Santa Cruz highway was completed, and railroads were pushed through to the Brazilian and Argentine borders. With major transportation routes now available, Santa Cruz could look beyond its own boundaries toward national and international markets for its agricultural products.

Since colonial times, Santa Cruz agriculturalists concentrated on the production of two marketable items, sugar and rice. Many secondary crops were cultivated, such as corn, bananas, manioc, coffee, pineapple, and peanuts, but sugarcane and rice have been the traditional mainstays of the regional marketing system. Sugar was produced on the finca; the cane was pressed and the juice rendered into sugar and other by products in the huge *pailas*, earthen cauldrons fired with dry kindling. The sugar was then stored in pottery urns called *hormas*, with a layer of moist clay spread on top to bleach out some of the molasses. Until the 1950s, all of the sugar produced in Santa Cruz was made in this manner.

Bolivia imported 73,300 tons of sugar in 1942 and 1943; in 1946, the Santa Cruz region produced only 161 tons of sugar, most of which was consumed locally (Romero 1974:255). When the Corporación Boliviana de Fomento (CBF) was established in 1943 to spur economic development in the nation, one of its first tasks was to undertake a feasibility study of sugar production. It was decided in 1946 to acquire 1,000 hectares of land near the community of Saavedra, some 60 kilometers north of the city of Santa Cruz and only a few kilometers from Montero. The Montero–Santa Cruz road would have to be paved and the Cochabamba–Santa Cruz highway completed in order for the sugar to reach highland markets. In addition, an agricultural experiment station would be constructed in Saavedra to provide technical expertise to cane growers. But before the project got off the ground, political turmoil in La Paz brought the efforts of workers and engineers to a halt. It was not until 1957 under the MNR regime that the Guabirá mill at Saavedra finally went into production (Romero 1974:256).

In the meantime, private interests also were cognizant of the CBF feasibility study and were willing to gamble on the promising future of sugarcane in the Santa Cruz region. In 1952, the Gasser family, a group of Belgian immigrants, opened their mill, La Bélgica, between Santa Cruz and Warnes.

La Bélgica was followed by San Aurelio on the outskirts of the city of Santa Cruz and later by La Esperanza, north of the lowland capital. As each mill went into production, more and more land was planted to cane. In 1958, 5,800 hectares of land were in sugarcane, 24,600 hectares by 1964. The 161 tons of sugar produced in 1946 jumped to 93,600 tons in 1964 and peaked at 115,700 tons in 1969 (Reye

1974:13). Sugar imports dropped from 66,700 tons in 1956 to zero in 1964. Exportation began in 1960 on a small scale of only 500 tons but had risen by 1969 to 10,000 tons annually (Reye 1974:13).

The impact of commercial sugar production in Santa Cruz was far-reaching. More than 12,000 zafreros (cane cutters) were needed each year to harvest the crop (Reye 1974:14). Most Cambas were unwilling to hire out for the backbreaking work, so labor had to be sought elsewhere. Highlanders responded to the call for zafreros, many of them campesinos in search of off-season work to supplement their farm incomes. The cane harvest coincided nicely with the three-month fallow period preceding spring planting. There are no data available regarding the number of cane cutters who may have chosen to remain in the lowlands, but many of those highlanders interviewed in towns or on small farms throughout the Santa Cruz region confessed that it was the cane harvest that gave them their first glimpse of lowland life. They liked it and decided to stay.

The production of rice in Santa Cruz followed a pattern similar to that of sugar. At the time of the revolution of 1952, Bolivia was importing 53 percent of its consumption needs or 83,000 quintales (100 pounds) of rice per year (Romero 1974:257). Sixteen thousand hectares of land were under rice cultivation in Santa Cruz in 1955 and 35,815 hectares in 1964, when rice production reached 42,500 tons, exceeding national demand by 10,000 tons. In 1965, growers cut back cultivation 30 percent because of that overproduction (Zondag 1968:194).

The agricultural boom in Santa Cruz made lowland settlement seem more palatable than usual to many highlanders. There was money to be made, and land was available in large quantities at relatively low cost. Even colonization no longer appeared to be such an ends-of-the-earth proposition. The prospect of homesteading in the lowlands became increasingly interesting to non-Bolivians as well. In its efforts to encourage the development of the Santa Cruz region, the Bolivian government granted large tracts of land to foreign migrants who demonstrated a willingness to become permanent and productive agriculturalists. To the north, in the center of prime rice-producing terrain, Japanese established the colony of San Juan. To the east, Okinawans set up a colony of the same name to engage in cane and rice production. In 1980, they were also experimenting with tropical wheat, a staple that still must be imported. A group of Old Colony Mennonites have been allotted land to the south of Santa Cruz, and their small settlements are well on the way to prosperity.

Coincidental to the great awakening of agriculture in Santa Cruz during the 1960s was a growing interest in the region's oil reserves. Before the full value of lowland petroleum and gas deposits was understood, the Bolivian government agreed in 1938 to return to the department 11 percent of oil revenues. This agreement was updated in 1956 and remains as part of the Petroleum Code (CORDECRUZ 1979a:55). It was not until the early 1960s, however, that the first revenues were turned over to the locally autonomous public development agency, Obras Públicas (Public Works). During its first decade of operation, 1963–72, approximately $24 million were spent on water and electrification projects, paving, and sewers in urban areas and schools, hospitals, and health posts throughout the department (CORDECRUZ 1979a:55). In the late 1970s, Obras Públicas was reorganized to become CORDECRUZ (Corporación Regional de Desarrollo de Santa Cruz), although the objectives for development remained the same. Just as with its predecessor, the 11 percent oil revenue income has given CORDECRUZ an enviable advantage over the other eight departmental development agencies in Bolivia. As a result, not only has Santa Cruz surged ahead of the rest of the nation in terms of infrastructure, but it also has had the advantage of attracting the country's brightest young architects, planners, and engineers. The fact that CORDECRUZ is one of few government bureaucracies that pay well and on time and have adequate funding for projects no doubt has contributed to this attraction.

The beginning of the 1970s witnessed a decline in sugarcane cultivation brought about by several droughts, sugarcane blight, and progressively lower prices. Cultivation dropped from 35,000 hectares in 1970 to 27,000 hectares in 1971 (Reye 1974:15). During this decline, many growers switched from cane to cotton, which was getting high prices on the world market and which had demonstrated good adaptability to the soil and climatic conditions of the region. Formerly, cotton had been grown in the lowlands by only one enterprise, the Algodonera, a privately owned, government-subsidized monopoly. A new administration in La Paz opened up cotton production, and everyone, farmers with large and small holdings alike, jumped in. From the 6,000 hectares controlled by the Algodonera in 1968, cotton cultivation spiraled to 60,333 hectares in 1974 (CORDECRUZ 1979b:27). Most of this cotton was destined for export, producing income which in 1973 assisted Bolivia's balance of payments by $19 million.

Aside from the economic impact on the region, the shift from cane

to the more lucrative crop of cotton occasioned demographic repercussions throughout the nation as well. Unlike sugarcane, which
during harvest makes use of small groups of primarily male laborers
to cut, clean, and load the cane on trucks, cotton harvesting is highly
labor intensive and a good deal less strenuous. Thus it requires large
numbers of pickers, not necessarily restricted by age or sex. Once
again, the lowlands were unable to meet the demand for labor, and
contractors were sent into the highlands to hire individuals, families,
or even entire villages and to ship them down to the cotton fields of
Santa Cruz. In 1974, 34,000 pickers worked in the cotton harvest and
it has been estimated that over half may have remained in the lowlands (Federación de Campesinos 1975).

The boom-bust situation that has characterized the Santa Cruz
economy in recent years continued its pattern with cotton. After only
four years of expansion, production began to drop off. Several factors
contributed to this decline, perhaps foremost a shortage of labor.
At first highlanders were eager to work the harvest. Then stories of
abuses by farmers and labor contractors spread rapidly through the
highlands. Soon it became almost impossible to find laborers who
were willing to risk the chance of virtual imprisonment on cotton
farms or the withholding of pay until the entire crop was harvested.
Some growers mechanized their operations, although prices paid for
machine-picked cotton tended to be lower than for that picked by
hand. In addition to labor shortages, however, the world market price
dropped, there were several consecutive years of insufficient rain,
soils were becoming depleted, and the insect population was rapidly
becoming resistant to pesticides. All together, these problems proved
too much for many small producers. Between 1974 and 1976 the
60,000 hectares under cultivation dropped to 28,545 (CORDECRUZ
1979b:27).

By 1980, another shift was apparent in the boom-bust economy
of Santa Cruz. Although sugarcane had begun to recover somewhat
after cotton production bottomed out, a deterioration in world market prices thrust production costs above market value (CORDECRUZ
1979a). There was also concern that diminishing oil reserves would
begin to threaten economic collapse not only in the department but
in the nation as a whole.

While Santa Cruz struggled to make agriculture a paying venture,
the economic situation in the highlands continued its downward spiral. Despite the fact Bolivia enjoyed relatively high prices for tin on
the world market, during most of the 1970s lower and lower produc-

tion could not keep abreast of the mounting external debt. By the first quarter of 1980, this debt was calculated at $3.5 billion (U.S.), the interest on which alone was absorbing 30 percent of Bolivian profits from exports (*Le Monde* 1981).

The worsening economic situation throughout the nation no doubt contributed to what was, even for Bolivia, growing political instability. Several palace revolts and coups resulted in the president of senate, Lidia Gueiller, taking over as interim president of the Republic in 1979. She was Bolivia's first woman president and the sixth person to hold this office since General Hugo Banzer stepped down in 1978. A call for free elections resulted in thirteen candidates. With so many contenders in the race, none received a clear majority although former president Hernán Siles Suazo a leftist, was the front-runner. Although accusations were made from the right that election fraud had occurred, it was expected that the Bolivian Congress would name Siles to succeed Gueiller. Before this could occur, however, General Luís García Meza led the army in a preemptive takeover. This move infuriated the Carter administration, which, through its ambassador to Bolivia, Marvin Weissman, had supported the Bolivian people in their holding of free elections. Ambassador Weissman was recalled to Washington; U.S.–Bolivian diplomatic relations were interrupted and military assistance and new development projects funded by AID suspended.

The withdrawal of U.S. monetary support, long a factor in Bolivia's economic viability, set off a chain reaction by other Western nations. Credit was curtailed and the national debt ballooned to $4 billion by the second quarter of 1981 (COHA 1981). The economic situation in the nation was so chaotic that many observers were led to speculate that the Bolivian government might be bankrupt. In April 1981, for example, *Newsweek* reported that certain heads of government were paying government salaries from personal savings and private loans. It was also intimated that much of this money may have come from the illicit cocaine trade (*Newsweek* 1981).

The production of cocaine in Bolivia, legal or otherwise, did not begin to proliferate until the MNR gave land to the peasants and the road to Santa Cruz was completed. Until that time, coca was grown by the landed elite on plantations in the *yungas* of Cochabamba and La Paz and shipped to the highlands for consumption primarily in leaf form by indigenous peoples. Because the lowlands east of La Paz and Cochabamba traditionally had been coca-growing regions, the opening of these areas for planned and spontaneous settlement after the 1953 Agrarian Reform led to expansion of coca production. In spite of early efforts by the Ministry of Agriculture and agricultural advisors from other nations to interest colonists in food crops for income, coca soon emerged as the most dependable cash crop for the small farmer (Henkel 1971). Since most farm produce in many areas of the colonies had to be taken out on the backs of people, coca was the only item that was worth the effort.

In Santa Cruz, the planting of coca bushes had been prohibited in new agricultural colonies in an effort to limit production. Because Cambas had never adopted coca-chewing as part of their culture and in fact ridiculed it as being "Indian," there was little lowland interest in growing the plant. Coca leaves in small amounts could be purchased in local Santa Cruz markets, but these were usually prepared in a tea to be used for stomach ailments. What Cruceñans did cultivate, however, was an interest in extracting cocaine from coca leaves for the illicit drug market. The opening of the Santa Cruz–Cochabamba highway in 1954 made large quantities of coca accessible for the first time to lowland cocaine producers.

Through the 1960s and early 1970s the production of cocaine in Santa Cruz increased slowly. Apparently what held it back was the generally favorable economic environment of the region spurred by oil discoveries and profits from sugarcane, cotton, and rice. During this period, migration of highlanders to the lowlands increased steadily with land accessible to most and wage labor readily available in urban areas and on farms. This influx of primary labor brought additional migration of merchants, craftsmen, artisans, and others ready to ride the crest of free-flowing money.

By the late 1970s, Santa Cruz had entered an agricultural slump with poor export prices, wildly fluctuating national markets, soil depletion, and a variety of other reverses (CORDECRUZ 1979a). Precisely at this point occurred a meteoric rise in the cocaine trade. Reported at about $1.5 billion annually, the income from illegal cocaine must now be considered the major economic mainstay of Santa Cruz. In the past, one heard little comment about the drug. Now it is an open topic of conversation. Conspicuous consumption in the form of expensive homes, cars, television sets, clothing, and appliances has become part of lowland life. Most of this spending occurs outside of Bolivia or is in the form of imported products, adding fuel to the 50 percent inflation rate and the balance of payments problem (COHA 1981).

Despite indications that most cocaine money eventually leaves

Bolivia in one form or another, there is evidence that there is some trickle-down. If one is dealing with what is conservatively estimated at over $1.5 billion a year, even a small percentage of that amount remaining in the department would have significant economic impact. Many of the imported items are purchased from local stores, which are thriving. Contraband from Brazil, Panama, and Miami is openly hawked on street corners, and people have money to buy it.

The drug trade also employs people directly, in all phases of production. One informant, a Kolla, claimed that he had stopped agricultural work at $4.54 (U.S.) a day because he could earn $22.72 (U.S.) for an evening's work pressing coca leaves in kerosene (the first step in the extractive process). Several farmers who were interviewed complained bitterly that it was impossible to find field laborers because the cocaine trade offered them so much more than farm wages.

Whether through the promise of land, employment, or the profits from cocaine, the Department of Santa Cruz continues to attract highland migrants at a rate of about 22,000 per year (INE–NN.UU. 1980). Because the migrants must employ new strategies for survival, they tend to be highly creative entrepreneurs. Thus while the promise of economic prosperity may bring them to Santa Cruz, highlanders themselves contribute to that prosperity. Lowlanders have not been overly enthusiastic about this recent invasion of their homeland by highland Bolivians, but they are fully aware of the positive impact it has had on the growth and development of the region. The deeply embedded prejudices held by the Camba no doubt will eventually be eroded by time and by the sheer numbers of Kollas moving into Santa Cruz.

3

Santa Cruz de la Sierra: Migration to a Primate City

Santa Cruz de la Sierra, or simply Santa Cruz as the city is commonly known, is the capital of the department of the same name. The largest urban center in the lowlands, it contains nearly a third of the department's 710,724 inhabitants (Bolivia 1976); and although other smaller cities such as Montero are rapidly gaining in prominence, it is Santa Cruz that remains the center of all governmental and commercial activity in the region.

The precipitous growth of the city, from 43,000 inhabitants in 1950 to 256,000 in 1976, may be attributed largely to internal migration in Bolivia. A survey conducted by the Instituto Nacional de Estadística in 1979 indicated that almost 44 percent of the city's residents were migrants, primarily highlanders and lowlanders from outlying areas (INE–DDE 1981). For the highland migrant, the enticement of the lowland capital has been overwhelmingly the promise of economic gain. At present, the department boasts the highest per capita income in the nation, and the city continues to attract about half of those highlanders seeking better income opportunities in the lowlands (Arze 1979). Lowland migrants have several motives for leaving the countryside, including, of course, higher wages; but educational needs and the desire to live in an urban setting—the so-called bright lights syndrome—also enter into the decision to migrate.

Santa Cruz is very much a reflection of the great numbers of migrants who have settled within the city's boundaries. The lowland migrant is quickly assimilated into the resident population; the highlander is adding an entirely new dimension to traditional Cruceñan society.

The City

The city of Santa Cruz began as a typical Mediterranean-style settlement of streets set out in a grid pattern with a central plaza. The physical orientation, whether by plan or accident, is almost true to the cardinal axes. Dominating the south side of the main square, the Plaza 24 de Septiembre, is the Santa Cruz Cathedral. It is frequently photographed by tourists in search of colonial architecture, but actually the building is only fifty-five years old. On the north side of the plaza are banks and the mayor's office (Alcaldía). To the east and west are public and private buildings, including the police department (Intendencia), the departmental offices (Prefectura), restaurants, tourist shops, bookstores, and a movie theater.

Unlike many urban centers in other parts of the world, the inner city has not degenerated into a slum but remains the hub of social and commercial activity. Many of the older Cruceñan families continue to live there. The buildings for the most part are single-story masonry or wattle and daub that has been plastered and whitewashed. Roofs are almost uniformly Spanish tile. A few multistory buildings have been completed in recent years, the newest and tallest rising fourteen stories. Still, when viewed from a high vantage point, the city presents a calm surface of curved, red-orange, lichen-splotched tile only occasionally interrupted by a concrete structure that rises above roofs.

Prior to the installation of sewer lines and the paving of the first streets near the main plaza, Santa Cruz was characterized by two extremes—dust and mud. During dry weather, winds off the plains of Grigotá drove sand and silt down every thoroughfare in town. The tile roofs of older homes and business establishments trapped pockets of soil that propagate spiny cactus plants along the eaves. Torrential rains brought momentary respite from the billowing dust, but the streets soon became flowing rivers of mud. In 1966 paving was begun, and gradually the sand was pushed back onto the plains. Gutters now carry away the street overflows from heavy downpours, making the rains only a temporary nuisance.

The outskirts of Santa Cruz, however, remain much as the inner city was in earlier years, although changes are being made. As money becomes available, CORDECRUZ, the regional development corporation, lays a few more meters of sewer pipe and seals the roadbed with *locetas*, hexagonal-shaped interlocking concrete blocks. (Aside from their curious honeycomb appearance, the locetas are also well adapted to the needs of the city and to the lowland environment: they reflect the intense tropical heat rather than absorbing it as will an asphalt surface. They are also practical. Because they are movable units, there is little loss of material if additional street excavation becomes necessary. The locetas are simply placed to one side of the roadwork and then repositioned when the task is completed.) As paving moves gradually toward the perimeter of the city, neighborhoods vie for political favors in order to be the first in the area to have sewers laid and streets improved. In recent years, CORDECRUZ has made concerted efforts to provide as few services as possible to new neighborhoods on the periphery of the city. One urban planner explained that these measures had been taken to curb spot development and to force people to develop designated areas of the city in an orderly manner. These efforts to direct growth patterns have been ignored as migrants rush in to claim peripheral land, which is always more affordable than developed areas.

Settlement Zones

Four concentric circular throughways, called *anillos* (rings), have been superimposed over the basic quadrilateral plan of the city. Three of these roads are wide and fast, enabling travelers to circumnavigate Santa Cruz without having to pass through the congested downtown area. The fourth has yet to be completed. Like rings on a tree, the anillos mark the outward growth of Santa Cruz. Various types of settlement patterns are evident within the confines of each anillo, and the nature of each pattern is greatly determined by the regional origins and economic status of the inhabitants.

The area enclosed by the first anillo, designated for the purpose of this study Zone 1, is the oldest part of Santa Cruz. As mentioned, this sector continues to be inhabited predominantly by the old Cruceñan aristocracy, wealthy or otherwise. The area immediately contiguous to the main plaza has become primarily a commercial center, although many of the owners of downtown establishments live behind their stores. Alongside the old Camba families in Zone 1 are foreign immigrants engaged in commerce and a few campesino families

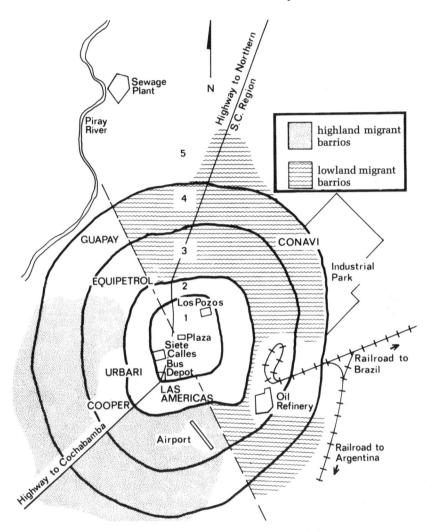

Santa Cruz: main plaza and intendencia

which have accumulated adequate capital to permit them to acquire a town house. The only highland stronghold in this section of the city is centered around Los Pozos market, in the northeast. Like every open market in Santa Cruz, Los Pozos has been taken over by highland entrepreneurs. While most live in the migrant *barrios* outside of the second anillo, many have purchased homes in the immediate area and others reside in the market proper, sleeping in their small stalls. Two other markets situated within the first anillo, Siete Calles and Mercado Nuevo, are both dominated by highland merchants. Unlike Los Pozos, however, highlanders have not settled around these markets, for Siete Calles and Mercado Nuevo are located closer to the center of town than is Los Pozos and are hemmed in by established Camba businesses and residences. Hence, most of the highland vendors have been unable to buy or rent in this area and must commute from the periphery of the city.

Built to connect the road from Cochabamba to the Montero highway, the second anillo was constructed of asphalt rather than locetas and for many years was the only paved road in the city. Although the other anillos were part of the city's master plan, the second anillo was the only major route around the city until well into the 1970s. At the time it was called simply the *circumvalación*, a name that persists to the present day. The residents living in the area between the first and second anillos (Zone 2) are also primarily lowlanders, although some highlanders have begun to acquire homes and shops within this perimeter. The Cambas occupying Zone 2 are for the most part lower-middle- and middle-income residents and campesinos who migrated to Santa Cruz a number of years ago when this area constituted the outskirts of the city. Also within the zone are the stadium, half of the university (the other half is in Zone 3), and the majority of entertainment facilities such as restaurants, nightclubs, and movie theaters. Homes here tend to be single family dwellings and, aside from being new, look very much like those of Zone 1. Because the second anillo was once the termination point for the Santa Cruz–Cochabamba highway, Zone 2 became the service center for the transportation industry. Mechanics, parts shops, steam cleaning, and lubrication pits are concentrated in this sector of the city, primarily along the second anillo, even though the highway now ends at the first anillo where the new bus station is located.

Crosscutting both Zone 1 and Zone 2 is the Avenida de las Américas, leading from the central business district to the airport. Along this avenue and for several blocks on either side is situated one of the three upper-income residential areas in Santa Cruz. Homes in the Américas district are large and expensive, and several are of unusual design. Wealthy Cruceñans, as well as foreign immigrants and the resident diplomats in the city, own or rent dwellings along the avenue.

Two similar areas exist outside of the second anillo, in Zone 3. The first, known as Equipetrol, began as apart of the Gulf Oil camp where well-to-do oil executives built large American-style houses. When the holdings of Gulf Oil were expropriated in 1961, the American colony vacated the site. Equipetrol became a second residential area for the city's elite, and it has continued to expand rapidly because of the vacant tracts of land available nearby. A middle-income housing project called Guapay has been tacked on at the rear of Equipetrol. These houses sell for $25,000 to $30,000 (U.S.) and may be purchased on a twenty-year loan after a modest down payment. Young professionals and middle-level bureaucrats, mostly Cruceñan, make their homes there. The other upper income residential area located in Zone 3 is the Urbanización Cooper, located just south of Equipetrol. It began as a planned development in the 1960s but never managed to get off the ground. The cotton and cocaine booms of 1975 and after inspired renewed interest in the old development, which was finally completed. Another contiguous urbanization, Urbarí, begun in the late 1970s, consists of Miami-style cluster homes. Unlike the early years of growth in Santa Cruz, which represented mostly a continuation of traditional adobe, brick and tile buildings, the decades of the 1970s and 1980s witnessed a trend toward more progressive architecture. Because of the cocaine trade and the contrabanding of high technology goods that accompanies it, Cruceñan society is now in continual contact with other areas of the world, particularly South Florida. One informant who makes several trips to Miami each year to buy trade goods commented that Santa Cruz was becoming a Miami suburb. There are direct flights daily between the two cities, leaving late at night and arriving early the following morning. Late model cars bearing Florida license plates are common on the streets of Santa Cruz, and "cruising" in them has replaced the evening walk around the main plaza.

The city of Santa Cruz has now stabilized within the confines of Zones 1 and 2. All of the streets in these two zones have been paved, and most of Zone 3 has been completed. As mentioned, urban planners are attempting to control patterns of growth by holding back the provision of streets and sewers to outlying areas until those sectors closer in have been fully settled. Although sound in logic, the plan is for the most part ineffectual. The nearer one travels toward the center of town, the more expensive are building lots. Recent arrivals in the city look for homesites beyond the third and, in the last three years or so, even beyond the fourth anillo. The extent of urban sprawl in Santa Cruz was so underestimated that Zone 3, in addition to being the major migrant settlement area, is also the site of the oil refinery, airport, railheads for both the Brazilian and Argentine lines, half of the university, and the San Aurelio sugar mill. Until the late 1960s, most of this land was pasture or forest and seemed at the time an appropriate location for industry and transportation.

For the present, the major function of Zone 4 is to catch the spill from Zone 3. Much of the area is in the process of being subdivided into lots, with water and electricity available only to those who are able to meet the expense of paying for lines to be run out that far. In recent years, a new type of entrepreneur has emerged in Santa Cruz as the result of increasing pressure from migrant families to secure homesites. These individuals, known as *loteadores*, locate a piece of land and then collect "subscriptions" from migrants looking for urban lots. Once a substantial number of subscribers are enlisted, the loteador begins the process of expropriation under the Urban Reform Law. This process is costly and not always effective, but if the loteador is successful, his or her clients will have acquired a 13-by-30 meter homesite for about $500 (U.S.). The same lot purchased through conventional negotiations would run about five times that amount.

There are two exceptions to the rule of unplanned and sporadic development in Zone 4. The first, Guapay, which is actually an extension of Equipetrol, has been discussed. The second is the CONAVI project. The Bolivian counterpart of the U.S. Department of Housing and Urban Development, CONAVI (Consejo Nacional de Vivienda) granted funds to the city of Santa Cruz for the construction of low-income housing. However, even with low-interest loans, the cost of these homes—in 1975 from $3,000 to $3,500 (U.S.) and now well over $10,000—is beyond the reach of most of the city's poor. Consequently, CONAVI-built homes have been inhabited primarily by middle-income residents and a few in higher income brackets who, for one reason or another, desired to live there.

After the CONAVI project began, adjacent land was purchased by several private development corporations and trade unions, such as the Cooperativa Orgullo Camba (Camba Pride Cooperative). These private concerns built homes similar in design to those in CONAVI and offered the same provisions for long-term payment. The cooperatives and corporations, however, did not keep to the same specifications as the government project. As a result, many of the homes were sold and occupied before water and electricity were brought into the area. The cost of installing these services was assumed therefore by the new owners in addition to their house payments.

All of these corporations, cooperatives, and even the CONAVI program are owned or administered by lowlanders who have attempted to bar highlanders from settling in these projects. A few Kolla families are evident in CONAVI, which was supported by national funding, but the private developments are uniformly Camba. One informant mentioned that there had been a struggle to exclude highlanders from the area and that the Cambas had prevailed. Incidents such as this no doubt have contributed to the segregation of Santa Cruz by regional origins. Many highlanders confessed that they would rather live in their own barrios where they are not subjected to the scorn and ridicule of lowlanders. Lowlanders complain that they do not want highlanders intruding in their neighborhoods. Even so, housing shortages in the city are so acute that often one must settle where one can, regardless of origin or preference.

The Migrant Barrios

Except for the old Gulf camp, now Equipetrol, the residential areas in Zones 3 and 4 are new settlements. Most have been carved out of former landholdings of the Cruceñan aristocracy. The Urban Reform Law prohibited the private ownership of more than one hectare of land within the four-kilometer radius of the city, so landowners were faced with the options of losing their holdings to the loteadores or having them surveyed into lots for subsequent sale. Most made the decision to subdivide and sell, and in most cases owners profited substantially from the transaction. It is in these newly formed residential tracts that recent arrivals to Santa Cruz have settled, creating a series of migrant barrios beyond the second anillo.

The migrant barrios contain either Camba or Kolla concentrations, with one or the other dominating in any single locality. In addition, the barrios themselves are clustered in accordance with the regional origins of the inhabitants, and this clustering has occasioned the bisection of the outer rings of the city. If a line were to be drawn from the airport through the center of the plaza to the Equipetrol section, all of Zones 3 and 4 to the west of the line would be predominantly Kolla, and all of the same zones to the east would be Camba.

The pattern of migrant barrios emerged initially from the location of major transportation routes. When the Brazilian and Argentine railroads were constructed, they opened communication along the routes with many inhabitants who were living in relative isolation. The inevitable outcome of this increased contact was migration from the hinterlands. Since both railroads terminate in the southeastern part of the city, it was here that many of these Camba migrants found themselves settling. Because of heightened commercial activity in the railroad areas, Santa Cruz began to grow toward the railroads. When the limits of outward growth had reached the terminal yards, the urban spread began to move toward the northeast section of the city. Much of the area to the south was already occupied by industrial centers such as the oil refinery and the San Aurelio sugar mill. The airport also constituted a considerable barrier to settlement toward the southwest. At the same time, lowland migrants were arriving from the north via the Santa Cruz–Montero highway. These new arrivals acquired property on either side of the northern entrance to Santa Cruz, but settlement toward the west was inhibited by the presence of the Equipetrol-Guapay complex. Migrants from the north were therefore forced by circumstances to expand housing areas toward the northeastern sector of the city. Thus the zones situated between the airport and Equipetrol on the eastern side of Santa Cruz became predominantly Camba migrant barrios.

Coinciding with the settlement of lowlanders in the eastern half of the city was the establishment of highland migrant barrios in the west. The Santa Cruz–Cochabamba highway enters the city from the southwest, so early migrants from the interior sought homes in this area. A large open market, Las Ramadas, also began to develop near the entry point of the highway adding further incentive, among Kolla women in particular, to settle in this sector of the city. Thus the western half of Santa Cruz as bounded by Equipetrol and the airport became a highland stronghold.

Recent settlement in these areas can no longer be attributed primarily to the migrant's point of entry. Once the new barrios began to grow, additional residents were recruited largely as the result of chain migration. Either through family networks or by word of mouth, both Kollas and Cambas contemplating the move to Santa Cruz have a good idea of where they would prefer to establish residence. In many instances relatives or friends provide temporary housing for the newly arrived migrants and their families. If these supports do not exist, migrants in need of shelter tend to search first in those barrios where people from their particular region make their homes. However, because of the present housing shortage in the city, many migrants now are forced to rent a room or house in any area that offers a vacancy. One informant said that it had taken her three weeks to find a small room to rent. In the meantime, one of the barrio residents where she first arrived let her sleep in a corner of the kitchen—for a small fee. This pressure for inexpensive housing has led to the opening of land beyond the fourth anillo although most is still sparsely populated. In these "urban pioneering" sectors the population is heterogeneous, with both Cambas and Kollas occupying contiguous homesites. Although Camba or Kolla ethnic barriers no doubt will continue to persist, current trends indicate that as housing demands increase, newer migrant settlement zones will be more integrated than the older ones.

Similarities in Migrant Barrios

Although ethnic differences have tended to dichotomize highland and lowland migrant barrios, both districts exhibit important similarities in settlement patterns and processes. One of these is the sequence of settlement. As a general rule, property owners in the migrant barrios who live closer to the center of Santa Cruz are the older residents in the neighborhood and have the better homes. This effect appears to be simply one of time and space rather than one of social ranking. Because the city grew outward concentrically, the areas nearest the center of Santa Cruz were settled first, and subsequent settlement gradually moved toward the outer fringes of the neighborhood. Barrio stabilization also follows this pattern. Greater numbers of permanent structures are evident in areas where settlement began, while temporary dwellings dominate the more recently settled parts of the barrio.

In addition to similar settlement sequences and stabilization, both migrant areas exhibit an economic heterogeneity of residents as inferred from differences in housing. In the older sections of migrant barrios, or those nearer the urban center, the disparity in housing between the more and the less affluent is not so pronounced. Most housing is brick construction with tile roofs. Wealthier residents built their homes at the outset of settlement and may have added on to them over the years. Poorer residents also have brick homes, but they are usually smaller and less complex in design and took longer to build. For this segment of the barrio population it has been time rather than wealth that has permitted the transition to a permanent structure. Many inhabitants spent years acquiring brick, cement, and other building materials before they finally were able to construct a better home. The same succession of events is occurring in the more recently settled areas of the migrant barrios where stabilization is still in process. On any street in a newer section of the migrant neighborhood, a variety of housing types is evident.

In 1975, the highland barrio called 4 de Noviembre had been in existence for about six years and represented the outward expansion of another barrio, Villa San Luís. Because the barrio was a newer settlement and still in a state of flux, it was a good example of migrant housing progression. On one street consisting of twenty lots, ten on either side, the following assortment of houses was in evidence:

Three large, substantial brick homes with tile roofs and such amenities as mosaic tile floors, curtains at the windows, lawns and flower beds, one home boasting a small swimming pool, all three surrounded by high masonry walls

Two large, substantial homes, tile roofs, unfinished but inhabited, neither walled or fenced and only partially furnished

Four smaller brick homes consisting of two or three rooms, one house with a surrounding wall

One adobe brick house with tile roof, one room

Two combinations of two houses, one small masonry and one wattle and daub with thatched roof

Five *lámina* houses, one or two rooms. "Lámina" is the term used for the refuse of the veneer factory. The thin sheets of wood are used like shingles to cover a rude frame. The lámina will last for only two or three years; it begins to deteriorate and must be replaced in part or in whole, but it does offer the advantage of quick, inexpensive housing.

One combination of two houses, one lámina and one small brick still under construction; the owners live in the lámina house.

Two vacant lots for sale

The owners of the three large, uncompleted homes constructed their residences soon after the lots were purchased. Of the two large homes still unfinished, one was used as rental property by the owner who lived in a barrio nearer to the center of town. The rent for this home, which was still greatly lacking in comforts (walls were unfinished mortar and there was nothing but bare dirt surrounding the exterior) was $175 (U.S.) a month. The price was steep by any standard but is indicative of the housing pressures being experienced by Santa Cruz. The other unfinished home was being built in stages by its owner, a mason, and superseded a lámina structure which earlier housed the family. Owners of the remaining residences were gradually working toward property improvement, with the exception of those involved in the business of renting.

By 1980 this same barrio had undergone a remarkable transformation. The streets had been paved with locetas and all temporary housing had disappeared. While the renting of rooms was still prevalent, most homes were occupied by the owner as well. The overall appearance of the barrio had changed from one of rude housing and muddy streets to a settled, working-class neighborhood.

It is not uncommon for migrants to rent a room or rooms in their home from time to time for the purpose of increasing family cash income. For many, it is a convenient way to accumulate money for the further improvement of their dwellings. However, there also is a certain amount of slumlording in the migrant barrios, especially in Kolla settlements. These property owners have built inexpensive housing for the express purpose of financial gain. Their primary interest, like slumlords everywhere, is not in improving their property but in extracting as much profit as possible from it. A few of these landlords may live on the premises, but most reside in a separate home in the same barrio or in another. As the neighborhood begins to stabilize and more permanent homes are constructed, property values increase. Ultimately it becomes more profitable to sell the substandard dwellings than to maintain them. (A "standard" home as defined by CORDECRUZ is masonry or finished lumber construction with a permanent roof, not thatch, flooring, piped-in water, electricity, and sanitary facilities.) The second or third owners eventually tear down the old rental housing and replace it with a single-family masonry home.

Despite individual efforts to upgrade living environments, migrant barrios are usually classified as peripheral city slums. However, as indicated, when such areas are permitted to follow the natural course of their development, substandard housing is eventually eliminated. John Turner (1970) has described a similar situation for the barriadas of Lima, which, like Santa Cruz, begin with low-cost, poor quality housing but evolve over time into residential areas of at least standard if not above-standard homes. Because of high motivation and initiative, migrants work toward the betterment of their property, contributing both time and materials to the effort. Unfortunately, this improvement may take as long as twenty years, which most urban planners find unacceptable. Hence, many cities have become involved in costly projects of instant development. Turner argues that large expenditures of public monies are basically unnecessary and even wasteful when applied to urban renewal projects for a city's migrant population. Not only are these programs costly, but they operate on principles that do not necessarily apply to the situation at hand. He proposes that

> The principle of minimum modern standards is based on three assumptions: that high structural and equipment standards take precedence over high space standards; that households can and should move when their socioeconomic status has changed so that they can afford to have a larger (above minimum) standard dwelling; and that the function of the house is, above all, to provide a hygenic and comfortable shelter. While these assumptions are valid in the United States, they do not hold true for such countries as Peru, Turkey, and the Philippines. (1970:2)

Given the opportunity, he continues, most migrant families "show that they prefer to live in large unfinished houses—or even large shacks—than in small finished ones" (Turner 1970:2).

Turner's observations are true for Santa Cruz as well. Over time, what was initially an area of lámina shacks and mud houses becomes a residential sector of primarily standard housing which in the long run is better constructed, has more living area, and was probably less expensive to build than the typical mass-produced urban renewal unit. The problem, of course, is time, and Cruceñan city planners continually ponder various urban development schemes to replace the migrant barrios with CONAVI-type housing.

Aside from the problem inherent in the disruption of an orderly and positive progression of development, the removal of the existing migrant settlements would have other far-reaching repercussions. Much of the vitality of the migrant barrio lies in the socioeconomic diversity of the inhabitants. A renewal project would tend to level this diversity, resulting in a homogeneous population based primarily on poverty. A sure outcome of such a program, which has numerous worldwide precedents, is the creation of a newer and more expensive slum but one with little hope for improvement. The migrant barrios of Santa Cruz are testimony to the belief that the individual initiative of migrants and their willingness to work and sacrifice for a larger, nicer home are perhaps better answers to problems of urban development than instant housing. It is certainly a much less costly proposition and one that holds some promise of creating a more viable and enduring social environment.

In looking at the great socioeconomic diversity in the Santa Cruz migrant barrios, one is struck with the inevitable question of site selection by the more affluent residents. Some barrio inhabitants were from the outset financially capable of moving into established neighborhoods, so why did they choose to build their homes in a raw, underdeveloped sector of Santa Cruz? For many, ethnic solidarity is an important factor: they simply prefer to live in areas where fellow villagers or people from the same region reside. But additional possibilities must also be considered when dealing with the financially elite of any barrio.

When asked why a particular lot in a migrant barrio was chosen, several informants replied that cost was a major consideration. They wanted a spacious homesite at a reasonable price, and it did not really matter where the lot was located. This type of situation exemplifies some basic differences in attitudes among the city's population toward space allocation. The middle- and upper-income residents of Santa Cruz who have purchased homes in the Americas district, Equipetrol, Guapay, and even the CONAVI project have adopted the middle-class North American model of externalizing space. There is a conscious effort to expand the visual field of exterior space: the homes are usually built in the center of the lot, surrounded with wide lawns and flower beds, and if a security barrier is present, it is normally an iron fence rather than a wall. The more traditional custom is to internalize the use of space, the prevalent pattern in migrant neighborhoods. Houses are built either right to the property limits with inner courtyards or are surrounded by a high masonry wall. Once an affluent barrio resident has entered the privacy of his home compound, it does not matter who his neighbors are or what their living conditions may be.

The existence of a handful of relatively well-to-do residents in each migrant barrio may also be related to prevailing attitudes regarding the achievement of a high status position in society. On a city-wide income scale, the affluent barrio dwellers probably would not fall into the upper-income bracket. If they moved into a typical middle-income Cruceñan neighborhood, it would be difficult to distinguish them economically from the other residents. However, in the barrio the contrast is immediately apparent, and persons of only average income are "wealthy" compared to the majority of their neighbors. Often the affluent members of the barrio are entrusted with or assume numerous leadership responsibilities and soon occupy positions of power. One stated that he was often asked to be the compadre of neighbors and that they sought his advice on important personal matters. He also expressed the belief that the barrio needed him and that it was his responsibility to respond to this need. Borrowing money is not encouraged, but many barrio "patróns" will furnish a small loan from time to time. Thus it becomes evident that although migrant barrios represent a disruption of previous life-styles and patterns of interaction, the continuity of traditional social institutions such as the patron-client relationship remains basically undisturbed.

Differences in Migrant Barrios

While all migrant barrios demonstrate certain similarities in settlement patterns and characteristics, there are also recognizable differences between highland and lowland residential areas. These differences may be attributed in large part to the cultural traditions and adaptive strategies intrinsic to each group.

Although highland housing types are not particularly suited to the lowland environment, they are much in evidence in the migrant barrios of Santa Cruz. For many recent arrivals, the rapid construction of an inexpensive shelter is of paramount importance, and most are not concerned with whether what they consider to be a temporary structure may be the ideal design for their present habitat. Too, many newly arrived migrants from the interior have little or no knowledge of lowland technologies or simply may not perceive the disadvantages of traditional highland architecture. So each highland barrio has numerous adobe brick homes, in contrast to the Camba neighborhoods which tend toward mud-and-wattle construction of non-permanent dwellings.

The primary objection to adobe brick is that after the foundations have been continually soaked by the Cruceñan rains, the entire building becomes unsound. The mud-and-wattle house, on the other hand, has embedded wooden posts, and even if the mud walls eventually melt away, the original weight-bearing structure remains intact. Another problem with adobe houses in the lowlands is the builder's failure to recognize the need to extend the roof overhang. In the interior of Bolivia, where humidity is low and rain infrequent, it is not necessary to protect adobe walls from rain wash. But in the lowlands, even permanent masonry structures have ample roof coverage to combat the erosive effect of constant dampness. After experiencing the problems of deterioration of walls of traditional adobe dwellings, many highlanders modify the design by raising foundations and extending the roof overhang.

For these and other reasons, lámina houses are not popular among lowland migrants. Not only do they leak and get soggy after long periods of rain, but they are also overrun by all manner of pests. Highlanders are accustomed to a relatively dry and insect-free existence; by building a lámina house, they magnify all the problems of a moist, bug-ridden environment. After only a few months of habitation, lámina dwellings with all their cracks, crevices, and overlapping shingles become infested with cockroaches, spiders, scorpions, centipedes, and ticks. Yet they are the cheapest, fastest house to build and require little construction expertise, so they have become abundant in the Kolla barrios. Cambas prefer to remain with their mud-and-wattle pauhuichi. It may take somewhat longer to build and require a good bit of skill, but most males and females as well have knowledge of the techniques involved and can erect at least a frame with roof cover in a matter of days.

Another basic difference in the housing patterns of the migrant settlement zones is the existence of two-story structures in the highland neighborhoods. In many villages in the interior, it is common to find two-story adobe buildings, the upper floor a sleeping area and the ground floor reserved for family activities and perhaps cooking. In the highlands, cold rather than heat is the dominant climatic feature, and a two-story home maximizes warmth from below that is trapped on the second floor. Needs are reversed in Santa Cruz, and ceilings and roofs are high in order to dissipate heat from within. In addition to heat buildup, a two-story structure in Santa Cruz must be able to withstand strong rains and wind, which cannot be accomplished with traditional lowland construction materials. Consequently, design requirements combined with a lack of cultural precedent have inhibited the building of two-story dwellings in the Camba barrios.

The few highlanders who have erected two-story homes in the migrant areas are the affluent residents. By necessity, these are masonry structures with reinforced concrete roof and wall supports, massive and expensive to build. Whether anyone has ever attempted to build a two-story adobe brick house in the city is unknown, but the absence of this common highland type of dwelling indicates that at some point its lack of feasibility became apparent.

The most noticeable contrast between the two migrant areas is the high population density of the highland barrios, manifested both in housing types and in the number of dwelling units per lot. Camba neighborhoods exhibit a fairly uniform pattern of a single house per lot, inhabited by a nuclear family or a group of extended kin. As noted, a spare room may be rented to a recent arrival, but this person is seldom unrelated to the homeowner. There are few cases of additional housing having been built to accommodate renters. Conversely, the highland migrant barrios are filled with rental complexes composed of numerous small lámina shacks or other small buildings, or one or two "long houses" with separate rooms which house several families, or a combination of both. Rents are high and space at a premium.

Along with the highland practice of filling all available space with some type of rentable shelter, it is common to find large numbers of individuals living in a single room. One rental complex of four rooms, each measuring approximately 3 by 4 meters, was occupied by twenty-two persons. The lot, 15 by 20 meters, also contained a covered shed where cotton mattresses and pillows were made. The inhabitants of this complex were unrelated families and were all employed at the bedding factory. A similar situation had three separate dwellings: a small brick kiosk where the property owner and her family lived, a lámina house of three rooms rented by two sisters and their families and an unmarried seamstress, and a third building that demonstrated some building ingenuity. It would have to be classified as a type of wattle and daub, except that the "wattle" consisted of lengths of clay sewer pipe which had been placed vertically side by side and the interstices filled with mud. This structure housed two families, unrelated to each other or to any of the other residents in the complex.

There are several possible explanations for the high population and housing unit densities among highland migrants compared to the Cambas. Because of the scarcity of arable land in the highlands, settlements tend to be located on terrain that is least suited for crops. When houses do occupy arable property, they are densely clustered so as to take up as little room as possible. It is common to find dispersed homesteads but ones that may combine several nuclear families of one kin group into a single living compound. William Carter (1967), writing on the Aymara, refers to these kinship groups as *unidades domesticas* (domestic units); Daniel Heyduk (1971) speaks of homesteads consisting of extended Quechua families. There is no doubt that a parallel can be drawn between the domestic unit or extended kin compounds found among Kollas in the highlands and the complex prevalent in the highland migrant barrios of Santa Cruz. However, as will be discussed, most migrants in the city of Santa Cruz did not come originally or directly from a rural situation, and information is generally lacking on urban life styles among the lower-income groups, in which may be found the majority of migrants. All that can be said of this aspect of residence compounds is that there are precedents in the highlands, but any direct relationship would be difficult to substantiate. The tradition is there, but it may be a generation or two removed from those who actually migrate.

That lowlanders do not encourage numerous related or unrelated individuals living together is evidenced not only by their housing preferences but also by their persistent sense of independence. Self-reliance is a cultural ideal among the Camba, and it is a great part of individual pride, *orgullo personal*, to be able to establish a household separate from familial assistance and interference. Even many of the elderly, if they are not infirm, choose to remain alone in their own homes rather than be taken in by a younger member of the family. It is only when no other option is available that an extended family will occupy one place of habitation. The idea of intentionally structuring one's dwelling so as to invite residence from persons who are not part of the nuclear family is incomprehensible to the Camba. They are still people of the frontier, and like other frontiersmen begin to feel uncomfortable when their relatives and neighbors are too close at hand. Highlanders and lowlanders seem simply to differ in their personal space boundaries, so what is unbearable crowding to a Camba may be a desirable and comforting existence for the Kolla. During the course of interviews in 1975 and 1980, highland migrants mentioned dissatisfaction with their physical environment but were generally unconcerned about the number of people who surrounded them. Only when personal animosities prevailed was there any expressed desire to seek a new social environment. Cambas, on the other hand, frequently complained about having to share their home with a renter out of financial necessity.

Another factor that must be considered in analyzing the disparity in settlement densities is the growing number of highlanders coming to the lowlands. The study of migration trends carried out in 1979 by the Instituto Nacional de Estadística indicates that almost 44 percent of the population in the city of Santa Cruz can be classed as migrant. Of this percentage, 38 percent are highland migrants, 51 percent are lowlanders who have moved to the city, and 11 percent are from nations other than Bolivia. Although Camba migrants still outnumber their Kolla counterparts, it should be noted that rates of migration for the groups are unequal. The lowland migrants have been moving into the city of Santa Cruz over several decades, a process that actually began with the city's founding. The advent of intensive immigration to the lowlands by Kollas is a relatively recent phenomenon. Most Cruceñans place the beginning of large flows of highland migrants into the area at about 1969, coincidental with the cotton boom. Since that time the number of highlanders in the city of Santa Cruz has continued to increase steadily. It may be, then, that simple housing pressures combined with a desire to locate near one's kin or countrymen are creating the notable population and dwelling unit densities in the highland migrant zones.

If Cambas suddenly were to embark upon construction of rental units in their neighborhoods, it is reasonable to assume that most would profit from the venture. The scarcity of housing is such that even the Kollas' tenacity in staying with their own people would be overcome. Two factors have inhibited the entrance of lowlanders into the rental market, at least until now. Cambas do not want to live with Kollas and generally have a greater animosity toward highlanders than the latter have toward Cambas, and lowlanders do not conceive of their homes as primarily a source of income. A small store may occupy a front room, but it is uncharacteristic of Cambas to threaten the sanctity of their home by allowing strangers, let alone Kollas, to reside there.

On the other hand, entrepreneurship and commercial enterprise are very much a part of the highland migrant experience in Santa Cruz. As noted, the majority of those migrating from the highlands to the city of Santa Cruz are not rural people. They may have been born in a small agricultural community but have long since traded that existence for urban life in one of Bolivia's highland cities before migrating to Santa Cruz. In many ways these migrants are similar to the Peruvian criollo/cholo described by Ozzie Simmons. According to Simmons, "The term cholo is reserved for those 'Indians' who are rapidly acculturating to the mestizo culture group but have not yet 'arrived.' A cholo may be classified as more or less criollo, depending on the degree of his orientation to the criollo outlook." This criollo outlook is characterized by "shrewdness, ingenuity, guilefulness, and the ability to be very good at verbal persuasion" (Simmons 1955: 108–11). Simmons also notes that the criollo businessman is always on the lookout for a better way to turn a quick profit and will stop at little to achieve this end. Many of the highlanders arriving in the city of Santa Cruz appear to exhibit the same propensity for shrewd business dealings as the Peruvian criollo. Lowlanders often relate the tale of the little highland woman sitting on a street corner selling oranges who, after ten years of manipulating her income, bought several new cargo trucks and opened her own transport company. Although these rags-to-riches stories are well publicized, in reality such occurrences are rare. Even so, it has become an integral part of highland migrant existence to approach any situation as a potential business opportunity. Thus rental housing is simply another way to expand one's earning capacity. To the highlander a piece of property in the city of Santa Cruz has negotiable value and is not necessarily perceived in terms of its intrinsic worth as a sacrosanct place of habitation.

As an outgrowth of the rental/nonrental dichotomy between highland and Camba barrios, stabilization of the two migrant zones is proceeding at an unequal rate. Because most properties in the lowland sectors do not have to go through the rental transition, permanent structures tend to be built earlier. In comparing one highland barrio with a lowland neighborhood of approximately the same age, more masonry homes were evident in the Camba neighborhood. In both areas informants did not demonstrate any appreciable difference in levels of income that might account for earlier stabilization in the Camba area.

Finally, the highland barrio remains distinct from its lowland counterpart in one additional aspect—the presence of the chichería. The drinking of corn beer, or chicha, is an important tradition among rural as well as urban highlanders. Although some Cambas will admit to liking chicha, they do not know how to prepare it and do not patronize the establishments where it is served. (Lowlanders prepare a nonalcoholic chicha made from boiled cornmeal, sugar, and flavoring, but it is a rare Camba who is familiar with the three-day-long procedure of making alcoholic chicha.) The chichería remains a stronghold of highland culture, where Quechua and Aymara may be spoken freely, highland music is enjoyed, and traditional dancing occurs. Rowdiness and violence often accompany the gaiety and song that characterize the business hours of the chichería—hours that conform only to the whims of the patrons but which reach maximum popularity on Saturday and Sunday nights. Although Cambas certainly are not parlor-sitters when it comes to drinking, they complain bitterly about the raucous behavior of Kollas in their chicherías. In many Camba neighborhoods, the informal negative sanctions against chicherías are so strong that local police officials are instructed to put pressure on any individual attempting to open an establishment to cater to the few highland residents there. Perhaps because Cruceñans are excluded by their own prejudices as well as by highland censure from participation in beer festivities, the chichería has taken on almost satanic dimensions. In 1975, after the owner of an uncompleted structure intended for chicha sale died without beneficiary, the city fathers expropriated the building and posted this sign:

> Este local antes fue una chichería. Ahora será una escuela, dentro de la campaña de moralización emprendida por la H. Alcaldía Municipal. Desde hoy este local cumplirá una función altamente social. (signed) Intendencia

> (This site previously was a chichería. Now it will be a school, as part of the moralization campaign undertaken by City Hall. From today on this expropriated site will fulfill a highly social function. [signed] Police Department.)

As a result of the criticism levied against chicherías by Cambas, many urban highlanders, in their new cultural context, began to look askance at this institution. Much of this debate was advanced by women, many of whom resented the weekly spending by husbands in the neighborhood chichería. One woman, referring to her spouse who was still unconscious from a previous night's drinking bout, stated in disgust, "Los hombres son unos chulupis; no sirven para más que tomar chicha. Las mujeres son las que tienen que trabajar" ("Men are cockroaches; they aren't any good except for drinking chicha. Women are the ones who have to work").

The negative sanctions directed toward chicherías by the Cruceñan community and by increasing numbers of highland migrants have resulted in certain building design modifications, but only of the chicherías within the city of Santa Cruz. In outlying areas the social pressures and official harassments are not so great, and the traditional building style has prevailed. In the highlands, there is no attempt to conceal the chichería: the drinking areas are built facing the street, with the family living quarters located above or to the rear of the property. Efforts are made in Santa Cruz to hide the existence of a chichería, but they are usually unsuccessful. In many instances the concealment only serves to attract more attention to the establishment. Most Cruceñan chicherías have the appearance of a fortress, with an extremely high masonry wall and telltale wide wooden door at the entrance. No simple homeowner would go to quite such elaborate efforts to protect his privacy, and it is not common to use a solid wooden door as an entryway, an iron gate being preferred. The wide wooden door at the chichería entrance not only marks the desire to keep out prying eyes but also is the passageway for trucks and carts laden with firewood and the huge casks used to store the brew. In spite of ongoing problems with the local population, chicherías continue to thrive in Santa Cruz and probably will as long as there are Kollas to sing, dance, and drink chicha.

By 1980, some of the public resentment toward chicherías was being redirected to the *pichicateros*, or dealers in cocaine. With the increase in the production of cocaine for international markets, local consumption of the drug, never widespread, was becoming recognized as a social problem of some magnitude. Juvenile use of cocaine, particularly in the form of *pitillos*, cigarettes laced with the drug, became an issue to be discussed by parents, the church, and the press.

Pitillos, which sell for about $4.00 (U.S.) each, are commonly produced in migrant neighborhoods, both Camba and Kolla, as a cottage industry. Because the makers of pitillos are normally connected only peripherally to big cocaine producers and are in a sense free agents, they enjoy little protection from police raids. They are frequent targets for drug busts which make good copy in the local papers but do little to threaten the industry. The use of pitillos, particularly by youth, is decried in public but has become very much a part of the Santa Cruz life-style. Among the upper classes, pure cocaine is frequently offered at parties along with food and alcohol. In Santa Cruz, cocaine is viewed from a morally ambivalent stance. As one Camba explained the dilemma, "If we keep talking about how bad it is to be involved in the cocaine trade, perhaps the world will overlook the fact that we are the producers, and we will forget as well. Then we can get on with the business."

The Santa Cruz Migrants

Since my introduction to the city of Santa Cruz in 1964, I have had many opportunities both to observe and to study the changes that have occurred over the years. My first research of the phenomenon of highland migration to the city was carried out in 1975. Five years later I had the good fortune to participate in a research project sponsored by CORDECRUZ which built on much of the data presented in my 1976 dissertation. The major distinction between the two studies was the inclusion of Camba migrants in the CORDECRUZ subsample. While my earlier work took lowlanders into account in the migration

Table 3.1. Location of Santa Cruz Informants, 1975

Barrio	Number	Percent
4 de Noviembre	17	25.8
Villa San Luís	17	25.8
Santa Rosa	14	21.2
Alto San Pedro	13	19.7
Villa Santa Rosita	5	7.6
Total	66	100.0

process, especially in the city of Santa Cruz where they presented a valuable contrast to highland migrants, the focus of the research at that time was the Kolla migrant. The later CORDECRUZ study therefore presents not only an update of the migrant process in the city of Santa Cruz and elsewhere but adds an in-depth look at the Camba migrant as well.

To ascertain the characteristics of highland migrants coming to the city of Santa Cruz in 1975, interviews were conducted in every major highland barrio, a total of sixty-six informants in five neighborhoods (table 3.1). A limit of four months was allotted to this portion of the study, and since there were no recent census data available to determine the population size of any barrio, the figures represent only the number of interviews it was possible to conduct in that time. However, subjective decisions were made about the comparative settlement density and population size of each neighborhood, so a greater number of interviews were completed in the larger barrios than in those with seemingly fewer inhabitants. Thus Villa Santa Rosita, which consisted of only four square blocks, received much less attention than Villa San Luís which covered an area of over two square kilometers.

A purposive sample was used, taking into account type of residence and distance from the city's nucleus. Informants included residents of both permanent and temporary dwelling types and migrants who lived at varying distances from downtown Santa Cruz.

An interview guide developed in the field after pilot testing was used to structure each interview to provide comparable data. But if an informant deviated from the original format, he or she was permitted to follow the line of discussion to its conclusion. A great deal of pertinent information was often elicited spontaneously by this technique.

A preponderance of females served as informants. Because interviews were conducted during the daytime, most of the males were at work elsewhere in the city, leaving females and children at home. The fact that I am a female was no doubt of considerable importance in gaining entry to many migrant residences. Most of the women were initially hesitant to admit a stranger into their homes, but once some preliminary conversation ensued, their suspicions gave way to open friendliness. A male colleague engaged in research in the same area mentioned to me that he was having difficulty being admitted to homes where only females and children were present.

Migration to lowland Bolivia has dichotomized into rural and urban flows that have tended to remain discrete units. Both groups of migrants have chosen different destinations in the lowlands: the city of Santa Cruz has attracted the urban-oriented individual while the rural migrant has headed into the northern Santa Cruz area. Santa Cruz is the focal point for both rural and urban migration among Cambas, however. Thus the majority of Kollas in the city are either not rural in origin, or, if their origins are rural, they have had exposure to an urban center in the interior before moving to the lowland capital. Of the sixty-six informants in the 1975 sample population, only seven—about 10 percent of the total—came directly from a rural highland situation; about 82 percent had either urban origins (38) or urban experience (16) prior to their taking up residence in Santa Cruz. Five informants (about 8 percent) were from road towns, semirural communities located along the Santa Cruz–Cochabamba highway. These localities are a special case: they are secondary and tertiary marketing centers with a primarily agricultural economic base. More important, contact with other urban centers via the highway was an influential factor in community organization. Road town residents were rural as well as urban in orientation, so these five informants necessitated a fourth category of migrants.

The reasons for the rural-urban settlement dichotomy in the department of Santa Cruz are several and will be discussed at varying points in the study. With regard to the city of Santa Cruz, urban highlander migrants are inclined to choose another urban setting. For rural highland migrants, the city offers no great attraction partly because of the relative ease with which rural people may obtain land in the lowlands. The rural Kolla is more likely to opt for the familiarity of an agricultural setting than chance the double jeopardy of both a new environment and a new life-style. Those migrants who do ultimately leave the lowland countryside in favor of urban residence apparently do not choose the city of Santa Cruz, however. Their af-

finities lie with family members and other rural migrants who have
made the city of Montero the center for rural-urban migrations of
Kollas in the lowland region.

The sample Santa Cruz migrant population was young. The average age of the sample group was thirty-one. Seventy-three percent of
the informants fell between the ages of eighteen and thirty-five; 4
percent were below age eighteen. Once in the lowlands, the desire to
return to the interior seems to diminish rapidly, and it was only the
older, recently arrived migrants who expressed a longing for their
mountain homes. Three of the five migrants who stated that they
would like to return to the highlands were over forty years old, a finding that also correlated with recent arrival in Santa Cruz. In each
case, the older migrant who expressed dissatisfaction with lowland
life had been there for less than two years.

For many migrants, arrival in the city of Santa Cruz was only one
of a series of successive moves. More than half of the informants in
migrant barrios reported migrations prior to the move to Santa Cruz.
For some, movement from place to place was considered an unacceptable life-style but one necessitated by economic pressures. Many,
however, expressed no concern with their seminomadic existence
and perceived continuous migration as a means of optimizing available resources. When a new opportunity arose in another locality,
the migrant household simply packed its belongings and moved on.

Chain migration was found to be an important factor in population
movement into the city of Santa Cruz, as would be expected in any
case where migration has continued over an extended period of time.
A significant number of migrants, nevertheless, made the move without the assistance of friends or relatives. One-third of the sample reported that their first place of residence in Santa Cruz was a rented
room, a hotel room, or a rented house, and that these accommodations were necessary because of a lack of known kin or other suppor-
tive networks in the region (table 3.2).

The Department of Cochabamba, the nearest highland neighbor of
Santa Cruz, supplied over half of the sample immigrant population
(table 3.3). About 17 percent originated in the Sucre area, also relatively close to the city of Santa Cruz, and the more distant highland
centers of La Paz, Oruro, and Potosí together furnished only 15 percent of the migrants.

Commercial activities by far outweighed other occupational specialties of the female informants (table 3.4). Twenty-nine of the fifty-
one women interviewed listed marketing or related activities as their

Table 3.2. Santa Cruz Migrants' First Place of Residence, 1975

Place	Number	Percent
Relatives	24	36.4
Rental	15	22.7
Friend/employer	14	21.2
Room	7	10.6
No data	5	7.6
Fictive kin	1	1.5
Total	66	100.0

Table 3.3. Santa Cruz Migrants' Origins by Region, 1975

Origin	Number	Percent
Cochabamba	37	56.1
Chuquisaca (Sucre)	11	16.7
Other	8	12.1
Oruro	4	6.1
Potosí	3	4.5
La Paz	3	4.5
Total	66	100.0

Table 3.4. Female Informants' Occupations, City of Santa Cruz, 1975

Occupation	Number	Percent
Commercial activity	29	56.9
Home employment	12	23.5
Servant	1	2.0
None	9	17.6
Total	51	100.0

principal source of income. Among highlanders, it has become a tradition for women to engage in much of the marketing activity. The market itself is an integral part of highland life, with certain days of each week set aside at particular localities for buying and selling. For lowland inhabitants, however, markets are a somewhat alien experience. The area has not been entirely devoid of markets, but until there was a substantial increase in highland entrepreneurs, the only open marketplaces in the department were in the city itself. Other communities depended in large part on small household stores, the pulperías, for foodstuffs and merchandise.

The marketing system in the lowlands differs qualitatively from the highland system of produce exchange in that goods are carried

into Santa Cruz by men and wholesaled to vendors who do the resell-
ing. In the highlands this system may also occur, but it is also common for females to grow, transport, and market their own produce,
giving up no profit to a middleman. At the same time, until the advent of highland migration, there were no special market days in
Santa Cruz, or *ferias*, as these temporal markets are known in the interior. The two main markets in Santa Cruz, Los Pozos and El Mercado Nuevo, operated continually during the week and on Saturday,
with only a few vendors engaging in commerce on Sunday until the
arrival of highlanders. Santa Cruz now boasts several ferias, open on
specified days and on Sundays. The custom of Sunday market, so
popular in the highlands, has had an enthusiastic reception in the
lowlands. Whereas Sunday was never considered by Cambas to be a
big market day, most lowland women now eagerly board buses and
taxis to shop on that day. Along with the ferias, Los Pozos and other
markets do their best business on Sundays. Three streets near the
second anillo are closed to traffic on this day, and the area is converted into a huge shopping mall. A multitude of cargo trucks from
Cochabamba and other highland areas arrive in Santa Cruz every Saturday night. By dawn the next morning they are parked in streets by
the downtown markets and throughout the area closed to vehicular
traffic. Fresh produce, fish from highland streams, dried llama meat
and mutton, herbs, and medicinal cures are all dispensed from the
beds of trucks to the throng of Sunday shoppers.

Kolla success in marketing may be attributed not only to the preference of highlanders, especially women, to pursue commercial activity but also to the lack of lowland participation in open markets.
Even in the city of Santa Cruz, where the open market has existed for
some time, going to the market was not a daily or even weekly occurrence among Camba women. It had always been more convenient to
patronize the neighborhood pulpería where credit buying could be
done. Pulpería owners traditionally did business with the large markets, since they were the source of wholesale items, but until recently the average Cruceñan homemaker stocked her kitchen from
the neighborhood food store, not from the market. The arrival of
highlanders in the city brought the introduction of bargaining in
markets, more competitive prices, and a greater selection of foodstuffs. Many Camba women realized that they could save a good deal
of money by going to a market when cash buying was done. Highlanders also initiated the daily shipment of fresh vegetables and other
produce from highland truck-gardening centers. The Camba diet had

never included such items as lettuce, tomatoes, carrots, bell peppers, cucumbers, radishes, and green beans, but the exclusion of these foods were due to lack of availability, not to lack of dietary acceptance. Kollas began transporting fresh produce on a large scale, and lowlanders as well as the migrant population from the interior flocked to the markets to buy it.

Lowland vendors in the Santa Cruz markets are now few in number since most of their *puestos* (stalls) have been taken over by the more astute highland entrepreneurs. It is only in such lowland production as beef, manioc, and bananas that the Camba still prevails. Every other type of merchandising is now controlled by Kollas; even the transport industry into the lowlands and within the Camba region is largely dominated by truckers from the highlands.

The open market idea has begun to diffuse as a consequence of highland migration to the Cruceñan lowlands. Warnes, a community just north of Santa Cruz, now has two thriving open markets, run by highlanders. Montero has one large market, on a par with any in the city of Santa Cruz, and a second smaller market has been constructed in another section of the city. Camba villages as well are beginning to consider the possibilities of setting aside space for an open market to be held on specified days. In San Carlos, for example, an old Camba settlement to be discussed, funds were collected from the townspeople for the construction of a market. These monies were matched by Obras Públicas (now CORDECRUZ), and the market building was completed in 1977. By 1980, the market was dominated by highland women, except of course in the area of meat sales. The rapid takeover of the market by Kollas was met with some disgruntlement by local residents, however, who conceived the idea with thought of their own gain.

Male informants generally fell into two occupational categories: mason (*albañil*) and home employment (table 3.5). The latter included such specialties as ceramic work and the preparation of food additives and condiments. Today, the manufacture of pitillos would also fall into this category.

When female informants were asked about the occupation of their spouses, 23 replied that their husbands were employed as albañiles. Thus, 49 percent of the males who enter into the survey are employed in the construction industry. Although the literal translation of "albañil" is "mason," the term has become a generic one for anyone employed in the building trades. A man who loads and unloads bricks at a construction site will consider himself an albañil just as

Table 3.5. Male Informants' Occupations, City of Santa Cruz, 1975

Occupation	Number	Percent
Albañil	5	33.3
Home employment	5	33.3
Transport	1	6.7
Industry	1	6.7
Other	3	20.0
Total	15	100.0

will a master bricklayer. It was the flourishing construction industry, encouraged by economic surges in the past two decades, that allowed absorption of highland as well as lowland male migrants. Without this source of employment requiring little skill or training, most migrant men would have had great difficulty in establishing themselves in the city.

Another area of investigation concerned dress patterns of migrants. All males in the sample wore mestizo apparel—cotton pants and shirt—generally produced commercially. The females wore either the traditional *pollera*, a wide gathered skirt with a tie band, or mestizo clothing such as a straight skirt and blouse or a cotton dress. Many women mentioned that their Santa Cruz–born children were exerting pressure on them to discard the pollera for mestizo clothing. Those women who still wore the pollera after more than ten years' residence in the lowlands stated that they maintained the traditional clothing because they felt more comfortable and were concerned about their neighbors' criticisms of trying to "put on airs."

One woman viewed the dress controversy in economic terms. She explained that it was good business to continue wearing the pollera, especially at the market or while selling, so as not to alienate much of the migrant population. Potential Camba clients expect to see highland women in their polleras—conforming to the lowlander's stereotype of the Kolla. The female informant also related the tale of two highland women who had stores next to each other. One began to use mestizo dress. Her business began to drop off until most of her customers were patronizing her neighbor. The Kolla shopkeeper was forced to reinstate her pollera in order to salvage her business.

The illiteracy rate among the migrants sampled in 1975 was almost 60 percent (table 3.6), much higher than that of the general population, according to the 1976 census. Although illiteracy in Bolivia dropped from 68.9 percent in 1950 to 32.39 percent in 1976, there is

Table 3.6. Illiteracy in Santa Cruz Sample Population, 1975

	Literate		Illiterate		Total	
	No.	%	No.	%	No.	%
Male	10	75.0	5	25.0	15	100.0
Female	17	33.4	34	66.6	51	100.0
Total	27	40.9	39	59.1	66	100.0

a discrepancy between highland and lowland figures. The oriente of Bolivia has the lowest rates of illiteracy at 19.15 percent; the altiplano and valley regions are 32.79 percent and 40.80 percent, respectively. Illiteracy among females, particularly in the highlands, has historically been much greater than among males. The migrant survey population, consisting primarily of people from the highlands and heavily weighted with females, could be expected to be above the national average in illiteracy, which in fact it was. Those whose command of Spanish was negligible or limited had a much higher illiteracy rate than those who had a functional use of Spanish, likely a reflection of a greater incidence of illiteracy among rural-born people and females who did not have equal access to an education where Spanish use and literacy are usually linked. Although there was a general trend toward the use of Spanish as length of habitation in Santa Cruz increased, many individuals who had been in the lowlands for ten years or more continued to be monolingual speakers of an indigenous language, usually Quechua. Many others had only limited ability in Spanish, a likely result of the lack of integration between the highland and lowland populations of the city. Highlanders live in relative isolation in their own barrios where Quechua is heard more often than Spanish. Even outside of the barrio, only a minimal amount of Spanish is needed to engage in trade.

The children of migrants who were attending Santa Cruz schools were striving toward bilingualism and, in many cases, monolingual use of Spanish. Forty-one of the sixty-six informants had children, and a large majority of these claimed that their children were unable to speak the indigenous language of their parents. Many immigrants stated that their sons and daughters could understand Quechua but refused to speak it. Parents of these children believed that peer pressure by Camba playmates at school inhibited their offspring from using the language spoken in the home. Some informants resented the situation, but most seemed pleased that their children were choos-

Table 3.7. Santa Cruz Migrants' Motives for Migration, 1975

Motive	Number	Percent
To find work	36	54.6
To accompany relative	11	16.7
Contracted to work harvest	6	9.1
Contracted to work	5	7.6
Visiting	3	4.5
Runaway	3	4.5
To accompany spouse	2	3.0
Total	66	100.0

ing the lowland life-style, thereby hastening the acculturation of the younger generation of highland migrants.

The reasons given for migration to Santa Cruz fell into six categories (table 3.7). Economic incentives were named by over half of the total sample population, and although other motives may have been offered, often they too were related to some economic purpose. For example, thirteen informants stated that they came to the lowlands to accompany a spouse, parents, or other relatives. The spouse or parents, however, were often lured to Santa Cruz by the promise of economic gain. Another eleven informants came to the lowlands as contract workers, either as harvesters or as employees of private individuals. The only categories that cannot be linked with economic interests are "runaway" and "visiting," and the latter is suspect in that all three informants admitted that while they were in Santa Cruz visiting relatives, they had taken advantage of the time to look for employment. In the case of Santa Cruz, economic incentives were foremost in the decision to migrate from the interior. One young informant, when queried as to why she had left the highlands, could reply only with a look of amused disbelief. The implication of her response was that the reason should be obvious. Finally, in exasperation, she said, "Para ganar, pués!" ("To earn money, of course!").

As might be anticipated in a situation of constant flux such as is found in the migrant barrios of Santa Cruz, those among the sample population who own homes rank only slightly higher than those who are renting (table 3.8). Another segment of the sample, approximately 20 percent, lived with other family members. There was a moderate relationship between length of residence and homeownership; residents who had been in Santa Cruz longer tend to own their homes. This finding was not unexpected: few migrants arrive in

Table 3.8. Santa Cruz Housing, 1975

Type of Housing	Number	Percent
Own	27	40.9
Rent	26	39.4
Live with relative	13	19.7
Total	66	100.0

the lowlands with sufficient capital to allow for the immediate purchase of a home or a building site. Most of the migrants questioned
did not own homes until after the fourth or fifth year of residence in
the city.

Another ratio emerged between those who had prior contact with
the lowlands and those who had no previous knowledge of the area.
Over 59 percent of the sample population had never been to Santa
Cruz before deciding to migrate, though a large segment of the migrants reported prior acquaintance with the region. Several of the
male informants and spouses of female migrants gave military service in the lowlands as the reason for initial contact. Others had
come on marketing trips, and a small number had worked the harvests. Although migrants with previous knowledge of the area stated
that familiarity with Santa Cruz made the decision to leave the highlands easier, over half of the sample made the trip blindly or with
secondhand information.

Finally, two-thirds of the 1975 informants stated that they had relatives in other areas of the lowlands. While these kin were often distant in degree as well as location, migrants seemed concerned with
keeping track of as many relations as possible. They knew that as city
residents they might be called upon to provide shelter for a variety of
visiting uncles, cousins, or fictive kin from the hinterlands of Santa
Cruz. At the same time, country kin could provide work as well as
diversion for the city-bound children of Santa Cruz migrants. Family
networks are a strategic factor for the migrant in successful adaptation since employment and housing often may be obtained only by
word of mouth. Even the most casual acquaintance is carefully nur-
tured for possible future utilization.

In 1979 the Dirección Departamental de Estadística (DDE) of Santa
Cruz undertook a study of migration based on surveys of 1,574 households selected at random from census tracts, about 7 percent of the
city's population as enumerated in the 1976 national census. From
this sample, another subsample of 53 households was selected ran-

domly for in-depth interviews in 1980. Fortunately I was in Bolivia
at the time and was able to participate in the second segment of the
study. Forty-four of the 53 households chosen in the subsample for a
return interview were locatable. Of the four localities we surveyed
(Santa Cruz, Warnes, Montero, and Villa Busch) Santa Cruz, the
largest and most urban population center, had the lowest number of
missing cases, 17 percent. Although the subsample was small, its re-
sponses supported the view that when migrants reach the city of
Santa Cruz, it is ideally their last major relocation although additional moves may occur within the city itself.

The DDE study added another dimension to the migrant picture in
that Cambas as well as Kollas were interviewed. And, because the
sample was taken randomly from the whole city, the inner city received greater representation than outlying migrant barrios because a
larger number of census tracts are located in the core area where population is denser. My 1975 study had been concentrated mainly on peripheral migrant neighborhoods and therefore showed less diversity
in population characteristics, particularly in such areas as occupation. Of the forty-four completed interviews in the DDE study, eighteen informants were highlanders, seventeen were lowlanders, and
nine were of foreign birth. Once again, Cochabamba, the highland
city nearest Santa Cruz, represented the place of origin of most Kolla
migrants (table 3.9).

Several factors may have caused the increase of 16 percent in migrants from the Cochabamba area between 1975 and 1980. First, I
may have greatly underrepresented the relative number of Cochabambinos in 1975 since I did not take the entire city into account as
did the DDE. Then, distance must be considered a major factor in migration patterns. Step migrations from smaller to larger cities frequently take place in the highlands before the move to Santa Cruz is
attempted. As the closest highland city to Santa Cruz, Cochabamba
has been a jumping-off place for lowland-bound migrants. Finally,
and perhaps most important, the apparent rise in the number of Cochabambinos could also be caused by chain migration, always a significant factor in any ongoing migration process. Having family in
the lowlands is an incentive to migrate and lowers the risks for a prospective migrant. The importance of chain migration in the case of
Santa Cruz is borne out by the fact that all of the Camba and Kolla
migrants sampled claimed relatives in the lowland region, 64 percent of them living in the city of Santa Cruz.

The pattern of urban-urban migration for Kolla migrants was in

Table 3.9. Santa Cruz Migrants' Origins, 1980

Origin	Number	Percent
Kolla		
Cochabamba	13	72.0
La Paz	3	16.0
Potosí	1	6.0
Chuquisaca (Sucre)	1	6.0
Total	18	100.0
Camba		
Santa Cruz	14	82.0
Beni .	3	18.0
Total	17	100.0
Foreign		
Brazil	4	44.0
Argentina	3	33.0
Hong Kong	1	11.5
Rumania	1	11.5
Total	9	100.0

keeping with 1975 figures in that 91 percent of the highland informants claimed urban residence prior to moving to Santa Cruz. In the case of the Camba migrants, however, the reverse was true, with over 87 percent having come from rural villages. Since Santa Cruz until recently was viewed by most lowlanders as the only true city in the department, it remains in their minds as the only possible "urban" move. Santa Cruz is still referred to by many villagers as el pueblo (the town), and when one goes "to town" it can mean only the city of Santa Cruz.

The main motive for migration—economic reasons—continued to outweigh others (table 3.10). Between 1975 and 1980, Bolivia's economic situation continued to deteriorate, but Santa Cruz felt these pressures to a lesser degree, and many highlanders continue to regard eastern Bolivia as an economic mecca. It is notable that in 1980 neither "contracted to harvest" nor "runaway" showed up as categories. In addition to sampling differences, this may have happened because the cotton boom, which in the 1970s attracted people as contract laborers and offered employment and housing to minors, had bottomed out.

Because the city as a whole was surveyed in the 1979 and 1980 studies, occupational categories are more diverse than they were for 1975 (table 3.11). Those migrants living in the city's core areas have generally been in the city longer than those living in migrant barrios

Table 3.10. Santa Cruz Migrants' Motives for Migration, 1980

Motive	Number	Percent
To find work	30	68.2
To accompany spouse	5	11.3
Visiting	4	9.1
To accompany relative	2	4.6
Contracted to work	2	4.6
Political problems	1	2.2
Total	44	100.0

Table 3.11. Migrants' Occupations, City of Santa Cruz, 1980

Occupation	Number	Percent
Commercial activity	8	18.0
Service (seamstress, beauty parlor operator, salesperson, etc.)	8	18.0
Transport	7	16.0
Servant	4	9.0
Unemployed	4	9.0
Professional (lawyer, dentist, etc.)	3	7.0
Administrator, public agency	3	7.0
Home industry	3	7.0
Administrator, private company	2	4.5
Construction (albañil)	2	4.5
Total	44	100.0

on the fringe of Santa Cruz. Many of the former arrived in the city with some type of profession or learned one over the years. On the other hand, unskilled laborers tend to concentrate in the poorer fringe areas. Informal interviews in three migrant barrios indicated that the occupation "albañil" or construction worker is still important, especially among recent arrivals. Nonetheless, the DDE survey places this job category in a somewhat minor position city-wide, pointing to inconsistencies that may arise from differing sampling techniques.

As the 1975 and 1980 migration data have shown, most highland migrants in the city of Santa Cruz had urban backgrounds prior to their move to the city. The rural-urban influx of migrants is confined primarily to Cambas coming in from the countryside. The major flow of rural highlanders is directed toward the northern Santa Cruz region, where commercial farming and colonization of new lands are occurring, rather than the city. In recent years, more and more urban highlanders as well are choosing to settle in the small northern cities and towns rather than in the city of Santa Cruz. They find the cost of living lower and the competition less than in the city.

Although increasing numbers of highlanders in Santa Cruz have become part of the city's fabric, Cambas still resent what they regard as an intrusion in their territory. There is only one route to the agricultural lands of the north, and its exit from the city is marked by a huge stone statue called the Cristo Redentor. The arms are upraised with the palms thrust outward in a gesture that Cambas say, only half-jokingly, means, "Halt, no more Kollas!"

4

Warnes: Cane, Cotton, and Contract Harvesting

More than any single factor, the economic promise of Santa Cruz has encouraged the exodus of highlanders from the interior of Bolivia. Crop failures and economic stagnation certainly contributed to the desire to leave the highlands, but without some hope of a better life it is probable that the urban poor as well as peasant farmers would have continued their marginal existence with stoic acceptance. For many migrants, however, the decision to move east is not an instant one. Among those who come for the harvests, the choice to remain in the lowlands may be made only after several years of seasonal migrations. Others may decide to stay after their first trip down. Still others may continue to come year after year with no intent of ever leaving the highlands on a permanent basis. But for all, the assurance of steady wages and the security of traveling in a group with one's family and friends make harvesting the least risky of the possible options for migration to the Department of Santa Cruz. Opportunities in the region such as seasonal fieldwork provide a testing ground for those migrants who may be examining the pros and cons of leaving the highlands.

The role of the agricultural enterprise that employs Kolla migrants on contract is important in the scheme of migration and population movement in the lowlands. It is during the harvest that the highlander will be faced with many of the factors that are part of the decision to remain or not. The varied experiences that accumulate during the three to five months' labor in Santa Cruz will also have a bearing on the life-style chosen by those who decide to stay in the lowlands. For many migrants, harvesting is the springboard into a series of new and diverse strategies for adaptation.

Farmers and Harvesters

Most towns and villages in Santa Cruz have participated at least marginally in the agricultural transformation of the region, but Warnes has been in the forefront of all major farming trends in recent history. Named after the Independence War hero Ignacio Warnes, the town is located just 30 kilometers north of the city of Santa Cruz. It lies in what was originally rice country but later was converted to sugarcane, cattle, and then cotton. Prior to the 1950s, the town did not differ much from other horticultural communities in the lowlands. A great deal of the land was in forest, cut and burned on a rotational basis to plant primarily subsistence crops such as rice, manioc, and plantains. The grasslands interspersed among the forests were home to the rangy criollo cattle found throughout the region. Some sugarcane was grown and processed on family farms, primarily for local consumption. Ox-drawn presses, or *trapiches*, squeezed out the juice, which was then boiled in huge clay cauldrons, or *pailas*. The end product was a light brown sugar kept in an urn with a hole in the bottom so the molasses could run out.

It was generally known that sugarcane did well in Santa Cruz, and in the early 1950s two privately owned refineries were built. These were San Aurelio, located outside of the city of Santa Cruz, and La Bélgica, near Warnes. Within a very short time, large amounts of land went into the commercial production of sugarcane. Some of this land was cleared by bulldozers so it could be worked with tractors. Gradually, many of the small-scale farmers were bought out to consolidate their land into larger, more profitably managed holdings suitable for mechanization. The problem of *cupo* also arose as cane production began to outpace the mills' capacities for processing sugar, even in a twenty-four-hour workday. Since the refineries could not accommodate all of the cane produced, tonnage allotments, called simply "space," or *cupo*, had to be negotiated with the mill in advance of the season. The owners of the large holdings, making use of family ties and political patronage, were able to secure most of these allotments.

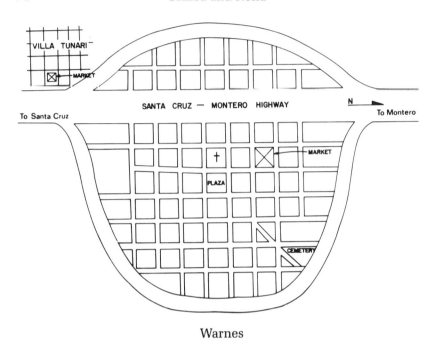

Warnes

Even today, with the Guabíra mill in operation in Montero, having cupo is imperative to successful cane growing. Few small farmers can compete on these terms.

The land around Warnes is also different now. Most of it has been cleared, and cane, cotton, or pasture dominate. To the south, near the city of Santa Cruz, much of the soil has been severely eroded by wind and rain, leaving it of little use to anyone. It supports a few head of cattle on the sparse grasses that tolerate the poor soil and drought conditions. Little is done to conserve cropland, and once yields begin to drop, the land is allowed to go to grass. Most farmers see ranching as a natural succession to crops as a way to deal with lowered soil fertility.

With the completion of the Guabirá sugar mill in Montero, the road from Santa Cruz to the refinery was paved, bypassing Warnes. As a consequence, Warnes began to grow in the direction of the highway, and many storekeepers abandoned their shops in town to set up stands along the roadside. A new market was also built in the hope of attracting passing traffic. Even today, the center of town remains quiet and dusty—a shady plaza, a well-kept church, and a cluster of houses with tile roofs, relatively unaffected by the highway to the west. Older residents point proudly to sections of Warnes that are well over a century old and have remained unchanged.

The outward quiet of the town belies the intense agricultural activity that engages many of its residents. Fortunes have been made, and continue to be made, on the land surrounding this community. Much of the profit goes to agribusinesses whose owners live in the large urban centers of the country or perhaps in foreign countries. The Warneño farmers who have done well by their land generally have not invested in their town. Instead, the money is put into homes in Santa Cruz or into farm equipment, or it is simply salted away for future need.

Warnes has weathered the vagaries of commercial agriculture in the region and has been agile in responding to market fluctuations. When blight and low prices threatened the prosperity of the cane growers, a substitute crop was found in cotton and a quick shift was made. But both cane and cotton demand hand labor for harvesting, and Santa Cruz has never been capable of meeting its own labor requirements. Most rural Cambas are themselves small farmers and have adequate acreage to satisfy their basic needs. They regard working the cane harvest as brutal and demeaning and the cotton harvest as not much better. On the other hand, the highlands have always possessed an abundance of people who through necessity or desire are eager to take on any task for a day's wage. During the season there is always work available, and the more adventuresome highlanders merely climb aboard a truck headed for the lowlands and make their way to some community such as Warnes where they are hired on the spot. Most, however, are hired by labor contractors, or *contratistas*, who arrive in the highlands with trucks and cash advances. Once a cash advance is accepted, the individual is *enganchado*, literally "hooked," and cannot back out of the arrangement.

In order to bring people legally from the interior, a contratista must be registered by the Federación de Campesinos, a farm labor organization controlled by the national government. Clandestine labor operations are supposedly kept at a minimum through the maintenance of two gates along the Cochabamba–Santa Cruz highway where all incoming trucks are inspected. The Federación also sends out representatives to individual farms, ostensibly to ascertain if living conditions for workers are adequate. Bribery is common in both cases, making actual enforcement of the rules a rare occurrence.

The farm owners are required by law to pay 2 percent of the salaries earned by harvesters to the Federación, the money to be used in the construction of schools and hospitals for rural people. Rarely will the landowner pay the full amount, however, and the Federación is forced to take what it can get. In addition, the Federación requires each grower to fill out a work sheet (*planilla*), listing by column the name of each harvester, a few vital statistics such as age, sex, and place of origin, and the daily amounts harvested. Another column represents cash advances or food items taken on credit, which will be deducted from weekly wages. The last column lists the net income of each worker. These planillas must be turned in to the Federación office in Montero at the end of the harvest. The contratista is paid a percentage of the pounds of cotton or tons of cane harvested by each worker, but this fee is supposed to be paid by the grower and not by the fieldhand. Since many contractors will attempt to collect both from growers and workers while farm owners will take the fee out of harvesters' wages, the fieldhand frequently pays twice.

Contratistas may be highlanders or Cambas. They are usually engaged by a grower who needs a certain number of harvesters, and they go into the highlands to find laborers. Some try the cities, but most search the countryside for people willing to come to the lowlands as fieldhands. After a group has been "enganchado," the members select a leader—usually a young literate male who is believed to know the ins and outs of contract harvesting. For cotton pickers, a work agreement is prepared in which the harvesters are guaranteed that they will be paid a certain price per 100 pounds of cotton picked, that they will have adequate living conditions, and that the grower will provide transportation to the nearest town for "Sundaying." The workers in turn must pledge to remain for the duration of the harvest. Once the contract has been agreed upon by the laborers and the contratista, the harvesters are loaded aboard a truck for the trip east.

Harvesters for sugarcane may be engaged in a similar manner, but not as many cutters are required to harvest cane as to pick cotton. Cane harvesters also tend to be a somewhat specialized group and do not represent a potential or actual drain on the labor pool needed for cotton harvesting. The greatest competition for workers exists among the cotton growers, not between the cane growers and cotton farmers. It is in reference to the labor needs of these two primary crops that recent changes in migration rates and settlement trends may be understood.

The road from the highlands had been open since 1954, land was plentiful, and there was seasonal work available in the canefields and on the Algodonera cotton farm monopoly. Yet highlanders were leaving the interior at only moderate rates and were not particularly visible in the lowlands. Even government-subsidized colonization projects were failing to attract the large numbers of highland Bolivians that had been expected. Then in 1969 the movement east gained momentum, and highlanders began flowing into the Department of Santa Cruz. Carmelo Durán, a Warneño explained:

When the cane crop began to fail and prices were low a lot of us began to worry. [When sugarcane production reached export levels, prices began to level off and then drop. Almost simultaneously, portions of fields became infected with blight. The adventitious appearance of cotton as an alternative crop and its high market value convinced many growers to shift to cotton cultivation.] But then the government abolished the Algodonera monopoly and everyone started planting cotton. It is primarily an export crop so we didn't need to worry about national markets so much. And European buyers were paying high prices for good quality, hand-picked cotton. I had been growing cane and still do, but not so much anymore. Cane does have the advantage that you don't need as many people to harvest it as cotton. With cane mostly men work, in groups of four to six, with perhaps one or two women to help husk it and do the cooking. But mostly men come for cane. These men seldom stay on because their families are in the interior. It isn't so much trouble finding enough cane harvesters. Also, if it takes a little longer than expected or something happens so that you can't get all the cane cut in time, the crop can just wait until next year. With cotton you only have a few weeks to get the crop in, then you lose it all. And you need a lot of people to harvest. But just about anyone can harvest cotton, it doesn't take a lot of strength. Women and children can often pick as much as a man. Now instead of just looking for men, I hire whole families.

Thus the advent of cotton farming not only increased the number of laborers needed for fieldwork, but it also diversified the labor pool. Women, children, and the elderly could accompany young men into the lowlands, and once there the incentive to return to the highlands was not so great. Entire nuclear families, extended kin, and village members could make the move simultaneously, without having to leave family members behind. But even more important, there was work available to anyone willing to go into the fields, and previously unproductive or underproductive persons could contribute substantially to family incomes. In the late 1970s, when cotton production began to slack off, seasonal migration also began to diminish somewhat. Some growers, however, were already having trouble hiring pickers as the result of stories circulating throughout the highlands of dishonest labor practices and maltreatment of workers. Still, in 1979 it was estimated that 70,000 to 80,000 campesinos came to Santa Cruz to work in either the cane or the cotton harvests (Riester et al. 1979).

The relationship established between the grower and his pickers harkens back to the old pre-Reform days of the patrón and his peones. Once on the farm, many harvesters become virtual prisoners until the harvest has ended. Only the fear of retaliation by the Federación keeps some growers from actual physical abuse of their farmhands. However, those cotton farmers who acquire a reputation for brutality frequently find themselves short of labor the following year. The "typical" grower simply treats his workers like any useful animals, providing for their minimal needs and showing little concern for their well-being.

Melfy Moreno and her husband Luís (pseudonyms) operate a Warnes cotton farm but are far from typical in their dealings with farmhands. Consequently they have earned the trust and respect of the inhabitants of a small village near Sucre, and these people return every year to work on the Moreno farm.

On their way to their farm, 30 kilometers east of Warnes, Melfy talked about the cotton business. She and her husband are both Warnes-born and had worked for the Algodonera for many years before converting some family land to cotton and trying it on their own. As Algodonera employees they both learned to speak Quechua, not fluently but adequately for communication—an unheard-of occurrence among Cambas. Melfy and Luís have a certain sympathy for their Kolla workers, but they relate to the fieldhands from a consistent stance of paternalism. The Morenos feel highlanders are children and must be guided and cared for because they are incapable of caring for themselves. When hands fall ill, Melfy administers medicine or prescribes a remedy. She also instructs her workers in the virtues of saving money and admonishes them to beware of dishonest contratistas.

The main encampment of the Moreno farm consists of a new brick house with one room for sleeping and another for storage, a pauhuichi where the overseer and his wife live, a thatched kitchen, and to the rear the two *galpones* where the harvesters are housed. Built of wattle and daub with palm-thatched roofs, the galpones are approximately 20 meters long and perhaps 10 wide. There are no windows in either building, only a door at each end. The harvesters sleep side by side along both lengths of the buildings, and movement within is restricted to a small path down the center between the feet of the occupants. A few couples have erected woven palm dividers for privacy, but the majority of harvesters sleep lined up like soldiers in a barracks. Most have constructed *chapapas*, raised platforms of tree saplings, to avoid sleeping directly on the ground. All cooking is done on open fires in front of each galpón. There is a shallow well for water but no sanitary facilities other than the woods a short distance away. In later conversations with other growers, it was evident that the housing accommodations provided by the Morenos were about average for the area.

The first galpón houses the villagers from Sucre, and the second *voluntarios*, a mixed group of harvesters who have hired on individually without the services of a contratista. Both groups have a spokesperson, each a young male, bilingual in Spanish and Quechua. Although the galpones are separated by only a short distance, and all cooking and socializing goes on in the same open space in front of both, there is little interaction between the two work groups. This seems to be the preference of the villagers, many of whom are related and whose previous propinquity and shared experiences make them an "in" group. These people have been returning to the lowlands in contingents of about eighty persons per year, approximately 6 percent of the total village population. One harvester commented that perhaps twenty villagers and their families have chosen to remain in Santa Cruz to date. If a job opportunity should arise while the villagers are in the lowlands, it is often adequate incentive to remain. Each year the Morenos have also hired several of their fieldhands for off-season work on the farm. These people, explained Melfy, ultimately purchased land farther north or moved to Montero to live and work.

Melfy and Luís pay their workers every Saturday night. At first this did not seem extraordinary, but after witnessing the complexity of the all-night event it was obvious why most growers pay less often. Some refuse to pay their harvesters until the end of the season, excusing this practice with such comments as "If I didn't withhold their pay, these people would spend it all and go home broke." Actually, withholding salaries is a common method of forcing a worker to remain for the duration of the harvest or forfeit all wages. Once the picking season has begun and harvesters have more knowledge of prices being paid, they often prefer to move from farm to farm to take advantage of labor price wars among the growers. To prevent this, growers simply withhold pay, and most pickers are hesitant in giving up even a week's wages to move to another farm unless the working conditions have become unbearable. Pickers who have signed contracts and then vacate the farm are in violation of their work agreement, but enforcement is difficult—especially in a seller's market where labor is scarce.

Weekly pay periods mean that the Morenos must have cash on hand and in the exact amounts necessary to give to each harvester. Melfy, who does most of the bookkeeping, must add up the pounds of cotton harvested by each worker, subtract any outstanding debts, and then note this final amount on an envelope with the name of the picker. The wages go inside. When payday arrives, the Morenos load their pickup truck with foodstuffs and other items from their store in Warnes. It is common for growers to provide this service, although many take advantage of their harvesters by charging exorbitant prices for the goods they bring to the farm. Melfy charges the same prices that she does in Warnes, still making a profit and at the same time maintaining goodwill among her farmhands. She continues this practice not out of any great humanitarianism, but simply because she is an astute businesswoman. If her laborers are kept content, she feels, they will continue to return each year, and the farm will not be pressed for harvesters. She is also aware that word of working conditions is carried back to the highlands by seasonal migrants, and it is better to lose a little in trade goods than risk an entire harvest.

After each harvester has received a pay envelope, Melfy, Luís, and the overseer begin weighing out foodstuffs and noting the amounts in a ledger. From time to time a special request will be made for an *encomienda*, such as a shirt or a pair of shoes which the Morenos will purchase in Santa Cruz or Montero and bring out to the worker the following week. Salary and food dispersal usually ends early Sunday morning, after which the Morenos make their way back to Warnes, and the harvesters return to the galpones for a few hours' sleep before preparing for their trip to town.

Most pickers leave the farm on Sunday morning aboard the flatbed trailer pulled by the Morenos' farm tractor. They are taken into Warnes and dropped off and will be picked up for the return trip late in the afternoon. Some harvesters use this opportunity to buy items which the Morenos have not furnished or which might be purchased in Warnes at a better price. Others are interested in going to the market to browse, talk, and eat, and then on to a chichería for the remainder of the day. Melfy noted that most of her workers make the afternoon pickup but are usually drunk. Some prefer to remain on the farm—to avoid the temptation of spending their money and to relax and wash clothes for the following week.

Sundaying is an important event in the life of a seasonal migrant in many respects. On the farm, the harvesters are isolated from information flows which could affect their strategies to remain or return. They are in the center of the lowlands but at the same time are cut off from any wider understanding of the area. About all the farm experience provides is a developing awareness of learning to deal with Camba employers and a taste of the lowlands' natural environment. In order to acquaint themselves with life-style options, harvesters must get off the farm.

When the fieldhands arrive in Warnes on Sunday morning, some go to the two small open markets in the town or into the highland barrio to drink chicha. The majority, however, head immediately for the highway and climb aboard any available transportation going to Montero. Warnes presents an interesting and useful case in comprehending migrant Sundaying choices. The town is equidistant from Santa Cruz and Montero, 30 kilometers from each, so the selection of the smaller city of Montero over the capital cannot be attributed either to factors of distance or to travel costs. The preference to go to Montero lies in other domains that ultimately have a bearing on the migrants' successful entrance into lowland life.

The city of Santa Cruz provides no substantial attraction for the Sundaying harvester. First, the route from the north terminates in the city at a point fairly distant from the location of the highland barrios so that an incoming harvester must pay an additional sum to get from the bus station to a highland neighborhood and back. Second, the highland barrios may be located in one sector of the city, but they cover a large area. Chicherías are spread out in a similar manner, and a migrant who is a novice to the city would have to walk around a good deal to find a drinking establishment to suit his tastes. Third, the markets are likewise dispersed throughout the city and generally are not contiguous to chicherías. Hence several forays are necessary to satisfy drinking and shopping needs, and only limited time is available before the return trip must be made to Warnes. Finally, most of the Kollas in the city are from urban backgrounds, have little in common with rural people, and would not freely pass on housing and employment information in an already stressed situation. There is not much to offer the Sundaying harvester in the city of Santa Cruz.

Montero, on the other hand, provides for many of the needs of the migrant harvester on short leave from the farm. Since this urban center is the topic of chapter 5, only a brief overview is necessary here. Montero is a smaller city than Santa Cruz in population and in land area. Thus its service centers are more compact and closer together. Because of its central location in the agricultural zone, Montero attracts highland harvesters and farmers from the entire northern region and, consequently, has become a stronghold of highland tradition and culture. The establishment of a highland district on the eastern outskirts of the city, where over eighty chicherías are located within an area of twelve blocks, holds tremendous attraction for the harvester and farmer on a Sunday excursion. Then, too, Montero's main market is located directly across from the highland barrio, with the Santa Cruz–Montero highway running between them. An incoming harvester need only get off a truck or bus and walk a few meters to be in the heart of the marketing and drinking areas of town where Quechua is spoken freely and camraderie runs high.

Beyond the attractions of ethnic solidarity and diversion offered by the city of Montero, there is the even more significant aspect of oral exchange. Montero is a clearinghouse of information for the rural highlander: the harvester is brought up to date on job prospects, available land, possible housing, and the current status of family, friends, and countrymen. The chichería is the principal gathering place for the Sundaying crowd, and between drinking and dancing, important information is appraised and discussed. The marketplace is another source of news, and vendors who have arrived recently from the interior relate the latest highland events. The level of interaction on this one day is so intense that the week's isolation on a farm becomes tolerable.

Sunday in Montero also has a great psychological impact on the highland migrant. The city is bustling with buyers, sellers, people looking for work, and people in search of workers. It is a scene of almost frantic prosperity and eagerness in which the harvester is quickly caught up. Friends encourage him or her to stay in the lowlands; there is a good job available, or a piece of land is being offered at a giveaway price. Dreams suddenly become reality over a pitcher of chicha. The fieldhand returns to Warnes late in the afternoon encouraged and exhilarated by the carnival atmosphere of Montero on Sunday. When the farm tractor pulls into town, tired and intoxicated harvesters climb aboard the trailer to begin another week of labor and to ponder the prospect of remaining in the lowlands.

The Townspeople

People engaged in commercial enterprises in the town of Warnes have responded enthusiastically to the increased flow of money brought about by the recent surge in the agricultural sector. A spark of interest in developing Warnes has been kindled among the townspeople with the result that a new hospital was completed in 1975 with the financial assistance of Obras Públicas, and in later years the plaza area was paved with locetas. According to the Warneños, however, with every good there must come some bad—in this case, Kollas. All of the prejudices apparent in the city of Santa Cruz are magnified in Warnes. It is a small, family-controlled town, and memories and old hatreds run deep. Even the local priest, a foreigner, was uneasy about the addition of highland families to the town's populace. No small part of this ecclesiastical and secular disfavor is rooted in the presence of the chicherías.

Across the highway and contiguous to the new market is located the Warnes highland migrant barrio, about eight blocks in which the market vendors and chichería owners reside. Another group of highlanders have settled to the rear of the central market, perhaps five families, and several vendors live in the market itself, sleeping in their stalls. There are no chicherías in the central market area, however, as it is considered within the city limits and within Camba territory. The highland barrio has been named Villa Tunari, after a mountain near Cochabamba. "Villa" is the preferred term of highlanders to designate a barrio. In it there are now about ten or twelve chicherías, catering mostly to those harvesters who come to town on weekends, a smaller number than the twenty or so operating in the mid-seventies when the cotton boom was in full swing.

Villa Tunari is located outside the main settlement of Warnes and enjoys some autonomy. The chicherías are constructed along traditional patterns, with drinking areas situated facing the street and no high walls. Harassment by local authorities occurs from time to time,

but over the years tolerance toward these establishments has increased. In the past, however, a good bit of tension existed in Warnes
as a result of the activities associated with the Kolla bars.

The first chicherías were built in Warnes in 1974. Even though the
bars were located a good distance from the center of town, they were
well within earshot of most residents. It was a commmon practice
then as now for these establishments to use *amplificadores*, large
speakers, a record player, and a powerful amplifying system, producing music which easily traversed the one kilometer to downtown
Warnes. Cambas also made use of rented loudspeaker systems for
birthdays and other occasions, turning up the volume so that plaster
was jarred off walls and ceilings. It was important to make known to
as many people as possible that a party was in progress and that no
expense had been spared. But when Kolla celebrations in chicherías
kept the town awake, they were met with grumbling and threats of
violence—and chicherías operated almost constantly. Even worse, as
far as lowlanders were concerned, the traditional music of the highlands was monotonous. After several months of chichería activity,
tempers in town began to grow short.

The townspeople finally convened a meeting at the parish house,
presided over by the priest who was also alarmed at the changes occurring in once-peaceful Warnes. The "Kolla element" in town was
going to have to be controlled. Several thefts had been perpetrated on
the church, probably by highlanders, it was felt, and for the first time
in the history of Warnes the church doors were kept locked except
during devotions. Pressure was brought to bear on the chicherías as
the result of a series of maneuvers attempted by the town. The two
local policemen made several visits into the highland barrio but were
generally unsuccessful in bringing about any modification of chichería activities. Then the priest spoke to several highland parishoners
who, as faithful churchgoers, did not want to be associated with the
chichería scandal. They began to work through barrio networks in an
effort to coerce the chichería owners into submission. But the chichería owners were a numerous and tenacious faction and stubbornly refused to give in to the demands for silence. Finally, the town's power
group, the Consejo Parroquial (Parish Council), also created by the
priest, met to discuss the problem. This group consisted of representatives from all the major organizations in Warnes, which included
the Club de Leones, Club de Madres, Escuela Said, Hombres del
Pueblo, Junta Vecinal 15 de Noviembre, Cooperativa de Servicios
Públicos, Associación del Sagrado Corazón de Jesús, Central Cultural

Recreativo, Liga Deportiva, Escuela Mariano Saucedo Sevilla, Cooperativa de Ahorro y Credito, Comité Cívico Juvenil, Sindicato de Albañiles, and the Representante de la Gente de Habla Quechua. In a
town the size of Warnes in 1975, it could be safely assumed that almost every Camba adult in town belonged to at least one of these organizations. Until the advent of the chichería argument, the Consejo
was uniformly Camba. Then a highlander was added to the group. He
was selected by the priest because he was an active parishoner and a
member of the highland neighborhood, but he did not represent any
formal barrio organization per se. Placing a highlander on the Consejo was simply a means by which an information source in Villa
Tunari could be tapped. The young man was part of a large family
engaged in marketing and as such had limited power in the highland
barrio. As the sole highlander on the Consejo, his opinions and rec-
ommendations were heard but not necessarily heeded. This representative was used mainly as a means of carrying the proceedings
of the Consejo meetings back to the highland neighborhood. The
chichería owners responded to the Consejo's intrusion into their affairs by forming their own league, the Asociación Villa Tunari, and a
meeting was held at which both groups were in attendance. Amid
threats and flaring tempers, the chichería owners were outnumbered
and consequently outvoted. They agreed to keep noise at a minimum
level, and once again relative quiet reigned in Warnes. The Asociación Villa Tunari disbanded but no doubt will regroup if the need
arises.

Because of the chichería dispute, the schism between Kollas and
Cambas widened appreciably. At first, the mere presence of highlanders in Warnes occasioned some ill feelings among the residents,
but the chichería episode along with the market situation moved
highlanders into a position of extreme disfavor.

When highlanders first began to migrate to the Warnes area because
of its harvesting opportunities, a few migrants settled in the town
proper to engage in commercial activity. It involved mostly street
selling, which entailed the setting up of a small stall, often of cloth or
canvas. The vendors were selling primarily fresh produce and so did
not immediately offer any real threat to the pulperías, small stores in
the homes of many Warneños. As more harvesters were brought in,
the number of vendors also increased to cater to their needs. Soon the
downtown streets were crowded with highlanders selling fruit and
vegetables and other merchandise. The Camba stores were also doing
well by this business, but most townspeople considered the presence

of so many people selling and living in the streets of Warnes a nuisance and a health hazard. It was decided that street selling would be prohibited and that all vendors would be moved into an area set aside for marketing purposes. Although Warnes, like other lowland communities, had no tradition of either an open market or special days set aside for marketing as is common in the highlands, the abundance of so many Kolla street vendors inspired the building of the first marketplace in town. The controlling interests in Warnes, however, were not amenable to letting highlanders take over the market. Thus a series of brick kiosks were constructed around the periphery of the market area, and these shops were to be sold or rented to Cambas. The interior of the market, an open quadrangle, would be allotted to the highland merchants. In this manner lowlanders would be able to share in the expected profits from Sundaying harvesters as well as collect a rental fee from each vendor.

After four years of operation, many of the Camba-operated kiosks were bought out by highland entrepreneurs, and the market became Kolla-dominated. As in Santa Cruz, prices in the market were more competitive than those in pulperías since highlanders would settle for a slimmer profit margin in favor of volume sales. For cash transactions, most Warneños went grudgingly down to the market where a few pesos could be saved. Thus the pulperías in Warnes had to depend in great part on their credit customers for most of their business. By 1980, the main market in Warnes was totally a highland operation and some of the more successful market people had constructed two-story stores and houses in this area.

The introduction of large amounts of fresh produce, very much a part of highland dietary patterns, began to have an effect on the eating habits of Warnes Cambas as well. Salads and vegetables are now an integral part of lowland meals. Since Kollas control the sources of vegetable production in the cooler mountain valleys, there is no possible way a Camba can compete in the produce trade. Although the Warnes townspeople do not want to admit it, highlanders have carved out a permanent niche for themselves in the community's economy.

It is interesting that meat butchering and selling is the one area of marketing in Warnes and in other localities that the highlander has failed to dominate. Cambas continue to control meat production in the lowlands, and the marketing of beef is done through a rancher-butcher-seller network which, to date, has excluded the highlander. To sell beef in a small town and to have a steady and dependable supply of meat, one must have established relationships with butchers as well as ranchers. If enough highlanders become involved in cattle production, however, this one last bastion of Camba enterprise will no doubt become yet another victim of highland entrepreneurship.

A second market was built in 1974 in the Villa Tunari area near the highway. It began as a joint enterprise between a majority of Cambas and a highland minority, but this market also is now controlled by highland interests, with the exception, of course, of the Camba meat vendors. What began as a lowland effort to take advantage of the presence of seasonal migrants, permanent migrant residents, and the influx of highland vendors has been transferred to Kolla hands. The Cambas were quite effectively outmaneuvered and are still trying to figure out how it all happened.

The Warnes Migrants

The town of Warnes is a primary gateway into the lowlands for many highlanders, but it has not become a major center of migrant settlement. The land around Warnes consists primarily of large farms, 500 to 1,000 hectares in size, owned by agribusiness consortia and a few of the older families in town. Parcels of 40 to 200 hectares, usually farther out, belong to the town's small farmers. In the cultivation of cotton and particularly sugarcane (because of cupo restrictions), it is not economically feasible to farm much less than 40 hectares, making the small land parcel in this area virtually nonexistent. A prospective farmer from the highlands would be hard pressed to find a small parcel of land to cultivate in the Warnes area. The rural-oriented migrant must go north, into the zone where primarily rice and bananas are grown. Here land is still within reach of the peasant, and rice can be grown both for profit and subsistence. Furthermore, each tract can be multiple-cropped, giving the campesino a year-round income, albeit small, in contrast to the monocropping practices common to the Warnes region.

For most urban Kollas, Warnes also can offer only limited opportunities. Because it is located just 30 kilometers from the city of Santa Cruz, Warnes has never become either a commercial or a governmental center. The influx of harvesters on a seasonal basis allows for a substantial but temporary expansion of the town's economy, and a few of these migrants may decide to settle in Warnes. But because of the scarcity of farmland, Warnes has not attracted a continuous flow of rural immigrants, Camba or Kolla. As a result, growth in the number of urban highlanders involved in service and selling activities has also been affected negatively. From time to time the economic base may be expanded on a more permanent basis, accompanied by a short-lived spurt in the town's population. In recent years a milk pasteurization plant and a sawmill constructed near Warnes offer an additional source of steady employment. Many of the workers in these two new industries were Kollas, generally perceived by highlanders and lowlanders alike as being hard workers and more dependable than their Camba counterparts. Then, too, several of the administrators in the two plants are Kollas who tend to seek employees among *paisanos*, or their own countrymen.

Cocaine production has also affected employment patterns in the town, though to an unknown degree. During an interview in 1980 with a Kolla migrant who claimed he was at the moment unemployed, a friend stopped by to tell him there was "work" that night. The informant refused to discuss the nature of this work, but since most of the processing of cocaine occurs at night, it is probable that this individual was being contacted to *pisar coca*, literally "to step on coca." According to other sources, unskilled labor is used in this first stage of the extraction process where the coca leaves are placed in shallow vats filled with kerosene (which recently has become a scarce commodity in the lowlands). The leaves are then pressed into the kerosene by men who step on them.

Even with the new industries and the cocaine trade, which is probably of minor importance in Warnes compared to other parts of the region, the town's population has grown at a relatively slow pace. According to the national census of 1950, Warnes had 1,500 inhabitants. When the next census was taken twenty-six years later the population was 7,000. These figures can be compared with those from, for example, Montero, which grew from 2,700 in 1950 to 37,500 in 1976 (Bolivia 1951, 1976).

Most of the Kolla residents in Warnes continue to live across the highway in the Villa Tunari neighborhood. The highway is a definite social boundary, and most of the town's Cambas refer to the area as "Kolla territory." The highland barrio west of Warnes was carved from a large landholding in the area. Because of community pressures to locate those migrants intending to remain in Warnes outside of the town proper, the Urban Reform Law was invoked and the property owner was obliged to subdivide and sell. From the outset it was understood that the resulting lots would be allocated to highlanders. Some paid for their homesites outright, but provisions were made for those who did not have ready cash. Lots were sold at about 8 cents

(U.S.) per square meter in the Villa Tunari barrio, and some of the allotted area still remains unsettled.

Unlike the Santa Cruz migrant settlement areas, the Warnes highland barrio is in no way a reflection of urban growth trends, transportation routes, or settlement sequences. The barrio exists where it is simply because the land was available and was far enough out of town. The construction of permanent dwellings has also failed to follow any discernible pattern, primarily because of almost simultaneous settlement of the area. Hence there is no system of linear progression from nonpermanent to permanent dwellings in the Warnes highland barrio as was found in Santa Cruz. It is notable, however, that few of the houses in the barrio are of temporary construction. Outside the city of Santa Cruz, highland migrants in urban localities generally move rapidly toward the completion of a permanent structure. One reason for this is the lack of lámina factories in the department other than those in the city of Santa Cruz, so the inexpensive lámina dwelling is unknown in outlying areas. Also, rental housing, at least in Warnes, is not in any great demand. There is no continual influx of migrants seeking residence in the town, and those who live there have initially constructed small masonry dwellings. Some of the chichería operators are renters, but the buildings that they occupy are also of masonry construction. In the twelve-block area of the barrio, there is a noticeable lack of temporary houses. Some informants stated that they saved their money from fieldwork to build a brick house because they were tired of "living like animals." Others were very much aware of the desire to impress the Cambas in Warnes that highlanders are "better" than lowlanders. Finally, many migrants expressed interest in increasing the property value of their land should they decide to move elsewhere. Those Kolla migrants who live on the Warnes side of the highway are concentrated in the market area and in a new barrio to the south of town. This small Kolla neighborhood began to develop when the SOBOLMA (Sociedad Boliviana de Madera) lumber mill and the pasteurization plant were opened. Many of the residents work in these plants. Again, there are few temporary dwellings although several of the masonry homes that are inhabited are uncompleted.

In 1975, twenty interviews of highland migrants (fifteen females and five males) were conducted in Warnes, in both markets and in the Villa Tunari barrio. Informants in the markets were selected by availability. If a person was busy selling, another nearby who was not engaged was interviewed. Three return trips were made to the central market and a total of seven interviews obtained, representing about one-third of the permanent weekday vendors at that locality. Four informants were questioned in the new market, half of that day's seller population. Eight interviews were conducted in the Villa Tunari barrio; selections were made by location within the barrio to include each quadrant and both permanent and temporary dwelling types. Two of the eight interviews were in chicherías. The final informant was an old woman who lived in the town, although not in the central area, a folk doctor, a *curandera*, with a special position in the social scheme of Warnes. Her story will be related later.

Of the twenty persons contacted, only three did not enter Warnes via harvesting. One was an elderly man from La Paz who was sent to Santa Cruz by his doctor as a health measure. Although he had lived most of his life in La Paz, this informant was of rural origin and wanted to return to a small agricultural town. He owned a large store in the new market. The other two who did not work first in the fields were a chichería operator and a young girl employed in a chichería.

The proprietors of chicherías proved to be a unique group, not only in their fortitude in standing up against the entire town but also in their migration histories. Although they generally resisted interviews because of fear and uncertainty, the chichería owners and their life-styles were well known by other barrio residents. The owners were all women, of course, for the making of chicha is a woman's art. Many of them were also heads of matrifocal households which included any children of the owner as well as female help and their offspring.

In spite of appearances, most chicherías are not formal houses of prostitution. It is common for a chichería proprietor and her employees to "entertain" a client if they are so inclined, and children may result from these brief unions, but the chichería remains primarily a drinking establishment. These women are tough and shrewd and make good incomes. For many, the prospect of a permanent male in residence could be viewed only as a nuisance.

The female-headed households centered around chichería operation are also interesting in that they comprise a group of itinerant chicha vendors who continually move from place to place. A house is rented, the chicha cauldrons and vats are set up, and business commences. When the customers begin to decline in number, the household paraphernalia is loaded on a truck and transported to a more prosperous locality. One chichería owner reported that she was going out to the Yapacaní agricultural colony the following weekend to look the place over. Business in Warnes was beginning to slack off, there had been trouble in town, and word had spread that there was money to be made in the Yapacaní. This informant, the daughter of a chichería proprietor, said that she, her mother, brothers, and sisters had always moved from one highland village to another. When the agricultural boom hit Santa Cruz, they came east. These women were "professional" chicheras, not part of the group that may fall into the chicha business as an alternative to fieldwork.

The remaining chicheras in Warnes definitely chose the profession as a means of deriving income from some source other than harvesting. Many of these women had prior knowledge of chicha preparation and felt more comfortable in this domain than in marketing. Barrio residents confirmed that all the female highland migrants living in Villa Tunari were either unemployed, engaged in marketing, or associated with a chicha establishment. A few knew of women employed in town as empleadas (servants), living with their employers, but household service is viewed as only a temporary occupation. Two informants stated that they had also worked initially as empleadas after coming out of the fields, but only as a means of making enough money to begin marketing. Both were adamant in their dislike of the occupation and commented that what they hated most was being mandada (ordered around) by Camba women. Of the fifteen females interviewed, nine were market vendors and five were owners or employees of chicherías. The remaining female was the curandera.

Male informants' occupational specialties were seller, tractor driver, part-time mason/fieldhand, and fieldhand. Four of the five had spouses, two who remained at home in Warnes to care for young children and two who engaged in marketing. Of the female informants, seven had spouses, four were unattached but had previous alliances which resulted in offspring, and four were unmarried. Of those seven women with spouses, three had husbands who did not live in Warnes. They worked agricultural land to the north and visited their families on weekends. The women stayed in Warnes to engage in commerce and to provide schooling for their children. These three families were engaged in what I term "multiple-resource exploitation," a migration option outlined briefly in chapter 1 and to be discussed at length in chapter 5. By owning property in more than one locality, particularly a combination of rural and urban land, these families were able to expand their resource base considerably. At the same time, both spouses were able to draw upon complementary skills—the male in farming and the female in marketing.

As in Santa Cruz, illiteracy among the Warnes migrants was high. Thirteen of the fifteen female informants could not read or write nor could two of the five males. The disadvantages of being illiterate seemed to be strongly felt among the migrants, and the schooling of their children was of primary importance in their lives. A Warnes schoolteacher reported that absenteeism among the children of highland migrants was much lower than that among Camba children.

Unlike Santa Cruz, which continues to attract a predominance of urban migrants, Warnes and surrounding areas are recipients of individuals from rural situations. Fourteen of the 20 informants originated directly from a rural setting; three had rural highland origins but moved into a city in the interior prior to coming to the lowlands. Only three were urban-born people who entered the Santa Cruz region as harvesters but quickly reinstated themselves as urban dwellers in Warnes. One of the three was a woman married to a Warnes Camba. This couple represented one of the very few cases of regional intermarriage encountered during the course of the 1975 study. The other two were a brother and sister from Oruro. The sister arrived first with the mother and several siblings. When queried as to her reasons for remaining in Warnes rather than locating in Santa Cruz or Montero, she replied, "Hay mucha competencia en Santa Cruz y no me gusta vivir en Montero" ("There is a lot of competition in Santa Cruz and I don't like living in Montero"). The brother followed the family within a few weeks of their arrival. His flight from the interior was the result of some political difficulties. He was not fond of Warnes or of the lowlands but could not return to the highlands.

The sample population in Warnes did not differ significantly from that of Santa Cruz in terms of age. The latter's average age was thirty-one, that of Warnes thirty-seven. The Warnes population did have a wider range, however, with a standard deviation of 19.58 compared to 12.78 for the city of Santa Cruz. The greater variation of the Warnes population was due in large part to sample size but was also a reflection of a more numerous group of informants in the upper age range.

In 1975, regional origins of the Warnes migrants held to a pattern similar to that found for the city of Santa Cruz (table 4.1). Exactly 50 percent of the Warnes sample population originated in the Department of Cochabamba, as had 56 percent of the Santa Cruz migrants. Once the Cochabamba sector was eliminated from the Warnes sample, the remaining areas did not vary greatly in the relative numbers of migrants they supplied. Cochabamba, because of both its propin-

Table 4.1. Warnes Migrants' Place of Origin (department or district), 1975

Origin	Number	Percent
Cochabamba	10	50.0
Oruro	3	15.0
Potosí	2	10.0
Chuquisaca (Sucre)	2	10.0
Other	2	10.0
La Paz	1	5.0
Total	20	100.0

quity and its function as a jumping-off place for highland migrants, was providing a substantial portion of the migrant population, as was found in the city of Santa Cruz. With regard to Warnes, Montero, and other agricultural localities, however, an additional element must be taken into account in analyzing the Cochabamba concentrations. The majority of chicherías in the Department of Santa Cruz operate in the countryside, not in the city, and most chicheras are Cochabambinas. The possibility exists that the rural sample may not have been influenced entirely by differential regional volumes of migration but by the abundant presence of a particular occupational group. Those who migrated for the first time numbered four, or 20 percent; sixteen, or 80 percent, had migrated prior to their move to Santa Cruz.

Dress patterns among female migrants in Warnes differed from those of the Santa Cruz population in that thirteen, or 86 percent, continued to use traditional dress (pollera) compared to 62 percent for the city migrants. Since Warnes consists of a rural-oriented population, these numbers seem to be in keeping with the more conservative attitudes of rural people.

The Warnes sample also diverged from the Santa Cruz group with regard to housing. Primarily because of the lack of incoming migrants whose intention was to remain permanently in Warnes, there was little rental housing available in town. So the majority of the Warnes informants owned their dwellings.

Finally, fourteen of the twenty migrants interviewed knew or were aware of having other relatives in the lowland region. Kinship networks were maintained much as they would have been in the highlands. Informants frequently mentioned that some of their relatives had not been seen or visited in years, but their whereabouts were known. If necessary, these relationships could be rapidly reinstated to provide mutual aid.

In spite of findings both in 1975 and 1980 that Kolla migrants rely on chain migration and the presence of relatives in the lowlands as a major adaptive strategy, some migrants arrive in Santa Cruz virtually alone. Others may know of kinfolk in the lowlands but have been unable to locate them. Under ordinary circumstances, these individuals would eventually find kin or make friends who can be relied on in times of crisis. As new arrivals, however, they have not yet formed these necessary alliances.

The most common problem facing the new migrant is illness. Poor food and long hours in the field soon take their toll on many harvesters, especially those who are first-timers and unaccustomed to the lowland environment. Unless their illness is acute, fieldhands will rarely be taken to a hospital or to a doctor, first because of the expense and second because of a lack of trust: hospitals are places where people go to die, and doctors are viewed as simply helping the process along. Many highlanders would rather rely on a folk healer, or curandero. There are many Kolla curanderos in the lowlands now, particularly in rural areas where their skills are always in demand. I met a well-known folk healer in Warnes, a woman named Sandalia, and came to understand her role among migrants.

Sandalia Rosado Vega is an almost ageless woman who claims to be in her nineties. Her mother died when she was an infant, and a neighbor woman took her in, chose her given name, and taught her the art of curing. Sandalia is from Vallegrande and is therefore a "Camba-Kolla." Vallegrande is in the Department of Santa Cruz but is located in the area where the mountains begin to rise up off the plain. Many Vallegrandina women dress in the traditional pollera and wear their hair in double braids as does Sandalia, but they do not speak Quechua or totally identify with highland culture. At the same time, they are not lowlanders and do not regard themselves as Cambas. The Vallegrandino is *medio camino*, middle of the road, straddling both cultures but not actually in either. It is because of Sandalia's age, origin, and profession that she occupies what could be termed a broker position in Warnes society.

Sandalia lives in an adobe brick house with a tile roof which was built by a highlander and is the only dwelling of its type in Warnes. The house has three rudely furnished rooms, a separate kitchen to the rear, and an outbuilding where Sandalia's chickens spend the night. Sandalia and her daughter occupy only one room of the dwelling since patients are housed in the remaining two. Her patients are of all ages, some traveling great distances to seek her remedies. She is a successful healer, and much of her success may be attributed to her great concern for the well-being of others. Sandalia concentrates on healing the body and the spirit, taking in people who have given up hope and who have no one to care for them.

Often at her own expense, Sandalia will feed and nurse a patient back to health, even if the individual is suffering from no greater illness than malnourishment, neglect, or depression. In many instances these are highland harvesters. They have come to the lowlands alone or have become separated from their families. After working long hours in the heat and humidity of the lowland cotton or cane field, they return to a damp galpón to eat a miserable meal. They fall ill and are brought to Sandalia by the farm owner or a fieldhand friend. Using her curing practices and constant personal attention, Sandalia will have the average harvester back on the job in three weeks. Fees are charged according to the ability of the patient to pay, and Sandalia depends on her more affluent clients to cover the costs of those who are too poor to reimburse her for her services.

Sandalia came to the lowlands in search of her daughter, who had contracted to work for three months for the harvest at La Bélgica. The three months went by and the daughter failed to return. After six months the curandera packed her things and came to Santa Cruz to locate her only child. It took her almost two weeks to find her way out to the mill where she and her daughter were reunited. Sandalia's daughter had been hired for some additional work and had no way to inform her mother that she would be remaining in the lowlands. Sandalia decided to stay with her daughter and set up an eating establishment to serve meals to the harvesters. At the same time, she began to treat those fieldhands who fell ill or were injured. Gradually her curing business grew, and she and her daughter finally moved into Warnes where they purchased their present homesite.

Her healing business continued to prosper in the town, and Sandalia was soon able to discontinue most of her other activities such as selling along the roadside. She still makes bread every three days since she enjoys this activity and believes that her bread is much better than any made in Warnes. Perhaps she is right, for when Sandalia is baking there is a constant stream of townspeople stopping by her house to buy a few pesos' worth.

Sandalia cures with the baño seco (dry bath) method and depends upon purgatives, herbs, and good food. She claims that she can cure people who are enfermo de los pulmones (sick in the lungs) in three weeks. The first treatment involves a baño seco given every other day for three days. It consists of filling gourds with boiling hot water and placing them around the patient, who is covered with blankets. Profuse sweating results, and Sandalia must change her patient's bedclothes three times before the bath has ended. Afterward the ailing client is given broth prepared from white (meatless) beef bones. When the third and final bath has been administered, a purgative is given and the patient is allowed to rest. During the following days special foods such as eggnogs and gelatin are prepared. When recovery begins, heavier solid foods are introduced.

For illnesses not readily discernible, Sandalia makes use of a diagnostic method involving divination through a *shogma*, though she does not use guinea pigs as is common in other Andean areas. Sandalia's shogma must be a young chicken, which she herself raises. The patient is then told to blow in the bird's beak which, according to Sandalia, will cause the illness to pass from the patient into the body of the chicken. Then she kills the animal, opens it up, and begins to inspect the entrails of the chicken for signs of disease. Sandalia is normally concerned with the condition of the bird's blood and explains that there are three types of blood sickness: *sangre negra* or *enfuegada* (black blood or hot blood), *sangrasa de resfrío* (corrupt blood from a chill), and *sangre débil* (weak blood), which is light red or pink in color. All of these blood pathologies are cured primarily with the application of a baño seco—"con los baños se componen todas las sangres y se quedan en una" ("with the baths all bloods are made well and become whole").

The remainder of Sandalia's cures consists of herbal preparations and the sacred power derived from religious articles. Sandalia is a devout Catholic and believes that all of the successful treatments are a result of her faith in God and the support of the saints. She has a constant supply of bottles of holy water on hand and goes to the parish priest to replenish her stock when it runs low. The holy water is often mixed with the dust that collects on her numerous religious statues, and the potion is then fed to patients. This particular remedy is used for heart problems and nervous attacks. Sandalia will also have some of her homemade bread blessed by the priest to be used as nourishment for her patients.

The mystical number three, so important in Christian theology, has obviously been incorporated into Sandalia's healing format. Three baños must be given, the bed is changed three times, most curing is put on a three-week schedule, bread is baked every third day, and the blood diseases are tripartite in nature. In spite of all her curing expertise, Sandalia believes that it is the sacred power of deity and saints that pulls the patient through. "Primero ruego a Diós y a la Vírgen que pongan su mano y sobre esa pongo la mía" ("First I pray to God and the Virgin to lay on their hands, and over theirs I lay mine").

Sandalia views her role as primarily that of healing physical afflictions, but she is also attuned to the importance of dealing with illness whose origins would seem to be psychosomatic. Many of the Kolla migrants who cross her threshold are in need of emotional reinforcement. Because Sandalia is herself a "neutral" person, she is effective in assisting the disoriented migrant in making difficult adjustments to change. David Jones has written of a similar situation among Comanche Indians who also are making often painful adaptations to acculturative pressures. The folk healer here is a woman called Sanapia.

> Perhaps the most significant points this study has illustrated are the psychotherapeutic functions which Sanapia possesses in contemporary Comanche culture . . . [in treating] a conversion reaction whose negative emotional basis is founded in the cultural and personal confusion and tension produced by the increasingly efficient success of acculturation in corroding the traditional basis of Comanche society. It then appears that Sanapia is the curer of a dynamic and functional human disorder. Sanapia treats the individuals rather than a specific static human affliction. (1968:104)

Jones attributes Sanapia's continuing success, in spite of the presence of white doctors, to her holistic approach to healing. It is in this respect that Sandalia has also prevailed over the practitioners of "modern" medicine. She views the illness of each patient as something entirely idiosyncratic to that individual and as a disease that must be treated on various levels of understanding. In essence, Sandalia does not separate mental from physical illness. Hence a highlander suffering from some unknown sickness that has been treated unsuccessfully by a mestizo physician will often seek out Sandalia's aid and be cured. Her astounding success in many cases appears to be based in her ability to deal with depression and alienation as expected components of disease. For not a few highlanders, the decision to remain in the lowlands has been influenced in no small way by the careful ministrations of an aging Vallegrandina.

Recent Trends in Warnes

The migrants interviewed during the 1980 study carried out by the Dirección Departamental de Estadística (DDE) included six Cambas and seven Kollas. The randomly selected subsample of the 1979 migration study of 484 migrants called for sixteen in-depth interviews. With only three missing cases, Warnes ranked second to the city of Santa Cruz in terms of success in relocating those individuals contacted the previous year.

After spending several hours with each informant and his or her family, it was evident that Warnes was not considered an ideal location for settlement by either Cambas or Kollas. Most lowlanders had lived in the village for many years and considered it a permanent place of residence. Cambas averaged fourteen years in Warnes, the least number of years eight. Many believed the town was "going nowhere" but had built homes there and had relatives nearby and so felt compelled to remain. The Kolla migrants averaged only 4.8 years' residence in Warnes, the least number of years just over one. Cambas and Kollas alike expressed the feeling that Warnes was stagnating and there was too little opportunity to make money. The nearness of Santa Cruz to the south and Montero to the north makes Warnes somewhat of an anachronism in view of present-day rapid transit. During harvest, the town receives added impetus to its economy, but most harvesters still prefer to go on into Montero for their weekend activities. Then, too, the harvest lasts for only three to four months; once it is over, there is little commerce other than that supplied by the villagers themselves.

The highlanders we spoke with did not display the exuberance or sense of expectation found among Kolla migrants in the other research sites. Those employed at the sawmill and the pasteurization plant were content with their economic situation but were not at ease with the social environment. Informants felt a certain oppressiveness in the town and were concerned about the degree of prejudice toward highland people. Of the four localities visited in 1980, Warnes was the only place where Kolla informants repeatedly commented on Camba treatment of them. Although latent prejudice toward Kollas and outsiders in general has always been a part of Camba society, the Warnes situation appears to be more pronounced than is the case for the area in general. The fact that the town has become a funnel for a population that ultimately goes elsewhere has created a sense of frustration

Table 4.2. Warnes Migrants' Place of Origin (department or district), 1980

Origin	Number	Percent
Camba		
Santa Cruz	6	100.0
Total	6	100.0
Kolla		
Cochabamba	3	42.0
Chuquisaca (Sucre)	1	14.5
Potosí	1	14.5
Oruro	1	14.5
La Paz	1	14.5
Total	7	100.0

among many residents, particularly the Cambas, who expected greater economic returns from increased highland migration.

Migration histories of the Kolla informants did not differ significantly from the 1975 study (table 4.2). Cochabamba remains the major source of highland migrants primarily because of chain migration. All but one of the Kollas interviewed came to the lowlands at the insistence of relatives already established in Santa Cruz, and, interestingly, the same was true for the Cambas: four of the six informants came to Warnes because they had relatives living there. The other two were offered jobs at the sawmill.

For the highland migrants, harvesting remains the major source of employment upon entry to the lowlands. Five of the seven informants came to Warnes as harvesters and decided to remain in the town primarily because they had other relatives there. Two came to Warnes because of job openings at the sawmill and pasteurization plant.

Only one Camba and three Kollas were living in rental housing during the 1980 study. As mentioned, there is a lack of rental housing in Warnes primarily because most highland migrants settle elsewhere once they leave the harvest. The one Camba family renting a house had a Kolla landlord, and highland renters were sharing space with landlords from the same place of origin. The three Kolla renters were convinced that they would not remain in Warnes; they had been there just over a year.

Whereas most of the highlanders came from rural situations, the reverse was true for the Cambas. It seemed contradictory in light of pervasive rural-urban trends that so many of the lowland informants had moved to Warnes after migrating first to the city of Santa Cruz.

Table 4.3. Warnes Migrants' Occupations, Male Informants
(including spouses of female informants), 1980

Occupation	Camba		Kolla	
	No.	%	No.	%
Carpenter	1	20.0	0	–
Truck driver	1	20.0	1	7.0
Night watchman (city)	1	20.0	0	0.0
Laborer (farm)	1	20.0	2	33.0
Mill or plant	1	20.0	2	33.0
Unemployed	0	–	1	17.0
Total	5	100.0	6	100.0

Table 4.4. Warnes Migrants' Occupations, Female Informants
(including spouses of male informants), 1980

Occupation	Camba		Kolla	
	No.	%	No.	%
Marketing	0	–	3	42.0
Chichería	0	–	1	15.0
Housework	3	50.0	2	28.0
Laundress	1	16.5	1	15.0
Pulpería (store)	1	16.5	0	–
Seamstress	1	17.0	0	–
Total	6	100.0	7	100.0

While most stated that the reason for coming was to join relatives, further inquiry revealed that economic incentives were their primary motives. Since many had no other skills but farming, it was much more difficult for them to find work in the city than in Warnes, where agricultural labor is always in demand. Once in Warnes, at least two eventually learned skills that provided steady employment.

Occupational categories, particularly among Kolla migrants, reflect the lack of economic opportunity in Warnes (tables 4.3 and 4.4). Most males hold sporadic jobs that require few skills. The women are somewhat better off in that they can depend on chicha production and marketing as sources of relatively steady income.

For the majority of highland migrants who make their way into the lowlands as harvesters, Warnes is only a gateway to the oriente. Beyond that, however, it offers little to the upwardly mobile migrant. Even for lowlanders it represents an eddy in most migration flows.

Cambas who have selected Warnes have generally been unsuccessful at other migration attempts and move to Warnes as the result of their defeat in dynamic urban areas. Kolla migrants with a penchant for urban life and challenges may go on to Santa Cruz, but most select Montero, the center of highland activity in the northern Santa Cruz region.

5

Montero: Agricultural Crossroads of the North

National interest in opening the lowlands for exploitation resulted not only in the completion of the Santa Cruz–Cochabamba highway but also in the construction of an additional stretch of paved road leading north from Santa Cruz. Its purpose was to service the first government-built sugar mill, Guabirá, which began operations in 1957. The refinery was located just northeast of the town of Montero, 60 kilometers north of the city of Santa Cruz and in the center of the best agricultural lands of the department. This region soon was to become the focus of population relocation programs (foreign as well as domestic), multinational development projects, and large-scale commercial agricultural enterprises.

At a point near Montero and the Guabirá mill the asphalt highway terminated; the old dirt track continued a short distance and then split into two branches, one heading west across the Yapacaní River and the other east to the Río Grande. Along these two roads new colonization zones were opened, and highlanders as well as groups of Japanese and Okinawans were granted tracts of farmland. The paved highway along with the offer of free land brought more people into the north. Montero's good fortune in being situated near the junction of these roads meant instant prosperity, and as commercial agriculture took hold in the region the town's economy surged beyond even the most optimistic expectations.

The City

Northern Santa Cruz has a history of settlement as old as that of the department itself, but like most of the lowlands prior to the 1950s, life proceeded at a leisurely pace. Camba agriculturalists planted and harvested rice, coffee, bananas, and manioc and then loaded their produce on oxcarts to make the long trip into Santa Cruz. They often formed caravans to guard their cargoes and their lives against attacks by bandits who roamed the area in search of the unprotected traveler. At this time Montero was just another Camba village along the route to the urban center of Santa Cruz.

With the construction of the Guabirá mill and the asphalt highway leading to it, Montero was given unprecedented opportunity for economic development, and the town began to grow rapidly in area and population. In 1950 the town's population was 2,700; by 1967 the inhabitants numbered 13,500 (Solíz 1974:3). Located at the termination point of the Santa Cruz–Guabirá highway, Montero soon became the commercial and governmental headquarters of the northern provinces beyond. The National Colonization Institute (Instituto Nacional de Colonización) established its regional headquarters there along with the office of the Agrarian Judge in charge of resolving land disputes. Several banks opened branch offices in Montero, and many of the larger Bolivian chain stores such as Manaco shoes acquired plaza locations. To the south of the city, the U.S. Point Four program constructed a multimillion dollar experimental farm, Muyurina, with the intent of providing agricultural assistance to the newly developing region. After about ten years of operation, Muyurina was sold to the Salesian Order, which converted the complex into a boarding school for campesino youth to train them in modern farming technology.

North of the city the United Methodist Church established its lowland religious center and school. The Methodists also constructed a hospital in downtown Montero, which they still administer. In other areas of the city the Baptists and Jehovah's Witnesses also erected churches and together with the Methodists and Mennonites competed with Catholic missionaries for converts.

In 1968 the roads branching east and west from Montero were paved, opening these agricultural zones for more intensive settlement as well as providing them with all-weather market routes. Montero's growth was thus given additional impetus, and the once insig-

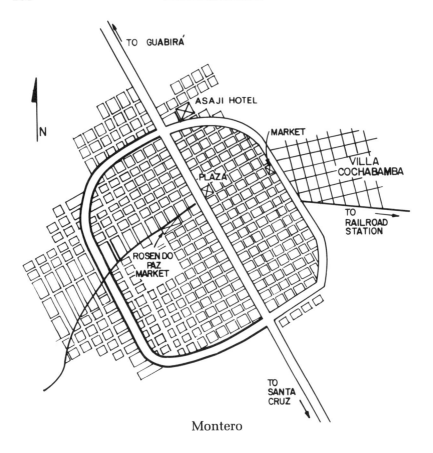

TO GUABIRÁ

ASAJI HOTEL

MARKET

N

VILLA
COCHABAMBA

PLAZA

TO
RAILROAD
STATION

ROSENDO
PAZ
MARKET

TO
SANTA
CRUZ

Montero

nificant Camba village was converted into a boom town rivaling even the city of Santa Cruz. By the 1976 census, Montero's population had reached 37,500 (Bolivia 1976). Today, Montero boasts telephone service with the rest of the nation, sewers, loceta-paved streets like Santa Cruz, and a poured-in-place concrete water tank with a million-liter capacity. Next to the Methodist school there is a new hotel financed jointly by the Corporación Boliviana de Fomento and the Interamerican Development Bank at a cost of $321,000 (U.S.).

Montero, like Warnes, was also bypassed by the highway that skirts the eastern periphery of the city before once again proceeding north five kilometers to the Guabirá mill. But, unlike Warnes, Montero was not adversely affected by the bypass. Within a relatively short time, the city had grown to the limits of the highway and has now extended beyond it. Also, as a road junction urban site, Montero has the advantage of being strategically situated, and its distance of 60 kilometers from the city of Santa Cruz makes it an important regional service center.

In spite of increasing marketing and commercial activity in the areas contiguous to the highway, Montero's central plaza zone continues to be the most desirable and prestigious business property in the city. A few old families still reside in homes fronting directly on the plaza, but even they have converted parts of their dwellings into commercial enterprises or restaurants. In many respects, the main square of Montero resembles its larger counterpart in Santa Cruz. The Catholic church dominates one side of the plaza along with the offices of the church-operated savings and loan cooperative. The remaining three sides are filled with banks, government offices, stores, and eating establishments.

Unlike the city of Santa Cruz, Montero is becoming a Kolla stronghold. Downtown Montero is lowlander territory, but it is surrounded by ever-increasing numbers of highlanders who are inexorably pushing their way into the center of town. When the first colonization projects commenced northwest and northeast of the city, a few highlanders moved into the city to begin trading. An open area just east of the plaza was converted into a small marketplace. Rice production, sugarcane, and, later, the cotton industries attracted more settlers and even greater numbers of harvesters from the highlands. The market area began to expand and was soon overflowing into neighboring streets.

The Montero Cambas were distressed at the numbers of highlanders pressing in around the plaza and also at the sudden appearance of chicherías within the town proper. Complaints by townspeople concerning the market and the chicherías in town brought about a city ordinance which effectively exiled both from central Montero. A new marketplace was secured by the *alcadía* to be situated along the highway on the inner periphery of the bypass. The chicherías were forbidden to operate within the boundary of the asphalt road and consequently moved into the highland neighborhood on the other side of the highway opposite the new market.

Although highlanders now live in most areas of Montero, the largest numbers of Kolla migrants are concentrated in several districts. The entire zone east of the highway, known popularly as Villa Cochabamba, is inhabited by highlanders. A Camba-Kolla continuum radiates from the center of town, with highlanders in the majority on the peripheries and Cambas still clinging to the sector around the plaza. It is the highlanders, however, who are gradually moving along this continuum as they acquire property vacated by the Montero Cambas. The lowlanders in turn are migrating to Santa Cruz. This same pattern of successive migration is occurring throughout the northern Santa Cruz region. As Cambas leave towns and countryside to migrate to the city of Santa Cruz, highlanders move in behind them.

To the west of Montero, a new market has been constructed and named after the man who donated the property, Rosendo Paz. Because of its location at a point distant from the highway and the competition presented by its counterpart to the east, the Paz market is struggling for existence. Unlike the large Villa Cochabamba market, which is totally controlled by highlanders, the western market has a few remaining Camba vendors. A scattering of highland families has settled around the Paz market in anticipation of its possible future prosperity.

As a lowland trade center, Montero is second only to Santa Cruz. In the past, prices in Montero were always somewhat higher than those of the capital, but for many the saving of a few pesos did not make the longer trip worthwhile. It was only when specialty items, such as mechanical parts, appliances or clothing, were needed that the journey into Santa Cruz became necessary. Now, however, there is very little that Montero cannot provide and at prices competitive with Santa Cruz. In fact, it is now common for many highland truckers to bypass Santa Cruz and go directly to Montero to sell their cargoes. Because of its function as a regional service center for primarily rural highlanders, Montero has many items that are campesino specialties and are therefore somewhat more difficult to obtain in Santa Cruz. The marketplace in Montero has a much better selection of hand-woven woolen articles and polleras, for example, than do any of the Santa Cruz markets.

Until the late 1970s, there was a coca vendors' street directly behind the main Montero market. The chewing of coca is practiced by a large segment of the highland population, men and women alike, but it is a tradition linked with the indigenous substrata. Hence, coca use tends to be more prevalent among the campesino group than among urban dwellers. Although at the time coca could be purchased in the city of Santa Cruz, selection was limited—a reflection of the relative lack of demand for the product in the city. For good coca in the lowlands, one had to travel to Montero. On the coca street, female vendors were lined up under their sunshades, each woman with a small table and a chair or box to sit on. Every vendor had several large sacks filled with coca from different areas of Bolivia. Prices varied according to freshness and place of origin. The most prized coca was from the La Paz yungas, east of the national capital, and it was more expensive than other varieties. The Paceñan coca was said to be more potent and sweeter to chew. Most coca trucks from the highlands reserved a large part of their cargoes for Montero. When they arrived at the market, there was a frantic scramble by the coca vendors and their helpers to purchase the best product ahead of their competitors. Prices for coca varied only according to quality so it behooved a vendor to have a good supply of the best. Rural highlanders appraised the coca at each stand before deciding on the type and the amount they acquired. For the highland campesino, a trip to Montero was incomplete without a stop at a coca vendor's table.

Today, the coca street is gone, just as are the few coca vendors in the Los Pozos market in Santa Cruz. Cocaine production has made coca for chewing a scarce commodity. Coca continues to enter Montero in large quantities, nonetheless, and the city's contribution to the illicit drug trade has given it the nickname La Diosa Blanca (the white goddess).

In addition to its importance as a marketing, service, and, of late, cocaine center, Montero is also the northern region's principal location for secondary education. Most settlements, including the agricultural colonies, have some provision for primary education; but until recently the inhabitants of the area were required to send their children into Santa Cruz for secondary education. Only the well-to-do of any community could afford this expense. Today Montero offers numerous choices in secondary schools, both church-affiliated and public. For those in nearby towns, daily commuting to a *colegio* in Montero is now possible. One group of Warnes parents formed a transportation cooperative to send their children to Muyurina each day. Those students who live a good distance from Montero will find their education expensive but still less than having to live and study in Santa Cruz. It is also important to note that at least two of the secondary schools, Muyurina and the Methodist colegio, are geared toward educating the children of campesinos and include agricultural studies in their curricula.

Agriculture, commerce, education, and light industry have all combined to make Montero the fastest growing urban center in the lowlands. Although the city has only 5 percent of the departmental population, it can lay claim to over 18 percent of the total number

Table 5.1. Selected Lowland Industries, 1975

Industry	Department	Montero
Sugar mills	3	2
Sawmills	43	6
Rice mills	19	5
Cotton mills	15	2
Beverages	1	12
Tanneries	5	1
Total	86	16

of selected industrial complexes in the Department of Santa Cruz (table 5.1)

In overall industrial development, the city of Santa Cruz still leads by a wide margin, and in many cases it is the sole location of a particular industry, such as the oil refinery. Still, in a region which has been dominated traditionally by a single central place, Montero is a fast-rising star and may prove a substantial threat to the economic hegemony of urban Santa Cruz. Optimistic Montereños and pessimistic Cruceñans believe that in the near future Montero may supplant Santa Cruz as the dominant urban center of the region. The highway leading westward from Montero will one day connect with another paved road pushing east from Cochabamba which forms part of the multinational Carretera Marginal de la Selva. When the two highways are linked, a new and shorter route to the highlands will be available, and Montero will be the jumping-off point.

Migrant Center of the North

Fanning out in all directions from Montero are the most productive agricultural lands of Santa Cruz. To the south are cotton and sugarcane, to the east and north rice and cane fields. The wetter zone approaching the mountains to the west is prime rice territory. Cattle are raised throughout the northern Santa Cruz region in areas where grassland has taken over the forest. Just ahead of the line of farmers and frontiersmen clearing land, loggers are moving relentlessly farther into the virgin wilderness in search of hardwoods such as mahogany.

All of these endeavors require people—men and women to farm and to harvest. There must be people to drive logging trucks and farm tractors, to haul cane, rice, and cotton, and to operate numerous mills.

Highland Bolivia furnishes the majority of laborers and settlers necessary to keep the lowland agricultural and extractive machine operating. At the hub of the labor pool is Montero, the region's manpower brokerage center.

Three blocks east of the Montero main plaza is the office of the Federación de Campesinos del Norte (Peasant Federation of the North), housed in an old building constructed of whitewashed wattle and daub with a tile roof. Behind the office is a large walled-in dirt courtyard with a few mango trees for shade. The clay patio serves as a holding yard for highland migrants who are waiting to be hired as harvesters or fieldhands. When night falls the area becomes a campground for those highlanders in search of work who have no other lodging place. At the front of the Federación office there are also groups of men and women standing or sitting next to their few belongings waiting in anticipation of a job contract. They too may be found at night sleeping in the open for want of shelter in the city.

The Federación de Campesinos is a multipurpose organization under the control of the national government and managed by the military. In 1974 it had 34,000 members who were classified as *flotantes* (seasonal migrants) and 20,000 *asentados* (settled farmers) (Federación de Campesinos 1975). By 1976 the cotton boom was over, and stories of ill treatment of workers by labor contractors and farm owners were circulating in the highlands. Migration appeared to slack off for about three years but picked up again as logging and the cocaine trade brought new impetus to the region's economy. Although fewer workers came under the jurisdiction of the Federación, it continued to function as a brokerage for farm labor, as a deliberative body for labor disputes, and as a political lever in the land allocation process.

Aside from its stated functions of labor management and worker protection, the Federación set out to undermine and eventually exterminate the labor unions or sindicatos. It is only one of five bureaucracies which together attempt to maintain control over highland campesinos in the rural areas of the lowlands. Linked to the Federación are the Banco Agrícola (Agrarian Bank), Desarrollo de Comunidades (Community Development), Acción Cívica Militar (Military Civic Action), and the Instituto Nacional de Colonización (National Colonization Institute). In 1975, the Federación was spearheading a movement to organize the highland campesinos into *nucleos*, or cell groups in each community or settlement area where migrants were present. The nucleos were reportedly a first step toward the creation of cooperatives in the farming community. The internal organization of the nucleos, however, did not seem to differ significantly from their sindicato predecessor. In fact, many of the same personnel were holding positions in the nucleo comparable to those held in the old union. One nucleo member stated that the reorganization of these campesino bodies had diminished some of the autocratic power previously held by union leaders and that members had a greater voice in the decision-making process.

The past history of union movements in Bolivia and their efficacy in revolutionary upheavals has given the national government some cause for concern. By bringing them under the direct jurisdiction of the ruling party and the military (actually one and the same), the government has reduced the threat of insurrection. Although union leaders worked diligently to unionize campesinos in Santa Cruz after the 1952 revolution, the idea never caught on among Cambas as it did among highlanders. Consequently, Santa Cruz remained relatively unaffected by organized labor movements in the nation, and the efforts of the Federación to transform the labor unions into cooperatives have been directed primarily at the highland campesino migrant.

Now, groups of migrants such as former harvesters commonly form leagues for the purpose of pressuring the government for farmland. These leagues are frequently called cooperatives in keeping with accepted terminology. Working through the Federación or another governmental agency, a cooperative presents a formal petition for the occupancy of a particular tract of land. Membership in the Federación does not guarantee settlement assistance, but it is one means of gaining access to the bureaucracies that control land allocations.

The larger the cooperative formed, the more power and money it will have for confronting the politicians who authorize land grants in the lowland territories. It is therefore a common practice for active recruitment to be carried on among prospective highland settlers while they are in Montero. Each new cooperative member must pay an initial quota of $50 to $100 (U.S.). For most migrants, this sum represents a substantial outlay; but if the organization is successful in its petition for land, the returns are worth the investment.

Along with their interests in organizing campesino cooperatives, the Federación offices preside over the exchange of labor in the northern Santa Cruz region. Since a large majority of voluntarios (farm workers not under contract) go directly to Montero and the Federación office to find work, labor contractors and other individuals in need of laborers frequent the establishment. Fees have to be paid for the use of this brokerage service by the person doing the hiring, but the newly arrived migrant ignorant of the rules of the game will often fall prey to the unscrupulous labor operative. Supposedly to prevent such occurrences, there is a work inspector (Inspector de Trabajo) present in the Federación office. His duties include the protection of laborers' rights, and a large portion of his day is spent in resolving minor disputes between management and labor or among groups of farmhands. In many cases equitable agreements are reached, but it is not uncommon for the inspector to pressure the workers rather than the employer to cease hostilities.

The Federación is the primary formal labor brokerage center in Montero, but there are numerous informal locations that serve as contact points for workers and farm management. Many migrants simply hang around the plaza waiting for a truck to stop and pick them up. Others stand across the street from the Federación office hoping to find jobs while avoiding bureaucratic red tape and membership fees. The market zone and highland neighborhood, especially in the vicinity of the chicherías, also provide meeting places for laborers and their clients. The latter method resembles a pattern in the United States where farm buses make morning rounds of all the town bars to collect the day's contingent of migrant harvesters. The same informal system of labor exchange occurs in other lowland localities, as in Warnes, but on a much smaller scale. For anyone in the labor market, buyer or seller, Montero remains the best brokerage center in Santa Cruz.

Montero attracts not only seasonal migrants from the highlands but also many Kollas who have become lowland farmers and are in need of work between harvests, especially the rice farmer, whose harvest in April and May will not normally conflict with the later cane and cotton season. The three-month slack period between the end of rice harvest and the next planting in September and October leaves many farmers idle and short of cash. Many head for Montero to hire on as day laborers. Again, it is primarily Kollas who avail themselves of the opportunity to supplement their farm incomes with outside work. The Camba generally does not participate in this activity, preferring instead to seek work locally or simply wait out the lean period by living on credit.

On the opposite side of town from the Federación de Campesinos office is the regional headquarters of the Instituto Nacional de Colonización (INC). This site is another focal point of interest for the migrant in Montero because it is through this office that recruitment of colonists for new agricultural settlements is conducted. In comparison to previous years, the administrative role of colonization bureaucracy has diminished significantly. From its capacity as sole controlling agent, the institute has now begun to withdraw gradually from its position of absolute autonomy in colonial matters. The older colonies presently are under the fiscal administration of the Department of Santa Cruz, and public officials are selected from among the resident settlers. The more recent colonies such as Buen Retiro (Antofagasta), Chané-Piray, and San Julián remain under the auspices of INC.

The Bolivian government and its settlement agency, INC, have had a long and somewhat torturous history of involvement in colonization projects and the expenditure of millions of dollars in loans without much visible result. Not necessarily having learned from its errors but no longer having the almost limitless funding for colonization efforts, the institute has been forced to reduce its activities. Now the major government commitment is to provide land in surveyed parcels with an access road and water pumps at 4-kilometer intervals. The colonists must rely on their own resources for any additional services or, in the case of San Julián, depend on other groups for assistance, such as FIDES (Fundación Interamericano para el Desarrollo), formerly the United Church Committee (Comité de Iglesias Unidas).

The United Church Committee of Montero arose as the result of the disastrous lowland floods of 1967. In an effort to coordinate rescue, shelter, and relocation operations, the major church groups of the city formed a combined assistance unit, later to be called the United Churches of Montero. The resettlement of flood victims eventually led to the involvement of this group in colonization.

In order to relocate the displaced victims, two new tracts of land were opened in 1968 for settlement. These became known as the Colonia Chané-Piray and the Colonia Hardeman (the latter named after the American road company whose camp was used as a temporary shelter site). Maryknoll nuns and Methodist and Mennonite volunteers worked with the colonists to start anew. Along with the flood victims, former harvesters were also recruited by INC and church organization to fill the settlements. From that point on, the Iglesias Unidas played an active role in colonial development. The Bolivian government was financially unable to provide comparable services, and the two groups began working in complementary capacities. When the new San Julián colony was initiated, the Iglesias Unidas was charged with planning and executing an orientation program for incoming colonists and providing them with volunteer technical assistance. INC supplied the infrastructure for the fledgling settlement.

Recruitment for San Julián was carried out at the institute office in Montero and at tables set up in areas of the city where highlanders tended to congregate. Rather than follow past precedents and recruit directly from the interior, the two agencies sought highland migrants who, because of their preadaptation in the lowland harvests, were considered to be better risks for the project. Thus a large majority of the San Julián settlers are former harvesters who were in Montero at the time of recruitment. Although very little land in the colonies is now available, migrants continue to pass by the INC office to inquire about colonizing opportunities. If none seems forthcoming, prospective agriculturalists must turn to a land cooperative or purchase their land from a private individual—both much more costly propositions than obtaining a plot from the government.

During the harvest season and to a lesser extent during planting and weeding times (what amounts to almost three-fourths of the calendar year), Montero becomes the meeting ground for the highland agricultural populace of the northern Santa Cruz region. Farmers in the area market much of their produce in Montero where prices paid for agricultural products are competitive with those of Santa Cruz. They also make use of the opportunity to replenish their larders, buy seed and equipment, and visit the chicherías. Most marketing activities are carried out on weekends, especially on Sunday when the city is overflowing with harvesters, merchants, farmers, hucksters, and hundreds of visitors eager to share in the festivities. Passenger trucks, buses, and private vehicles are filled to capacity transporting people to and from Montero on Sunday. At times the transient population reaches such proportions that crowds turn into angry mobs fighting for space on a truck or bus in order to return home by late evening. The renown of Montero on Sunday is such that persons from as far away as the city of Santa Cruz will eagerly make the 60-kilometer excursion into the northern province to participate in the marketing and drinking activities or to simply sit in the plaza and watch.

The carnival atmosphere of Montero on weekends pervades the entire city and is highly contagious to anyone who ventures into town. Migrants disembark from vehicles with eyes wide and mouths agape. Soon they are caught up in the swirl of buying and selling, drinking, dancing, and animated conversation. Nowhere is off limits to the migrant throng, much to the displeasure of the Camba residents. Highlanders sit and talk in the plaza and line the street curbs; hawkers are everywhere shouting and pleading with passersby to stop and survey their merchandise. This is the day when newly arrived migrants meet and talk with older town residents and settlers from the hinterlands. The neophyte Kolla is given information about land, business opportunities, employment, or perhaps news of a long-lost relative known to have traveled east. Cooperatives are organized, or already established groups seek to interest new members. Agriculturalists look for farm help and laborers search for possible employers. Widely dispersed families will often meet in Montero to renew old ties and exchange gossip. Even soccer games between rival communities of highlanders are often held in Montero. Business is conducted in the markets, on sidewalks, or in chicherías. By nightfall the city is ablaze with light and throbs with the sound of amplificadores pounding out strains of highland music.

The following morning a semblance of normality returns. Most of the visitors have gone to homes and farms for another week of work. A few chicherías remain open, serving the diehards trying to squeeze a little more mileage out of their Sunday. Many of the streets near the chicherías are littered with the inert bodies of the previous day's drinking casualties, Kollas who will later contend with the wrath of wives or employers or both.

The Migrant Barrio

The Methodist hospital, about four blocks east of the plaza, is the present Camba-Kolla settlement boundary in Montero. Dispersed highland families live in other areas of the city as well, but they have not yet formed any major barrio concentrations. The primary highland residential areas are east of the hospital and in Villa Cochabamba, which directly faces the market on the far side of the paved road.

Although highlanders are living within the inner boundary of the highway, the road here has become a social marker as it is in Warnes. Those highlanders west of the highway work in the market, own small stores, or are employed as day laborers. Buildings in this area are constructed of permanent materials and generally conform to the urban style of the surrounding Camba neighborhoods. Rental housing is common here, especially in the form of "long houses," single rectangular dwellings housing numerous families in individual rooms. Unlike those found in the city of Santa Cruz, these rental complexes are well constructed of brick and tile. Absentee landlords are also prevalent in Montero but are of a different genre than their

Santa Cruz counterparts. Many of the Montero rental housing owners are campesinos who maintain dwellings in the city to provide inexpensive shelter for themselves while marketing. In the interim, the
property is protected from abuse and provides a small additional income for the farm family. It is common for one or two members of an
extended or a nuclear campesino family to reside in one room of
such a complex while the remaining kin continue to work their land.

East of the highway lies Villa Cochabamba, unequaled anywhere
in the lowlands, and perhaps even in the highlands, for its multitude
of chicherías. Villa Cochabamba, like Villa Tunari in Warnes, is the
result of both highland pressure for living space and lowland desire
to remove the highlanders from central Montero. Again, the Urban Reform Law was invoked to obtain the property that was subsequently subdivided into urban dwelling sites. The barrio is concentrated in an area four by three blocks square, the longer side running
along the highway. There are other houses scattered outside of this
main settlement area, but they are few in number and many are in
various stages of completion. What is most notable about the central
district of the villa is the proliferation of drinking establishments. In
the entire twelve-block area there appear to be only two dwellings
that are not involved in the preparation or serving of chicha. One is a
pauhuichi inhabited by a Camba family, the original residents of the
property who have chosen to remain in their home. It is totally surrounded by chicherías and is definitely the neighborhood anomaly.

Within the confines of Villa Cochabamba are eighty chicherías
(Municipalidad de Montero 1975), an average of over six drinking
establishments per square block. The architecture of the Montero
chicherías seems to be a combination of traditional highland styles
and lowland adaptations. Many of the smaller chicha bars are built
directly facing the street with the drinking parlor visible to passing
traffic. Some of the larger chicherías have elaborate "fortifications"
consisting of high walls with broken glass along the top and impreg-
nable wooden or metal doors, a style commonly found in the city of
Santa Cruz. All are adorned with small hanging signs or painted wall
advertisements extolling the virtues of the brew served within—
"chicha buena," "chicha clizeña," or "chicha punateña." (Cliza and
Punata are villages in the Cochabamba Valley renowned for their excellent chicha.) The city of Montero collects a healthy tax from the
chicherías, so, for the moment, their presence is tolerated. It seems,
nevertheless, that many bar owners, especially the "professionals"
who have had previous negative encounters with the authorities, are

diligent in protecting their property and go to great expense in barricading themselves from unwanted intrusion. These women are taciturn and distrustful, not surprising since hostility and deceit directed from the dominant society are a daily part of their lives.

As in Warnes, the chichería owners are a mixed group of females: those who have come to Montero for the express purpose of opening a drinking establishment and others who entered the business as an alternative to fieldwork or farming. The structures that house chicherías are both owned and rented, the latter option preferred by the professional chicheras who will move on if business begins to drop off. Some chicheras who entered the business following other occupational experiences engage in part-time activities such as marketing. Since business on weekdays tends to be slow, chicha vendors often use this time to operate a market stall or prepare food to sell to shoppers.

Buildings are permanent in the main settlement area of Villa Cochabamba, as would be expected given the number of drinking establishments in the district. All are constructed of brick and have tile roofs. Many have minimal finishing, some lack windows or floors, and the brick walls have not been stuccoed as is the custom for a completed building. The major concern in many cases seems to be to erect a structure as quickly as possible to accommodate one's clients. Some chicherías will be completed as time and money permit, but others may remain much as they are since they serve their purpose adequately.

The villa is expanding to the east and south, so as one moves farther in these directions dwellings become more scattered and a greater number of temporary structures are evident. The prevalent nonpermanent building material in Montero is the rough, first-cut boards that are discarded by lumber mills in the area. Lap-sided shacks are erected from the refuse lumber; most have corrugated iron roofs, making them extremely uncomfortable during the warmer months of the year.

The southernmost boundary of the highland settlement is now marked by two parallel dirt roads leading to the new railroad station east of the city. The Santa Cruz–Mamoré railroad, still under construction, will ultimately reach the Department of Beni to export beef from the region. Along the two dirt tracks, numerous houses have sprung up, most of permanent construction but others of wood. Because of the transit through the area, several of these structures are chicherías, and others have a store in a front room. This zone has become the settlement site for many families from the agricultural colonies to the north, especially for those from the Buen Retiro Colony. Many of these inhabitants are females and children, the families of men who continue to work on their land. In other words, Montero has become an additional place of residence for many families rather than one that is subsequent to colonization.

Multiple-Resource Migration

Throughout the rural lowland area, highlanders are engaging in what appears to be a unique form of migration but one that, when viewed in terms of cultural persistence, is in keeping with traditional highland life-styles. As outlined in chapter 1, migration patterns take several forms—various combinations of rural and urban movement and seasonal migration, step migration, chain migration, and so on. All of these patterns normally have one characteristic in common: the migratory unit—the individual, the family, or a community—exploits its resources sequentially; that is, one habitat is abandoned in order to exploit the next. Granted, in many instances kinsmen and landholdings may be left behind, and periodic visits may be made, but in general the act of migration, in the words of British sociologist J. A. Jackson, "implies an element of disassociation from the usual and familiar world, a transition and an involvement with a new environment, a new context of physical space" (1969:9).

In rural Santa Cruz, a new dimension has been added to migration processes. Many highland migrants are embarking upon a system of multiple-resource migrations in which several economic niches are exploited simultaneously. As succeeding migrations are made, each preceding place of residence is not abandoned but is maintained as a source of income, and disassociation fails to occur. The following account is an example of this new pattern.

Jorge Mamani, his wife, Susana (both pseudonyms), and their two children contracted in their highland village to work in the cotton harvest. Jorge left his small house and one-half hectare of land in the care of his eldest brother, who held contiguous land. During the harvest the Mamanis were careful with their wages, buying very little food and no luxuries, and saved enough to purchase a small farm near the Yapacaní agricultural colony. After two years, Jorge joined a land cooperative and through this organization was able to acquire an additional 50 hectares of land in the colony itself. He worked both parcels simultaneously, and Susana moved the family back and forth to help with the planting and harvesting. After five years in the low-lands, Susana and the children, now numbering four, migrated to Montero where Susana set up a vegetable stand in the central market. She rented a room for a few months from another highlander while Jorge built them a house in Villa Cochabamba. When the two-room structure was completed, one of the rooms was rented to a migrant and his family who had recently arrived in the lowlands.

Jorge continues to spend most of his time on their land, and Susana periodically visits the farm to bring in produce to sell in Montero. Jorge comes into Montero on weekends to see his family and drink chicha in one of the many bars in their neighborhood. Recently the Mamanis purchased an additional urban lot in the villa and con-structed from scrap lumber a small shack which houses Jorge's cousin. Susana has secured a vegetable kiosk in the market area of the main settlement in the colony and pays her sister a percentage of the prof-its to run it for her. When Susana visits the colony she usually sleeps in the kiosk with her cousin rather than out on one of the parcels be-cause, she complains, "it's too buggy out there."

Although this case represents one of the successful migrant fami-lies which has been accumulating capital several years, many others are working toward similar goals and may be found at varying stages of property acquisition. Perhaps the most difficult transition for the migrant is from the initial single resource to that of multiple re-sources. One migrant family interviewed labored six years in an agri-cultural colony before accumulating enough capital to purchase an additional house in a nearby town where the wife set up a store. Oth-ers may never make that transition, but when one talks with newly arrived highlanders, it is evident that most have aspirations of mov-ing parts of the family to other localities in order to diversify and ex-pand their earning capacity.

Whereas the Camba may participate in the custom of having both a rural and an urban residence, it is rare that the city home is con-ceived of primarily as a source of income. Rather, the additional home represents both a convenience in that it provides an inexpen-sive shelter for children who may be studying in town and serves as a status symbol for an upwardly mobile farm family. The Kolla, on the other hand, is concerned primarily with the economic potential rather than the intrinsic value of the properties obtained. As ex-plained, entrepreneurship is a characteristic of most highland mi-grants regardless of age, sex, or social status. However, in analyzing the particular case of rural Santa Cruz, multiple-resource exploitation not only can be attributed to the tendency toward commercialization and capital accumulation but it seems also to be rooted in Andean culture.

Although conquered and subjected first by the Inca and then by the Spaniard, the highland Indian retained intact what John Murra (1972) has described as the vertical exploitation of numerous ecological niches. Thus a single village would have access to products from the humid lowlands, grazing land on the high puna, farmlands in the fertile mountain valleys, and perhaps an oasis along the Pacific coast. Murra emphasizes that each zone was exploited by a permanent colony, or archipelago, sent out from the original nuclear settlement and that a certain segment of the population remained in these archipelagos continually. Vertical ecological exploitation, then, was not a matter of seasonal migration or nomadic moves but a system of simultaneous control of ecological levels. Similar to Vayda and Suttles' interpretation of potlatching on the northwest coast of North America as a "functional response to the problem of minimizing the effects of seasonal and long-term fluctuations in the productivity of the local group" (Harris 1968:313), Andean verticality gave each community access to a variety of staple foods and other commodities.

The basic structure of multiple-resource exploitation as practiced in the Andes has been transported by highland migrants into the Bolivian lowlands, although with some modification. In a totally different social and environmental context, highland verticality has been converted to lowland horizontality. In Santa Cruz, the migrant is not faced with a need to exploit several ecological niches in different natural environments but rather utilizes various *economic* niches within the same natural environment. The migrant's resource exploitation is thus extended over a horizontal plane based on economic differentiation and not a vertical one of zonal ecological variation. The underlying structure, or that of permanent archipelagos, as Murra terms them, has not been altered. The highland migrant is not engaging in a type of seasonal migration or a typical rural-urban progression but rather has established permanent residences in different locations in order to exploit several economic niches simultaneously. A significant aspect of Andean culture has demonstrated not only persistence through time and space but also the ability to adapt successfully to a contextual change.

The system of multiple migration may follow any one of several strategies, combining urban and rural residence with variations in economic maintenance schemes. Numerous localities throughout the lowlands are participating as shared residences of highland migrants. It is Montero, nevertheless, that most often appears as an additional site of settlement in the phenomenon of multiple-resource migration. Because of the combination of available and inexpensive urban land, commercial potential, and growing concentrations of Kolla inhabitants, Montero is high on the list of collateral settlement choices (Stearman 1978).

The Montero Migrants

Twenty-six individuals, selected from four areas of the city, were interviewed in Montero in 1975. The large market at the edge of the highway provided nine informants, the smaller Rosendo Paz market five. Two female vendors selling in the streets near the plaza and ten persons from the Villa Cochabamba sector completed the sample population of twenty females and six males.

Informants in Villa Cochabamba were chosen to include residents in the central neighborhood as well as those in peripheral areas to the east and south of the barrio. Although it might have been more representative to have obtained a larger proportion of chichería operators, it was difficult to gain entry to these establishments. All outsiders are suspect and, if not actually denied admittance, are simply ignored. Only two chicheras were interviewed, and much of the information concerning chicherías in Montero was supplied by these individuals or by other neighborhood residents. In the market areas, informants were selected by availability of the vendors and diversity of selling activities. The main market provided various types of informants, including those selling produce, those engaged in merchandising, food and drink hawkers, and two coca sellers. Of the five individuals questioned in the Paz market, two were selling vegetables, two dealt in dry goods, and the fifth operated a small brick kiosk on the east end of the marketplace. Two street vendors working in the plaza area were also included in the sample. Both were females sitting on the curb hawking produce. They were doing an excellent business and were not burdened with the nuisance of having to share their profits with the city treasury as did their marketplace counterparts. One did comment, however, that street vending was illegal and that she was forced to move around a great deal to stay ahead of the authorities.

Because of its dual importance as a service center and as a gathering place for rural migrants, Montero is attracting both urban and rural highlanders. Although the 1975 sample may not be representative of the larger Montero population at the time, it did point to the mixed nature of Montero migrants. Origins of the sample population of twenty-six were evenly spread over the categories of urban highland (eight), rural highland (ten), and rural-urban highland (eight). The rural migrants slightly outnumbered urban individuals as would be expected for an agriculturally based community. The average age of the sample population was 33.5, mid-range between the Santa Cruz sample average of thirty-one and the Warnes sample average of thirty-seven. The standard deviation for the Montero informants was 9.1.

Half of the 1975 sample population of twenty-six entered Montero via the harvest, and three of the eight persons with strictly urban backgrounds came to the lowlands initially to work as fieldhands. Of seven farming informants, four went directly to an agricultural colony where they continued to hold land, but they also purchased or were in the process of purchasing urban dwellings in Montero; another three had lowland farms but subsequently disposed of them to migrate to the city. Five began marketing immediately, and one of the two chichería owners came to Montero expressly to set up a drinking establishment. The other is one of the three persons who began as agriculturalists, but she and her spouse liquidated their farm holdings to come to Montero to open a chichería.

Montero, like Warnes, has the disadvantage of a scarcity of agricultural land for the small-scale farmer. Once again, agribusiness has introduced the trend of consolidating small landholdings to permit the more efficient exploitation of agricultural properties. The small farmer in Montero now works only the marginal areas where, for one reason or another, plow agriculture is not economically feasible. Single males or heads of families interested in establishing a small farm must go elsewhere.

What Montero can provide is available employment for rural individuals desiring to settle in an urban situation. In 1975 the laying of sewers and streets was occupying much of the unskilled labor coming out of the harvests. Two of the six males interviewed were engaged in the loceta project, and five of the fourteen spouses of female informants were similarly employed. Thus one-third of the total male sample population was working on street projects. The remaining male informants and husbands of females interviewed fell into various occupational categories with farming (in absentia) and marketing (three) most often cited. It should be noted that, as in Santa Cruz, the word albañil (mason) is a generic term for anyone employed in the construction industry. Of the seven males who claimed albañil as a profession, only one was actually a mason, the others working in any capacity from ditchdigger to hod carrier.

Among the twenty females interviewed, seventeen were in part- or full-time marketing, two operated chicherías, and one was unemployed. The informant who was not working stated that she had been a market vendor, but that having four small children had curtailed her marketing activities temporarily. She added that her husband was also a vendor and at the time his income was adequate for their needs. This informant, however, was adamant that she would return to her profession as soon as the children were older and could care for one another. Four of the spouses of married male informants were engaged in marketing, and the fifth was unemployed. Thus twenty-one of the total female sample population of twenty-five were vendors in the markets of Montero.

Both chichería operators had a male in residence, one an ex-farmer who helped his wife in their drinking establishment and the other an albañil working on the street project. The latter was evidently a current paramour of the professional chichera since she did not once refer to him as her husband (*esposo, marido*) but employed more circumspect terms such as "el hombre que vive aquí" ("the man who lives here") or "él que me ayuda" ("he who helps me"). The professional chicha vendor confirmed that many of her chichera neighbors came to Montero not to harvest but to take advantage of the boom resulting from a large influx of seasonal migrants. She also stated that other barrio women had opened chicherías only after spending time on a farm or in the fields. It would seem, then, that Montero and Warnes were attracting both the itinerant chichera group and rural females who fell into chicha production and sale as an alternative occupation to field labor. According to other informants and the two chicheras, matrifocality and sequential monogamous unions seemed to be prevalent among many of the professional chichería owners in Montero, as was the case in Warnes.

Three of the female informants and their families were involved in some phase of multiple-resource exploitation. They owned a house and property in Montero but continued to work and reside periodically on the family's rural agricultural land. A fourth woman interviewed did not yet have a home in Montero but was in the process of purchasing a lot in addition to the farm holdings she and her family had in an agricultural colony. Two of the three resident females in this group rented out part of their dwellings to other migrants, and one owned another lot with a wood shack which was rented to a migrant family. All four informants were acquainted with or knew of other inhabitants of Villa Cochabamba who are also involved in multiple-residence ownership. One woman stood in her doorway and pointed to three houses nearby whose owners traveled among their various property holdings in town and country.

As one might surmise from the name of the largest highland barrio in Montero, Cochabamba is well represented in the city (table 5.2.). Almost half of the migrants sampled listed Cochabamba (city or department) as their place of origin. Eight persons were from other highland regions but had lived in the city of Cochabamba before coming to Santa Cruz, underscoring this locality's importance as the jumping-off place for many Kollas who make their way to the lowlands. The remaining departments were fairly evenly represented, with Chuquisaca (Sucre) contributing a few more migrants than the others.

For a large segment of the individuals interviewed in Montero, migration to Santa Cruz was not their first experience with moving. Sixteen informants stated that they had lived in other areas of the Bolivian highlands since leaving their place of birth. While these moves might appear to be "steps" in a geographic or in an economic sense, informants were not consciously aware of such a process. Although the migrant progression may be one that demonstrates a rural-urban trend or entails continual economic betterment, informants commented that they moved because their financial situation had begun to deteriorate. In other words, they viewed their moving as the result of negative factors rather than positive ones of economic improvement. Even so, many of those migrants interviewed who had experienced multiple changes of residence said that they would freely move again should the need arise. These individuals did not consider frequent migrations either pathological or undesirable.

Again, illiteracy was high among the migrant sample; fourteen of the twenty-six informants in Montero reported a lack of reading and writing skills. As was true in Santa Cruz and Warnes, females had a much higher rate of illiteracy than males, the result of differential access to education.

As has been reported, reasons for migrating to Santa Cruz were overwhelmingly economic. Almost half (twelve of twenty-six) of those interviewed in Montero entered the lowlands via harvesting, as would be expected for this area. Seven informants commented, how-

Table 5.2. Montero Migrants' Place of Origin (department or district), 1975

Origin	Number	Percent
Cochabamba	12	46.2
Chuquisaca (Sucre)	4	15.4
Oruro	3	11.5
Potosí	3	11.5
La Paz	2	7.7
Tarija	2	7.7
Total	26	100.0

ever, that they also had come to the lowlands to find work but that they preferred not to enter field labor; this group was composed of market vendors and the professional chichera. Four persons cited the availability of land as their principal incentive for moving east; three of them continued to hold rural as well as urban properties, while the fourth had severed economic ties with the hinterlands. Three had accompanied relatives.

Family networks among highlanders in the lowlands seemed to be well established, and only seven migrants in the sample reported no known kin in Santa Cruz. The presence of other family members in the lowlands may be attributed primarily to chain migration. It was common for informants to state that, during visits to the interior, they would interest an uncle or cousin in accompanying them on the return trip. These relatives were often successful in obtaining employment in Santa Cruz and would later send for the remainder of their families.

Dress patterns among women interviewed followed the rural orientation of Montero. In fact, a mature highland woman wearing mestizo dress is rarely seen on the streets of Montero. All of the men wore the mestizo-style cotton clothing customary among highland males in Santa Cruz. The pollera was preferred by the large majority of female informants, 70 percent, and in a city such as Montero, where highlanders are so numerous, there is little stigma in wearing traditional highland dress.

Rental and home ownership among the sample population in Montero were about equal, a situation similar to that encountered among the Santa Cruz informants (table 5.3). In 1975 both cities had received a large influx of new arrivals in the lowlands, and housing patterns seemed to reflect this change in the availability of rental properties. Both localities also offered those types of employment that permitted

Table 5.3. Migrant Housing in Montero, 1975

Type of Housing	Number	Percent
Own	12	46.0
Rent	11	42.0
Live with relative	1	4.0
Live in kiosk	1	4.0
Not a Montero resident	1	4.0
Total	26	100.0

continued urban residence for nonskilled laborers. Warnes, on the other hand, had little to offer in urban employment or farmland and could absorb only a limited number of permanent residents from the migrant ranks. Consequently, rental housing was not prevalent in Warnes and still is not.

The interviewing of migrants in 1980 as part of the DDE study further contributed to an understanding of the migration process occurring in Montero. The 3 percent randomly selected subsample of the 1979 survey of 1,023 migrants called for thirty-five informants. Of those, thirteen (38 percent) could not be located, placing Montero second only to the agricultural colonies in terms of population flux. Whether the thirteen missing cases went back to the highlands, moved elsewhere in the lowlands, or simply relocated in Montero is not known. Except for one case—that of a Camba migrant whose neighbors recalled the family having moved to Santa Cruz—the survey team was unable to ascertain their whereabouts. Part of the difficulty can be attributed to the degree of renting that prevails in the city. Of the twenty-two informants contacted, seven were living in rental property and one was squatting on city land designated for a future park; thus eight families, or 36 percent of the sample, were located in temporary housing. All of the renters claimed to be saving to purchase a lot, preferably in Montero. Based on this information, it might be assumed that many of the thirteen missing cases had been renters and had moved elsewhere in the city after acquiring their own home or property.

The 1980 study, which included Camba migrants as well as Kollas, also pointed to some interesting differences in housing patterns between these two groups. Of the twenty-two cases, nine were lowland migrants and thirteen highlanders. Three highland families (23 percent) and four Camba families (44 percent) were renters. Nonetheless, the average length of residence in Montero was longer for Cambas than Kollas, 10.2 to 5.8 years, indicating that length of residence, which usually correlates positively with homeownership and permanence of structure (Turner 1970), does not appear to be a factor in this instance. Again, the problem seems to be one of cultural differences in the attitude toward making and saving money. The highland propensity toward entrepreneurship, saving, and reinvestment means the average Kolla migrant will acquire capital for such things as housing more rapidly than a Camba counterpart and then will use that property for additional income. Of the nine Kolla families owning their homes, four were renting rooms to other highland migrants, most of whom were recent arrivals. None of the five Camba homeowners was earning income in this manner. One of the Camba renters was living in a house he had built and once owned but had sold to meet living expenses. The new owner is a highlander.

Motives for migration also differed between Cambas and Kollas, perhaps indicating not only cultural differences between the two groups but a different selection process as well (table 5.4). Cambas moving from one place to another do not really perceive of themselves as migrants because the social environment tends to remain constant. Thus moving is seen simply as that—a move—and not a major life decision. Of the nine Camba informants interviewed, six came to Montero to be with close relatives. Although financial betterment may have influenced the decision to move, family considerations were paramount. Two men came because they were hired in Santa Cruz to work at the Guabirá sugar mill. They had jobs waiting for them so there was little risk involved. The final informant liked Montero better than his home community of Portachuelo and moved because of the level of social activity found there.

For the highlander, however, moving to the lowlands represents a major decision and always involves risk. The move also means leaving one's natal culture for one that is alien and at times hostile. Thus the Kolla who decides to migrate tends to be the sort who will not merely seek to survive but will fight to get ahead. Among the highland informants all but two came for economic reasons. Of the two who did not, one was a child at the time and came with her parents and the other was a Protestant minister who gave up his mission in Potosí to work with harvesters.

Montero continues to attract both urban and rural highland migrants as it did in 1975. Six of the Kolla informants come from rural backgrounds and entered the lowlands through harvesting or field work (four) or as colonists (two). Three of the informants had made a

Table 5.4. Montero Migrants' Motives for Migration, 1980

Motive	Camba		Kolla	
	No.	%	No.	%
Find land	0	—	2	15.0
Work in harvest	0	—	3	23.0
Find work	0	—	6	46.0
Accompany parents	0	—	1	8.0
Missionary	0	—	1	8.0
Live with relatives	6	67.0	0	—
Work at Guabirá	2	22.0	0	—
More urban environment	1	11.0	0	—
Total	9	100.0	13	100.0

previous rural-urban move in the highlands and four came directly from highland cities. One of these four worked a season in the cotton harvest before renting a stall in the market.

Lowlanders were also about evenly divided between rural (four) and urban (five) backgrounds but, unlike highlanders, talked of eventually moving to Santa Cruz. Many Cambas in Montero resent living in a city so dominated by Kollas. Even though they admit that they may have steady work and a home, they feel obliged to complain about Kollas as a way of maintaining their ethnic identity. Cambas also consider Montero a poor substitute for the real thing, the city of Santa Cruz, which in their minds remains the cultural center of the lowlands.

Occupational categories among highland female informants remained constant between 1975 and 1980, with marketing the most often cited form of employment. Five of the Kolla women interviewed were engaged in either full- or part-time marketing, and three of the spouses of male informants were also so employed. The remaining two female informants and two spouses of male informants stated that they were staying at home temporarily to take care of young children. The Camba female informants tended to follow the lowland pattern of remaining at home to manage household affairs while the spouse supports the family. This pattern represents a major distinction between highland and lowland gender roles and one which again contributes to the Kolla family's ability to accumulate capital in a shorter period of time. The indigenous substratum present among highland people places a great deal of emphasis on the female's economic importance to the family in marketing or producing goods for sale. Among Camba women, the Mediterranean patriarchal model is prevalent, and it is expected that the male will take full responsibility in providing for the family. Among rural and urban Cambas who are poor, it may become necessary for the women to take on odd jobs such as laundering or becoming a domestic for a short period of time. Rarely is this work seen as important, however, and once the male begins to bring more money into the household, the Camba woman will return to being a full-time housewife. Kolla women, on the other hand, consider what they do as significant to their own well-being as well as that of their family. They often continue to work throughout their lives as a means of accumulating additional capital for investment in property or to expand merchandising operations.

Occupations of highland males changed in the five years after 1975, no doubt as a result of the completion of the sewer and loceta projects. While differences in sampling may account for these discrepancies, a wider variety of occupations was apparent among Kolla migrant males in 1980 than in 1975, and many of these were skilled or semiskilled in nature. Although some building continues in the city, there no longer is a need for large numbers of unskilled workers. Whether the unskilled workers of earlier years may have acquired job expertise necessary to remain in Montero as wage earners or simply moved elsewhere is unknown. Since the paving of streets continues in the city of Santa Cruz, it is conceivable that some of these workers may have migrated to the city to pursue the same work there.

Of the six rural highland migrants, two were engaging in multiple-resource migration, holding land in agricultural colonies simultaneously with their urban residence in Montero. In both cases, the male spouse was working the land and spending weekends in Montero while the female was a full-time vendor. In addition, both families were renting rooms to Kolla migrants in Montero.

All of the Camba migrants had other kin in Montero itself, and eleven of the thirteen Kollas made the same claim. Among both groups, chain migration continues to be an important factor in motivation for migration (especially Camba) and site selection (especially Kolla). The great majority of highland migrants come from Cochabamba, as was true in 1975, lending further support to the importance of chain migration in the migration process itself (table 5.5). Vallegrandinos are also beginning to appear in Montero; formerly their relocation was limited almost totally to the city of Santa Cruz. Vallegrande is a region in the mountains that belongs politically to the Department of Santa Cruz but is culturally a highland domain. The town of Valle Grande is an old urban center but one which, like

Table 5.5. Montero Migrants' Origins, 1980

Origin	Number	Percent
Camba		
Santa Cruz	8	89.0
Beni	1	11.0
Total	9	100.0
Kolla		
Cochabamba	8	62.0
La Paz	1	8.0
Potosí	2	15.0
Vallegrande	2	15.0
Total	13	100.0

much of the highlands, has increasingly less economic opportunity. As a result, many of the residents have chosen to leave the area and migrate to the city of Santa Cruz, about an eight-hour bus trip from Vallegrande. The fact that some have moved on to Montero may be an indication of housing shortages in Santa Cruz (more rental property is available in Montero), Montero's growing economic prosperity, and the booming cocaine market centered in this area. (The continued influx of migrants despite the relative lack of legitimate employment in unskilled areas may be partly explained in terms of the drug trade.)

In the settlement situations in Santa Cruz, Warnes, and Montero, Kolla migrants have maintained a certain distance from their Camba neighbors. Economically they have relied on wage labor or have occupied economic niches, such as marketing, that were only half-heartedly exploited by Cambas. In some instances, parallel economic systems have been set up which exclude Cambas entirely: selling chicha, traditional highland clothing, produce, or prepared food solely to other migrants. In each of these cases, intensive social interaction with Cambas is not necessary for economic success. In chapter 6, Kollas in a Camba village largely dependent on semisubsistence horticulture find that, in order to survive, they must participate in the already established socioeconomic system.

6

San Carlos: Highland Migrants
in a Lowland Village

Old Camba villages with their prejudices toward outsiders, especially toward Kollas, are probably the least attractive settlement opportunity available to the highland migrant. Yet for some rural highland migrants, village life is a comfortable alternative to the pressures of larger centers such as Montero, and it affords amenities that are absent in the agricultural colonies or on dispersed farmsteads. Any number of small northern Cruceñan communities would provide excellent insights into the process and impact of highland migration in a village situation, but because of my long involvement and familiarity with one particular locality it has been chosen to serve as an example of current settlement trends.

The township of San Carlos is situated 80 kilometers northwest of the city of Santa Cruz. It was once a point of embarkation for cattle drivers and rubber tappers heading north into the Beni and Pando regions. Now it must be content to be counted among the many small farming communities scattered along the western branch of the paved highway from Montero.

San Carlos was founded in 1797 as part of a missionary effort spreading outward from Santa Cruz. The inhabitants of the village are the descendants of Yuracaré Indians, blacks from Brazil, Spanish settlers, and other indigenous and European groups. The community's population at the time of the 1976 census was 2,010 (Bolivia

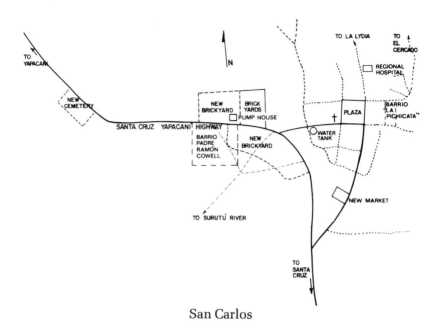

San Carlos

1976), almost all campesinos. San Carlos is not much different from scores of similar Camba settlements throughout the department. It has a main plaza, church, alcaldía (mayor's office), and streets set out in a grid pattern. The houses in the prestigious plaza area are uniformly of masonry or whitewashed wattle-and-daub construction with Spanish tile roofs. As one moves farther from the center of town, the houses become smaller and more rudely built. On the outskirts unplastered pauhuichis with thatched roofs are the rule. The proliferation of sawmills in the region has also encouraged hut construction using low-grade lumber for walls. Warnes and San Carlos are similar in appearance, but there is a significant difference between the two settlements. Warnes has become a town of commercial farmers tied directly to the agribusiness enterprises in the surrounding region and dependent upon contract harvesting and wage labor. San Carlos remains a community of small, independent farmers and ranchers, and only a handful of villagers have given up swidden horticulture in favor of mechanized agriculture. Cotton is not grown in the area, and only one agriculturalist is exploiting sugarcane commercially.

Before 1969, not one Kolla family lived within the three-kilometer radius of San Carlos. By 1975 seven highland households were present. Most took up residence along the highway on the periphery of town, but one family succeeded in purchasing a house on the corner of the plaza where they opened a small store. For highlanders to survive in a village which had no marketplace, chichería, or public projects to absorb unskilled laborers and had a limited need for fieldhands, they had to be competitive with Cambas in Camba areas of endeavor and their occupational options were largely limited to farming, storekeeping, or crafts. Since economic expansion in San Carlos existed at a negligible rate, most newcomers were replacements for urban-bound Cambas and not actual additions to the village population. Such a situation implied at least partial integration into the community's social and economic structure, not easily accomplished given the closed nature of San Carlos and the pervading prejudice against Kollas.

Those highland residents who secured small farms near San Carlos remained somewhat marginal to village life because the land filled many of their needs. Still, the vagaries of agriculture and limited cash reserves often required that food, medicine, or other supplies be acquired through a credit agreement with a storekeeper. The two migrant families that operated stores participated more fully in the established socioeconomic system of the community in order to make a living. Since there were only seven highland families living permanently in San Carlos at the time, the highland storekeepers could not depend solely on other Kollas for their clientele, as would be possible in Santa Cruz, Montero and even Warnes, where migrants were numerous. Whether store owner, farmer, or craftsman, then, the highland migrant in San Carlos by necessity had to break into existing socioeconomic networks.

For the migrant, participation in the socioeconomic system of a Camba village is both difficult and easy—difficult in establishing initial relationships which, for an outsider such as a Kolla, takes time and effort, relatively easy because of the highly integrative nature of village society. It is a complex model but one that is well adapted to the particular demands of the village situation in the northern Santa Cruz region.

Socioeconomic Integration

San Carlos rests on a hill of red clay which town lore says was once a bank of the Surutú River. That river now flows some five kilometers southwest of the village. To the north, west, and south of the town lie agricultural lands, covered with young, second-growth forest. The area to the east has been set aside for cattle ranching. Here, the forest breaks into pampa, extending for miles before the jungle closes in again. Most of the landholdings in this zone are larger than those owned by the horticulturalists. The pasture is unimproved and normally will support no more than one cow per three hectares. While ranching is an important part of the village economy, relatively few families are involved in this activity and the bulk of the population in and around San Carlos relies on horticulture for its livelihood. The principal subsistence and cash crop is dry rice. It is grown on land prepared by cutting and burning the vegetation, a process that serves both to clear the ground and to enrich the soil with mineral nutrients deposited in the ash. Only one rice crop per year is planted, usually during the wet months of September through December, to be harvested five months later.

Crops of secondary importance include corn, yuca (manioc), cacao, plantains, guineos (eating bananas), citrus, pineapple, and coffee. They are valuable both in the additional income they represent, especially between harvests, and in providing the family with some variation in diet. Nevertheless, rice is the economic mainstay of San Carlos, and the greater part of village life is ruled by the demands imposed by its cultivation; into the yearly planting cycle is woven the thread of village society, one inseparable from the other.

Although it is recognized that no person can exist without establishing a network of reciprocal relationships, the Sancarleños constantly guard against intrusion by others into what they feel is the sanctity of their individuality. Cooperation among groups of persons is uncommon. Only the dyadic relationship can be trusted because each partner is personally in control of the degree of obligation and responsibility. Dyadic relationships, or contracts, as Foster (1961) terms them, are established in San Carlos primarily through bonds of fictive kinship by means of the institution known as compadrazgo. Its manifest purpose was to give children godparents at baptism and thereby guarantee them a Christian upbringing should they be neglected or orphaned. The religious significance still remains in the ritual, but the social implications carry much more meaning. When a child is baptized, a bond is established between the child's parents and godparents. They become compadres for life. This relationship may form the basis for daily interactions, or it may be activated only occasionally, or even never. Sidney Mintz and Eric Wolf have de-

scribed compadrazgo as "a two-way social system which sets up reciprocal relations of variable complexity and solemnity. By imposing
automatically, and with a varying degree of sanctity, statuses and obligations of a fixed nature on the people who participate, it makes the
immediate social environment more stable, the participants more in-
terdependent, and more secure" (1967 : 188). In San Carlos, the choice
of godparents for a child is made only after much deliberation. A
chance to gain allies through recognized obligations of mutual aid
must not be wasted. It is through the bond of fictive kinship that merchants and farmers, whether Kollas or Cambas, provide for their re-
spective needs.

When a farmer requests that a merchant become the godparent of
his child, the storekeeper will seldom refuse. First, it is a breach of
tradition to turn down such a request. Second, by accepting another
godchild, the merchant gains additional clients. The farmer's interest
in the arrangement lies in the realm of the availability of a ready loan
or commodities on credit. Life in San Carlos exists on a day-to-day
basis, and economic disaster is a constant threat. When times are
lean or an emergency occurs, assistance is sought through the merchant. As Arensberg had stated, "The shopkeeper, as creditor, has the
whip-hand. As an urbanite, he has the superior status. Yet he is no
less under obligation to his debtor" (1968:157). This obligation is
even stronger if it has been reinforced by ties of ritual kinship. If a
compadre is in need, tradition demands that he not be refused. Thus
it is an economic safeguard for the farmer to have at least one compadre who is a storekeeper.

For the merchant, numerous ritual bonds of kinship assure him a
steady flow of customers. Much buying is on credit, which always
poses a risk to the storekeeper. If a creditor is also a compadre, however, there is greater likelihood that the debt will be paid because the
compadrazgo relationship is sacred and must not be diminished by
failure to comply with recognized reciprocal obligations. There are at
least ten stores in the village, all carrying almost identical stock in-
ventories. Prices between stores vary only slightly, and bargaining
does not exist. Upon first examination, then, one might question how
these shops manage to compete with one another, or why there is not
one large outlet to service the entire community. Part of the explana-
tion for the survival of these numerous small stores is to be found in
the system of credit.

Similar situations have been reported for other parts of the world,
and Barbara Ward's (1960) analysis of the credit system in Sarawak is

especially relevant to the case of San Carlos. In her study of the role of merchants and the multiplicity of traders, she found several factors influencing the continued success of the small store. First, numerous similar stores are allowed to exist, often side by side, because of the service they render in giving credit. Several clients are tied to each merchant through credit obligations, and the fact that every store carries the same goods is irrelevant. Each shop caters to a rather fixed set of customers, all with similar needs, who have established credit there. Second, since the shopkeeper is normally operating on a limited amount of capital, the extension of credit over too wide a range would carry the threat of insolvency. Third, merchants must depend on personal knowledge of their clients and their daily whereabouts as security for the investment. The number of debtors is therefore kept within the range of capital limitations and personal trust. As Ward has hypothesized, "In a population which depends upon a wide distribution of credit, no creditor can be expected to have more than a limited number of debtors; then necessarily that population must include (or have access to) a large number of creditors" (1960: 144). The case of San Carlos with its numerous small stores would seem to give further credence to this hypothesis.

As stated, credit buying enables the Kolla or Camba family to acquire food and other trade articles when cash income is only sporadic. While many items secured in this manner are not absolutely necessary for physical survival, they are important to the peasant's sense of well-being. Kerosene for light, tobacco and alcohol, patent medicines all contribute some measure of comfort to a life of hardship. Once credit has been established, the debt need never be paid off completely. A demonstration of good faith, that is, continually giving small amounts to the merchant, is all that is required. With numerous debtors paying in this manner the merchant can maintain enough capital to restock the store and still make a profit. Part of this dyadic relationship between merchant and farmer depends on the perpetuation of the debt. If the debt is canceled, there is no obligation for the merchant to extend more credit to the client or the client to return as a customer. The security of both would then be threatened. Arensberg notes that "any credit system exists upon a peculiar state of mind in which expectancies are roughly balanced. Should all the debts be called in and all outstanding obligations mature at a single blow, the system would perforce come to an end" (1968:155). Instances do occur, however, when credit extended is limited. If a merchant feels that a client has accumulated too large a deficit without at least a token payment, he will call in the debt. This act always presents some risk, for the client may simply refuse to pay the amount or promise payment at some future time. However, since the nonpayment of a store debt readily becomes common knowledge, it would be difficult for the farmer to secure credit elsewhere in San Carlos. It therefore behooves him to maintain himself in good standing with his creditors.

For the majority of highland and lowland storekeepers in San Carlos, sale of merchandise is but one facet of enterprise. While daily sales will maintain a steady flow of income, it is in rice speculation that most large profits are realized. Because of the labor-intensive nature of swidden horticulture, one man is capable of clearing, planting, and harvesting only about two hectares of rice per year. If the soil is fertile, the land may produce up to 12 *fanegas* (2,225 kilos) per hectare. However, most of the farmland in the environs of San Carlos has been cultivated year after year, and yields seldom exceed six or eight fanegas. Receipts from the sale of a season's harvest are often much less than what is needed to support a family. Coupled with the problem of poor harvests is that one has to sell when the market is glutted and prices are low. Most farmers cannot afford to hold their crop until prices rise enough to give them a wider profit margin, nor do they have adequate storage facilities even if they wished to do so.

In many cases, by the time a crop comes in, much of it may be owed to the merchant for credit or for loans received during the year prior to harvest. If the farmer needs cash, he may borrow a small amount from a merchant at no interest; a more common practice, however, is to sell part of a crop before it is planted. The storekeeper will pay only half the current market value for rice sold in this manner. If the farmer has an extraordinary run of bad luck, such as illness or injury, his entire harvest may have been sold to the merchants by the time the crop is actually brought in. Since the lowest market price for rice seldom drops below twice the amount paid by merchants to their clients and usually is much higher, shopkeepers are guaranteed at least double their money. The peasant does not have the option of selling his rice at the market price and then returning the money he borrowed, since the rice is considered property of the merchant and must be delivered in kind. If merchants can afford to hold the grain until the end of the season when rice becomes scarce, they are likely to triple or quadruple their investments. Since crops are often presold to pay existing or overdue debts, the merchant is profiting twice from a single transaction: the money received for unplanted rice is returned to the same shopkeeper to maintain the grower's good credit standing.

In defense of this apparent usury, the merchant is providing the peasant with a service unavailable elsewhere. Credit cooperatives have never had much success in San Carlos, perhaps because they offer no sense of *personalismo*. The campesino does not like to deal with large institutions where the formation of dyadic relationships becomes impossible. The shopkeeper, on the other hand, is an individual, most likely a compadre or comadre, and is in the position to supply cash immediately when the farmer is in need. The merchant also is taking a risk, albeit small, by purchasing a crop yet to be harvested or even planted. A drought or blight can leave storekeepers overextended and without any cash reserves to see them through to the next harvest season when there is hope of recouping their losses.

Few if any Sancarleños operate outside of this complex system of socioeconomic interrelationships based on patronage, ritual kinship ties, credit negotiations, and crop speculation. The fragile village economy, which is subject to the unpredictabilities of near-subsistence agriculture, makes participation in this system necessary for highland migrant residents as well. They are also campesinos, struggling to make ends meet at the conclusion of each harvest season. The Kollas in San Carlos are no more immune to the imminent threat of economic disaster than their Camba counterparts. To a greater or lesser degree, rural highlanders in a village situation must rely on the establishment of functional relationships with the dominant Camba sector to assure the continuation of their social and economic well-being.

Recent Trends in Migration

Between 1975 and 1980 the village of San Carlos continued to attract highland migrants. From the seven Kolla families consisting of 40 people in 1975, the village highlander population has grown to 26 families totaling 126 individuals (Solari 1978). Many of these continued to replace Camba families which have migrated to the city of Santa Cruz, although village size is increasing as well. Over the years, chain migration has played an important role in encouraging greater numbers of Sancarleños to move to the city, where they usually establish themselves within short distance of each other. As more migrate, more desire to do so, leaving the village open either to other rural

lowlanders seeking a progressively more urban existence or to highland migrants with essentially the same motive.

Some physical changes have occurred as the result of increasing
migration into the village. A new urban barrio built at the base of the
old community on the hill consists of both Cambas and Kollas who
have moved into the area primarily from the agricultural colonies or
from more rural settlements. The barrio was named "Ramón Cowell"
after the town's first resident priest, an American missionary who
worked in San Carlos for about ten years. Another new neighborhood
to the South, inhabited entirely by Cambas, is referred to locally as
the "Barrio de la Pichicata" since many of its residents are reported
to be involved with the cocaine trade. The older residents and even
some newer ones tend to look down on the inhabitants of this barrio
because of their illegal activities. In San Carlos, the value system is
still geared to agriculture as a hard but honorable existence; and although there appears to be some envy of the money to be made in
cocaine, most of the older Sancarleños consider it immoral. One
farmer I have known since 1964 was angry that it had become so difficult to find or afford field labor for his rice crop because of the high
wages paid by the cocaine producers.

In addition to the two new barrios, there is a large marketplace
built on the site of the old cemetery. As might be expected, most of
the vendors are Kolla women, with the exception of the meat sellers
who are Cambas. The appearance of a market in the village was no
doubt an attraction to many of the recent Kolla migrants to San Carlos. A new regional hospital has been built on the outskirts of San
Carlos, funded by CORDECRUZ, the community itself, and the Salesian
religious order represented by two Italian priests and several lay
people working in San Carlos. The cost of the hospital is reported at
$2 million (U.S.); much of the furnishings, such as stainless steel
kitchen equipment, machines for the laundry, autoclaves, beds, and
other equipment, has come from Italy as a gift from the Salesians.
The hospital officially opened in October 1980, and it is still too
early to determine what effect it will have on the village economy
and population.

The San Carlos Migrants

The sample migrant population for San Carlos in 1975 numbered
seven informants, representing each Kolla household in the village
that year. In 1980, eight interviews were conducted in as many

households, representing 30 percent of the 26 Kolla families in the community.

Other than the obvious increase in numbers of highlanders in San Carlos, the characteristics of migrants moving into the community have not changed markedly. The migrants interviewed in 1975 gave as their places of origin Cochabamba (three), Potosí (three), and Sucre (one). Of the 126 immigrants residing in the community who were counted in 1978 by Fr. Solari, most came from these three locations, with the other highland departments represented as well (Table 6.1).

Table 6.1. San Carlos Migrants' Places of Origin, 1978

Origin	Number	Percent
Potosí	41	32.4
Chuquisaca (Sucre)	28	22.2
Cochabamba	27	21.4
Tarija	12	9.6
Oruro	9	7.2
La Paz	9	7.2
Total	126	100.0

Source: Solari 1978

The migrants in both sample groups were overwhelmingly rural—six of seven in 1975 and six of eight in 1980. The three informants who migrated from cities (Cochabamba and Sucre) all came to work in the cane and cotton harvests and then secured their own land. Although the first Kollas to live in the community had no relatives there in 1975, all of the 1980 informants claimed they came as a result of having kinspeople in the community. Two of those interviewed were related to the original seven families.

Step migration and multiple-resource migration were also prevalent among both groups as strategies employed for social and economic betterment. For several informants, the move to San Carlos was viewed as a culmination of years of work to achieve a better life for their children. Although San Carlos lacks many of the opportunities found in larger towns, for the rural Kollas living there it represents a workable combination of both rural and urban existence. The proximity of San Carlos to the Yapacaní, Antofagasta, and other agricultural colonies in the zone makes it possible for a family to continue to work their land while they also begin to expand into an urban economic niche. In an effort to demonstrate how these migration strategies are employed, four case studies, three from 1975, since updated, and one from 1980, are presented.

The Batallanos family (1975 and 1980).—Sixto Batallanos (all names are pseudonyms), at age thirty-three, left his small village near Potosí in 1965 to come to the lowlands. He had spent his life trying to eke out a living on a few hectares of rocky soil which barely provided enough for himself, his wife, and their two children. Two years before Sixto decided to migrate, his elder brother left for Santa Cruz and was successful in obtaining a parcel of land in the Yapacaní colony. The brother returned to the highlands for a short visit, and his tales of bountiful land convinced Sixto that he should sell his farm and move east. He left his twenty-five-year-old wife, Aurora, and their children with her sister while he accompanied his brother into the lowlands. But Sixto was not as fortunate as he had hoped, and there was no free land being given out by the government. He began working in the colony as a day laborer and after six months had saved enough money to join a land cooperative which was trying to acquire some property near the Surutú River. It was successful, and by the end of his first year in the lowlands Sixto had 50 hectares of farmland and could send for his family.

Aurora and Sixto built a small house on their property and began to plant rice. They were fortunate in that much of the 50-hectare tract they owned was virgin forest and their crop yields were high. Both worked diligently on the farm along with their children, who now numbered four. Little was spent on other than absolute necessities, and Sixto saved enough to purchase another 25 hectares of land from a Camba in San Carlos. The Batallanos worked both properties, hiring helpers and living apart so that each could oversee one parcel. It took the family eight years to accumulate enough capital to buy a residence in San Carlos, and they were able to pay $1,500 (U.S.) in cash for a house on the southeast corner of the plaza. The Camba owner, Aníbal González, had decided to move permanently to the city of Santa Cruz, and the Batallanos were the first to appear with the money in hand. Later, Aníbal boasted that he had really "taken" the Kollas because the house was not worth much, but the house was centrally located and would be an excellent site for Sixto's wife's store. Sixto knew that as a highlander, he would not have much bargaining power with Aníbal and would have to pay what was asked.

Sixto and his family were the first highlanders to move into the central district of San Carlos but the second family from the interior to locate in the village itself. The town's overt reaction was minimal, but most of the Camba residents, when asked, were not pleased with the intrusion. Aurora opened a small store in the front room of their new house and slowly began to build her business. A core of creditors was established, and soon she and Sixto were asked to become godparents of a Camba farmer's child. The Batallanos have not yet been accepted fully into village life, but their presence in San Carlos is tolerated because they are recognized as hard workers and contributors to the town's economic well-being. Their participation in the community's socioeconomic system has assured the a stable position within their sphere of activity.

Although the Batallanos now have a town residence, Sixto continues to work their two parcels of land. He is absent from San Carlos during the week, returning to his wife and family on weekends to visit, rest, and drink. Aurora is pleased to be out of the *monte* (high forest) and to be living in a situation where their children can finally attend school. Her husband can read and write a little, but she is illiterate. The Batallanos' offspring still are taunted by their Camba playmates and called "Kollas," but Aurora and Sixto are confident that in time the children will be accepted by their peers. Although Quechua is often spoken in the home, especially by the parents, the children prefer to use Spanish. If a Camba is present, Spanish is always used by the Batallanos family. Sixto jokingly relates that his children are growing up Cambas, which he says is fine since they will probably never return to the interior. Both the Batallanos think that their offspring may marry lowlanders.

By 1980, Sixto and Aurora had further expanded their resources by purchasing a lot in Montero to be used as rental property. Because the children are now in secondary school, they required a place to live, Sixto explained, and a house in Montero was an ideal choice. It provides additional income for the family as well as shelter for the Batallanos children. Aurora also makes use of the house when she travels to Montero on buying trips, and since she may stay a few days at a time she can concentrate on selecting her merchandise. Aurora notes, however, that she has no intention of moving permanently to Montero. There is too much competition and too many chicherías where Sixto would be spending their money.

The Ferrofino family (1975 and 1980).—Claudina and Jorge Ferrofino were the first highlanders to move into San Carlos. They have lived in the village for over ten years and, of all the highland families in San Carlos, are the most integrated into village society. All three of the Ferrofino children were born in La Lydia, a small farming community near San Carlos. Their godparents are Cambas from San Carlos. In turn, Claudina and Jorge have been asked to serve as god-

parents for sons and daughters of Sancarleño lowlanders and have
established fictive kinship ties with twelve village families.

At age twenty-four, Jorge came to Santa Cruz from Cochabamba in
1964 to work in the cane harvest. He met Claudina, then seventeen
and also a Cochabambina, while she was marketing in Montero.
When Jorge had enough money put by to purchase some farmland, he
asked Claudina to marry him and they moved to La Lydia. For $300
(U.S.) Jorge was able to acquire 50 hectares of land which included
several mature cacao trees. At that time, he commented, property was
inexpensive and not in much demand. Another 50-hectare parcel
purchased several years later cost double the amount of the first. In
all, the Ferrofinos own three parcels of land, totaling 125 hectares.
After four years in La Lydia the Ferrofinos purchased a lot on the outskirts of San Carlos at a site known as the "Pico de Plancha" (tip of
the iron). Here the highway from Montero veers to the left and the
road into the village continues straight ahead, forming a triangle of
land between the two thoroughfares which resembles the pointed
front of a flat iron. The Ferrofino property is directly opposite the
Pico and so has the advantage of being located both at the town's entrance and near the main highway. Claudina and Jorge built a large
brick house and opened a well-stocked store. Many highland migrants in San Carlos buy from Claudina and in two cases have formed
ritual relationships with her family. Even so, most of the store's business is derived from Camba clients who have established fictive
kinship as well as credit ties with the Ferrofinos.

Jorge owns two trucks which he uses to bring in farm produce and
to collect the rice that has been sold to the Ferrofinos prior to harvest.
Much of the year these vehicles remain idle while Jorge is out working the land, since he does not want to wear out his trucks hauling
cargo on contract. Other than their primary use for bringing in produce and rice, the trucks are used to carry merchandise for the store
and to transport the Ferrofino rice to market when prices peak. Jorge
and Claudina are deeply involved in rice speculation, as are most
Sancarleño merchants who have been in business long enough to establish the necessary networks. Their creditors and compadres, often
one and the same, rely on the Ferrofinos for loans and a steady flow of
supplies. These debt obligations are most commonly met by presell-
ing crops to the highland couple. Jorge's trucks become a necessity at
harvest time when debtors find it difficult to transport the rice they
owe to the Ferrofino store. Not only a lack of adequate transportation
facilities but also a reluctance to part with the fruits of a year's labor

will keep many Sancarleño debtors from voluntarily surrendering their crops. Hence farm visits become vital if the Ferrofinos are to collect their due. Other storekeepers find themselves in the same predicament each year, and those without vehicles must pay the cost of renting a truck. One would think that with all the problems inherent in rice collection store owners would be reluctant to enter into this annual struggle, but the profits earned are large enough to ensure the perpetuation of the rice-credit system. The campesino will hold out as long as possible, making the harvest season an interesting drama of wits and tempers that all disparage but one that only whets the appetite for a return engagement.

The Ferrofinos have been in the lowlands for about the same length of time as the Batallanos but have spent less of their time in the monte among other highlanders. Consequently, Claudina and Jorge are more acculturated to the lowland life-style. Both wear mestizo clothing, and Claudina has given up the traditional double braid for a single braid down her back in the Camba style of hairdress. In contrast, Aurora Batallanos continues to use the pollera and double braid. The Ferrofinos have lost much of their highland accent and are adept at using lowland colloquialisms, but Claudina is proud of her highland origins and has insisted that her children learn to speak Quechua.

Although the Ferrofino family has been in San Carlos for several years now, they are still referred to as "Kollas." It is a label that they will always carry. In the same manner, a German who had married a Sancarleña and who had lived in the village for over thirty years before his death was called simply "el gringo" (the stranger).

The Acuña family (1975 and 1980).—West of the village and at the bottom of the hill are located the San Carlos brick factories. Most of the Santa Cruz region is composed of sandy, alluvial soils, but here and there are found deposits of heavy clay. San Carlos is situated near one of these infrequent deposits and is the only source of fired brick for many of the neighboring towns. Three Camba families traditionally held the rights to clay-bearing property in San Carlos, and these kin groups were also the town's brickmakers. Each brickyard employed two or three laborers who were paid by the piece if they were molding bricks or roof tiles or by the day if they were mixing clay, hauling sawdust for temper, or firing the kilns.

In 1972, Carmelo Acuña, a twenty-two-year-old Potosino migrant working in a Buenos Aires brick factory, had to leave Argentina and traveled to Santa Cruz. Like hundreds of other Bolivians he had crossed the Argentine border illegally, and after two years he began to have problems because of his lack of proper documentation. Many migrants in similar situations, especially those who had entered Argentina to work in the grape and cane harvests, were forced to return to Bolivia. But by this time word had spread that there was work in the fields of Santa Cruz and that the pay was good. Carmelo followed the harvesters to Santa Cruz, confident that he would find a suitable location for establishing his own brickyard. The road eventually led to San Carlos, and there Carmelo found some pastureland for sale across the highway from the old clay pits. Examination of the land revealed the presence of clay, so Carmelo purchased the site. It was somewhat of a surprise to the Camba brickmakers when Carmelo moved in and began to erect a kiln and dig holes in the middle of his pasture. By that time he had sent to Argentina for his wife and three children and had hired two men as assistants. Carmelo's Camba competitors took it all in stride, however, since they had never been able to keep abreast of the demand for fired brick nor had they actually tried. Carmelo's entrance into the field of brickmaking was not viewed as a threat, therefore, but as a curiosity.

Carmelo, his twenty-nine-year-old wife, Viviana, and their children have lived on the outskirts of San Carlos for six years. They have established credit ties with storekeepers in town, including the Ferrofinos and Batallanos. Carmelo has initiated economic relationships with several Sancarleños who furnish him with firewood for his kilns, and he is now on friendly terms with the other brickmakers who pass along customers they are too busy to serve.

In 1975 Carmelo purchased a plot of land adjacent to his pasture and expanded his brick factory. Viviana's nineteen-year-old brother, Eusebio Correa, arrived from Potosí and with Carmelo's help erected a small house on the new property for himself and his new wife. He is now in charge of the second Acuña brickyard. Although Eusebio initially wanted to purchase his own farm, the income from the brickyards has kept him working with his brother-in-law. Eusebio likes the village of San Carlos and plans to remain. He still talks about buying farmland nearby.

Although Viviana admits that the family is doing well in San Carlos, she complains of the heat, the insects, and the rude living conditions. She feels that she will be "stuck" in San Carlos for some time. The highlands have little to offer, and there is not much hope of returning to Argentina. Having had a taste of urban life in Buenos Aires, Viviana understandably finds the village close to intolerable. Carmelo also is discontented with the relative quiet of San Carlos after having experienced the noise and activity of a large metropolitan area, but he seems to be adjusting to his new environment more readily than his wife. This adjustment may be due in large part to his incipient efforts to participate in village socioeconomic networks. Viviana, however, has remained aloof from the Camba villagers and from the other highland residents as well.

The Antesana family (1980).—Miguel Antesana came to the lowlands as one of the early contingents of cane cutters brought to the region when the first private mills opened. In 1959 he left rural Potosí at the age of twenty-three to work the *safra* of San Aurelio. After three years of seasonal migration, he was employed on a private farm, "Las Habras," where he worked in the cane, corn, and rice fields as a day laborer for six years. The farm was in the area of the new Antofagasta colony, so when land became available, Miguel applied for and received 50 hectares. He and his wife, Modesta, whom he married in Potosí while a seasonal migrant, worked the land in Antofagasta for nine years. During that period he bought a cargo truck which he operated in addition to his farm. In 1977 he bought an urban lot in the new barrio of Ramón Cowell on the outskirts of San Carlos. He also rented three hectares of land near town on which he is establishing a chicken farm. The truck continues to provide income to the family since Miguel has hired a driver to work full time hauling hardwoods and other cargo. The 50 hectares in Antofagasta are idle. All of the forest has been cleared, leaving weeds and second growth. Miguel says the only way he can continue farming the parcel is to mechanize. He explained that he joined a cooperative which FENCA (Federación Nacional de Cooperativas Arroceras) organized, to which he and fifteen other Antofagasta colonists contributed $2,500 (U.S.) each to pay for a tractor to prepare the land for planting. The machinery failed to arrive, and Miguel and his colleagues lost the entire year. Miguel believes it unlikely that he will ever see his money or the tractor. In the meantime he has rented 10 hectares of land near Antofagasta for rice and corn, but he complains that the yields were low at only one fanega (185.5 kilos) of rice per hectare. High forest, he related, will yield 10–12 fanegas per hectare and in some areas as many as 20. Miguel also applied for a loan from the agrarian bank (Banco Agrícola Boliviano) to assist with his farming expenses. Although the loan was approved, the money did not arrive until after the harvest when it was useless. He vowed never to get involved again "in that mess."

In addition to their multiple sources of income from farming and trucking, the Antesanas also operate a store from their home in San Carlos. Modesta runs the *venta*, which is similar to most other small stores in the town. She continues to dress in the traditional pollera and wears her hair in a double braid. Located near the brickyards, Modesta's store draws many Kolla customers who find it easier to deal with someone who is also a highlander. She uses Quechua with her Kolla neighbors and says she would not insult them by giving up the pollera. It would appear, then, that among recent Kolla shop-keepers, ethnic identity overlies credit and fictive kinship ties in es-tablishing a dependable clientele.

Miguel and Modesta both attended school in Potosí but completed only three grades. Miguel says his wife has forgotten how to read and write but that he has retained minimal skills from having to do busi-ness. One of their incentives in moving to San Carlos was the pres-ence of a primary school and a new colegio, or secondary school. Ex-cept for their eldest child, a nineteen-year-old female now working as a domestic in Santa Cruz, all of the Antesana's four school-age chil-dren attend class in the village. The youngest daughter, only two, re-mains with her mother in the store. Both Miguel and Modesta feel it is very important that their children receive an education so that "they will not have to work in the fields to make their way in life as we have had to do." There was no shame in this statement, only a sentiment that their lives have been difficult and that they want better for their children.

Miguel has three brothers in the lowlands working land in the An-tofagasta and the Yapacaní colonies. He also has cousins in Santa Cruz but is not certain of their whereabouts. Most of his family has migrated to the oriente during the past ten years and has remained. Miguel still visits his elderly mother in Potosí, returning to the high-lands every two or three years. He wants her to come and live with them in San Carlos but said she is afraid of the climate and insects.

Modesta eventually would like to move to Montero or even Santa Cruz, stating her children's needs for higher education as a reason. She also admits that she is attracted to the cities by their excitement and opportunities for commerce. When queried about moving to a more urban location, Miguel simply shrugged and said he knows nothing but farming. He agreed that he would probably acquire some property in Montero or Santa Cruz so that Modesta could accompany the children there and also expand her storekeeping.

Summary

The continual movement of Sancarleños to more urbanized areas and especially to Santa Cruz has created new slots for both Camba and Kolla migrants from outlying areas. Although tensions between highlanders and lowlanders are still evident, the gradual change in village composition, particularly among Camba residents, creates an atmosphere of greater tolerance toward Kollas. Since so many of the lowland residents are new to the village as well, they are somewhat more reluctant to claim their ethnic preeminence than are their native Sancarleño counterparts.

There is opposition at times to the changes occurring in the old village, but the transition from a predominantly Camba settlement to an integrated community of highlanders and lowlanders is well under way. Small rural towns like San Carlos have a greater hope of achieving this integration because immigration is proceeding at a relatively constant pace. Unlike Santa Cruz, Montero, and Warnes, which have experienced a rapid influx of migrants adding to the overall population size and creating new and segregated neighborhoods, San Carlos is absorbing highlanders at a steady rate into existing village structure.

Although recent setbacks in agriculture have had a negative effect on seasonal migration as a strategy for gradual adaptation to lowland life, extensive kin networks are now serving the same function. The presence of family members in San Carlos creates an incentive for chain migration and also provides for a measure of security while the migrant adapts to a new situation. In this respect kinship ties are preferable to seasonal migration, which supplies employment and some experience in the lowland environment but little social support. It is probable that, as time goes on, more highlanders migrating to San Carlos and other lowland villages will do so as the result of direct rather than step migration. At present, however, data indicate that at least half of the town's Kollas arrive in the lowlands after having done fieldwork on commercial farms, worked land in the colonies, or both. In 1975, three of the seven migrant families interviewed in San Carlos came to the lowlands to work in the cane or cotton harvests. Of these, two eventually secured land in an agricultural colony and later migrated to the village. In 1980 the same pattern persisted; four of the eight informants had arrived to do fieldwork, and three of these had then taken land in the colonies prior to their move to San Carlos.

7

Agricultural Colonies

With the completion of the Santa Cruz–Cochabamba highway in 1954, the revolutionary government began in earnest its efforts to open the lowland territories for exploitation.

From 1954 to 1956, four agricultural colonies were begun in Santa Cruz. The first, Aroma, 15 kilometers northeast of Montero, was started by two individuals and later taken over by the Corporación Boliviana de Fomento (CBF), the agency superseding the military's Colonial Division which had previously been charged with lowland resettlement. Although the administration of colonial affairs was transferred to civil authority, the military continued to provide manpower and equipment for clearing land, and many of the officials appointed by CBF to administrative roles in the colonies were military or ex-military personnel.

Aroma colonists were required to volunteer three two-month terms of labor in land clearing, house construction, and road building in order to qualify for 25 hectares of land. During this initial settlement period CBF provided them with food and tools. Later, technical and medical assistance were made available. By the end of the decade, 200 families had settled in Aroma, but the attrition rate was high and "approximately 60 percent of these colonists returned to their place of origin" (Ferragut 1961:130). Those who vacated their land were replaced by others, and today Aroma continues as a small agricultural community of about 240 families (Crist and Nissly 1973:137). All assistance has been withdrawn from the colony, which is inhabited largely by highland campesinos working their land not as colonists but as individual, self-reliant farmers.

The colonies of Cuatro Ojitos and Huaytú were begun by the military in 1955 and 1956, respectively, soon after the establishment of Aroma. These ambitious projects were begun by four army battalions sent to build roads and bridges, erect houses and schools, clear farmland, and drill wells for drinking water. The highland soldiers who accomplished the task of clearing were to be the recipients of the tracts of land opened for settlement. Civilian highlanders working in lowland cane fields were also given an opportunity to claim a parcel in the new colonies. In 1958, CBF replaced the army but military advisors and 900 soldiers continued to administer the program. Attrition again was high, and only 10 percent of the conscripts actually settled on parcels. Over half of the colonists were civilians, primarily former sugarcane harvesters. Both colonies are now under civil authority with a total of 600 families in Cuatro Ojitos and 170 families in Huaytú (Crist and Nissly 1973:138).

In 1958, the Bolivian army began widening the trail from the Yapacaní River to Puerto Grether on the Río Ichilo with the intent of establishing another colony. This location had been an early settlement site for lowland agriculturalists, but the distance to market and the difficulty of crossing the unpredictable and flood-prone Yapacaní River had left the area virtually uninhabited. A few Cambas continued to live in the main settlement three kilometers from the river, most earning their livelihood by hunting animals for pelts and by fishing.

Highlanders at first were slow to arrive in the Yapacaní colony. Many quickly became discouraged and returned to their places of origin or sought farmland in less remote areas. As in other colonies at the time, CBF administered settlement procedures in the Yapacaní. Technical assistance and small loans were available to the colonists, but without market access they faced only continual indebtedness and incredible hardship.

During the initial years of government efforts at resettlement, foreign groups as well as Bolivian highlanders were encouraged to colonize the lowlands. Fifty Volga-German Mennonites arrived in Santa Cruz in 1954, followed by another 50 Dutch-German Mennonite families in 1958 and in 1964 by an additional 54. The Mennonites were guaranteed religious freedom, exemption from military service, the right to establish their own schools, and duty-free access to farm

equipment. In the late 1950s more than 3,000 Old Colony Mennonites arrived from a parent colony in Mexico (Lanning 1971).
These settlers located in the arid zone to the south of Santa Cruz
where, in spite of environmental difficulties, they established productive farms. All of the Mennonite colonies have resisted any form
of assimilation into lowland Bolivian society. Marriage outside of the
religious sect is prohibited, and only the males are taught Spanish,
for marketing purposes.

Several hundred Japanese and Okinawan migrant families have
also settled in the Bolivian oriente. On August 2, 1956, an agreement
providing 35,000 hectares of land for Japanese colonization was
signed by the governments of Japan and Bolivia (Thompson 1968:
201). By June 1965, the new San Juan colony had 262 households
and 1,546 individuals. In spite of its somewhat better location on the
near side of the river directly opposite the Yapacaní colony, the San
Juan settlement suffered many of the same problems as the fledgling
CBF project. During the early years of Japanese colonization in San
Juan, the farmers held much of the rice produced in homes and store-
houses, unable to ship it to market. The road out from the colony was
unimproved and virtually impassable when wet. Once the main road
to Montero was reached, another five or six hours' travel were necessary to arrive at lowland markets. In spite of tremendous obstacles the
colonists persisted in their efforts to wrest a living from the wilderness, and most have prospered. The improvement of the colonial
feeder road and the paving of the Montero-Yapacaní highway have
given the Japanese of San Juan expectations of further success. Most
farms are now mechanized, rural electrification reached the area in
1979, and large marketing cooperatives have been formed.

Another agreement among the Bolivian, Okinawan, and U.S. governments opened land east of Montero for Okinawan settlements. The
Okinawans founded three colonies, and the paving of the road through
Okinawan lands from Montero has assured the colonies' permanence. The Okinawans are engaged primarily in rice, cane, and cotton production. In the late 1970s they began experimenting with
tropical wheat, which shows promise. Unlike the Mennonites, the
Japanese and Okinawans have intermarried with Cambas as well as
with highlanders residing in the lowlands. Spanish is taught in their
schools, and children are socialized as Bolivians in addition to learning Japanese or Okinawan values.

By the beginning of the 1960s, efforts by the Bolivian government
to establish viable agricultural colonies of highlanders began to fal-

ter. In most instances, colonies had been opened for settlement before adequate market routes were made available, leaving the settler cut off not only from the marketplace but also from medical, educational, and social support. The colonies became options only for the desperate and destitute and were avoided by scores of prospective migrants searching for land. Colonists frequently used the settlements as temporary stopping places until they could acquire farmland with better market access.

The early 1960s also witnessed the failure of other projects initiated by the revolutionary government. In many cases, railroad construction was halted only a few kilometers from the starting point; hydroelectric dams were erected where water supplies were inadequate for operation; agricultural extension stations were built and abandoned because of lack of funding. Much of the fault lay with poor coordination among the various government agencies and the absence of a directive office in charge of long-range national planning. As a result of these deficiencies, the Junta Nacional de Planeamiento was formed in 1962 with technical advisors supplied by the United Nations. But, again, problems arose from a lack of articulation with other governmental bureaucracies, and a subsequent reorganization of the Junta occurred. The agency was removed from direct control by the president and placed under the direction of the Ministerio de Planeamiento y Coordinación, the Consejo Nacional de Economía y Desarrollo Social, and the regional planning offices (Zondag 1968: 263). The old junta became the Servicio de Planeamiento. One of the principal tasks of the new servicio was to implement the recently enacted ten-year plan for economic development, the Plan Nacional de Desarrollo Económico y Social, covering the period 1962–71. The plan dealt with all sectors of the economy, including the major problem areas, mining and agriculture. In order to increase agricultural production and at the same time provide an outlet for increasing labor pressures in the mines, the economic development program called for additional efforts to colonize the lowlands. An ambitious settlement program was devised that would be centered in three lowland regions: the Alto Beni east of La Paz, the Chapare east of Cochabamba, and the Yapacaní northwest of Santa Cruz. Loans were obtained from the Interamerican Development Bank (IDB) and from other nations, primarily the United States, to finance road building, land clearing, and resettlement of highland miners and campesinos. The program proposed to resettle 8,000–10,000 families over a ten-year period at an initial cost of $6.5 million (U.S.) (IDB 1970). The

Corporación Boliviana de Fomento was to administer the project (INC 1970:8). By 1969, settlement expenditures had reached $9.1 million, but only 4,984 families had been relocated (IDB 1970). In the meantime, CBF had been superseded by the newly organized Instituto Nacional de Colonización, brought into existence by supreme decree on June 28, 1965 (INC 1970:9). As a result, all colonization activities would be centralized under one agency whose only task involved the opening and settlement of new lands.

The three colonies were plagued from the outset by problems of unstable administration, graft, improper allocation of foodstuffs, and excessive paternalism. During one year, the attrition rate for the Yapacaní colony reached 90 percent (IDB 1971). The ten-year plan ended in 1971, at which time the lowland colonies lost financial support from the government. In the three areas combined, 5,055 families had been settled by 1970 (Galleguillos 1970:3). Abandonment rates for the period 1962–71 averaged from over 50 percent for the Alto Beni project to 33 percent for the Yapacaní (Galleguillos 1970: 4–6). Still, the figures for abandonment can be somewhat misleading: they represent a turnover in population, not vacant land. As of 1980, the colonies were filled to capacity. What is lacking is not settlers to occupy land but rather a stable population of colonists who remain on their land.

Colonization in Bolivia, as elsewhere, has been treated somewhat idealistically as a permanent form of resettlement, its success or failure measured in terms of the number of colonists who retain or abandon their property. Much of the frustration experienced by agency personnel working to stabilize populations in new settlements can be attributed to a lack of understanding of the true role that colonization plays in lowland frontier expansion. Because colonization is frequently only an intermediate stage in lowland development, as it is presently occurring, to expect the majority of settlers to remain permanently in these areas is a contradiction of the expansion process itself. Colonization is in most instances simply a catalyst that precipitates a series of events soon beyond the control of the settler and ultimately beyond control of the agency involved.

In Santa Cruz, land allotments to colonists have ranged from 10 to 50 hectares. The smaller allotments were increased after it was realized that parcel size contributed to population instability. Those settlers with only 10–20 hectares of land quickly used up their virgin forest and found themselves caught in what Simon Maxwell (1979) aptly terms the "Barbecho (second-growth) Crisis." Once the forest cover has been removed, weeds and shrubs are quick to take advantage of the open space. This second growth is what the Bolivian calls "barbecho," and the settler finds himself technologically incapable of combatting it. Using traditional methods of slash and burn horticulture, the peasant is soon overcome by weed invasions that sap strength from the crops and that require continual labor to control. In a short time, the cultivation of barbecho land simply does not pay. An even worse problem is the grasslands in many areas of eastern Bolivia; chances are strong that grass will invade the cleared land, rendering impossible any subsequent traditional farming. There are two avenues of escape: first, to convert to mechanization, which, for a time at least, makes farming barbecho cost-effective; or second, to let the grass encroach or to plant pasture and gradually convert to beef or dairy cattle. Because little thought is given to rotating crops and thus conserving fertility, much of the land now under plow will end up as pasture in a last-ditch attempt to make the land commercially viable. Either process requires substantial capitalization. Machinery and livestock both represent significant financial investments for the peasant who finds himself faced with the barbecho crisis. If his parcel is 50 hectares, the crisis will be postponed a bit but is still inevitable. Those few colonists who have been successful in managing their affairs find themselves able to make the necessary investments to move on to the next agricultural stage—either mechanization or cattle or a combination. Those not so fortunate must abandon their land to go even farther in search of new wilderness. The "worthless" land they leave behind is quickly acquired by their successful neighbors who consolidate it into their own holdings.

Thomas Royden and Boyd Wennergren, with the UTAH/USAID project in Bolivia, have stated that

> The settling and clearing of state land and the subsequent sale of the partially improved property is emerging as a way of life for spontaneous colonists, such as those who will have migrated successfully to new frontier areas twice in the last ten years. The colonist frequently has contributed to the development of someone else's production unit, while making limited progress towards improving his own economic and social status. While the commercial farmer expands his production, the colonist achieves little more than survival and a subsistence level of living. It should be noted, however, that such development patterns are not uncommon in opening and settling virgin land

areas. The spontaneous and mobile colonizer performs the role
of making the initial clearing and settlement of the new area.
(1973:72)

For the majority of colonists, then, their future as small farmers is
locked into shifting horticulture. Without capital to meet the barbecho crisis, most settlers move on to cut down more virgin forest,
crop it for a few years, and then sell out to those who can mechanize
or buy livestock.

According to government officials, Bolivia's current hope of break-
ing out of shifting horticulture is cooperativism, whereby groups of
campesinos are organized into production units capable of bearing
the costs of mechanized farming procedures. If cooperatives fail, the
succession leading to large-scale commercial farming is inevitable.
The eventual outcome of this trend would seem to be the formation of
an agricultural proletariat to absorb the frontiersmen who have exhausted their frontier. But until that happens, colonization will continue to spearhead the land settlement movement, and government
officials and loan agencies will persist in their unrealistic demands
that people stay put.

Since 1971 the Instituto Nacional de Colonización has continued
to supply administrative assistance to colonial centers, but there
have been no repetitions of the financially ambitious settlement
projects characterizing the 1960s. Colonization is now spontaneous
or semidirected whereby INC supplies secondary or tertiary roads,
some technical assistance, water, and schools in some localities.

In 1975 the U.S. and West German governments financed the construction of two graveled roads west of the Río Grande in the post-1969
flood victim resettlement location of Chané-Piray and through the old
San Julián Colony. In addition, USAID provided INC with $200,000
(U.S.) to fund the relocation of 4,000 highlanders over a five-year period in San Julián. This latter program officially began in 1976, although nine colony zones, or nucleos, had already been established.
In contrast to past projects, San Julián has received relatively little
monetary support, and the majority of the colonists are former harvesters with prior lowland experience rather than highlanders brought
directly from the interior.

In the Santa Cruz region, INC-sponsored colonization is occurring
only in the Chané-Piray and San Julián sectors. The remaining colonies, including the Yapacaní, have all become agricultural communities under civil authority and local control. As new lands are
opened in the future, INC will attempt to provide infrastructure and

initial technical assistance in concert with international agencies involved in resettlement programs. Even so, the primary emphasis today is on the provision of land and market access. Paternalism has been replaced by individual initiative. Prospective settlers are no longer dragged out of the highlands and thrust unprepared into the wilderness. Today's colonist tends to be from an agricultural background, a former harvester, and an individual eager to obtain a parcel of Cruceñan farmland.

The rapid expansion of the lowland economy, better market roads, and increasing numbers of people in search of farm property have bestowed value on much of the hinterlands of the northern Santa Cruz region. No longer are the colonies viewed as a type of purgatory but rather as areas of desirable agricultural land. Unlike the early days of colonial planning and strong-arm tactics used to obtain settlers, the active colonies have people waiting in line to receive property. Land cooperatives have become popular as alternative means to acquiring the always sought-after virgin forest by direct solicitation to the government. The great numbers of highlanders in the Santa Cruz region who are seeking arable land in the vicinity of market routes have brought about the introduction of "sooning" to the lowlands. As quickly as word or rumor spreads that a road is to be opened, cooperatives jump the land before actual allocation is made. The battle then begins to legalize their claims, but most cooperatives are able to rally their membership into paying additional quotas to provide for the necessary bureaucratic adjustments.

The situation in the agricultural colonies might be better understood by looking at specific cases. For this study, two colonies have been selected for analysis. One is the Yapacaní, which has the longest and most costly history of settlement. I visited this colony on numerous occasions from 1964 to 1968 as a Peace Corps volunteer and again in 1975, 1978, and 1980. The other is the more recently settled San Julián colony, which exemplifies current trends in colonization as well as characteristics of those settlers presently attracted to colonial life. San Julián's progress was charted in 1975, 1978 (during a USAID evaluation project in which I participated), and 1977–78 (by David Hess, a graduate student in anthropology).

The Yapacaní Colony

In 1964 the gravel-surfaced highway north from Montero forked near the Guabirá sugar refinery, the western road leading to the Yapacaní River, where it terminated. At the river's edge a few pilings could be

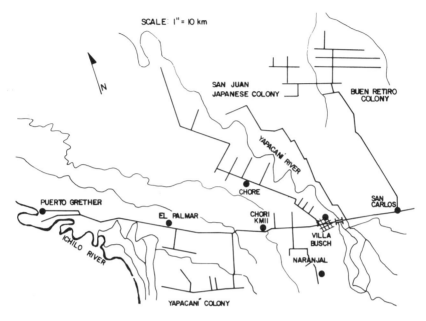

The Yapacaní settlement area

seen—remnants of unsuccessful efforts to span the waterway. On the far side lay the Yapacaní colony, consisting of 10-, 20-, and 50-hectare parcels strung out along a 62-kilometer road cleared by the Bolivian army. At several intervals along the trail, side paths, or *fajas*, had been opened into the jungle and additional parcels were surveyed for settlement.

The main camp, "Villa Germán Busch," was located three kilometers from the river. Colonists or administrative personnel wanting to reach its headquarters had to cross the Yapacaní River first. Individuals rode in canoes and paid the boatman from 10 cents to 50 cents (U.S.), depending on the condition of the river. Motor vehicles were loaded on large wooden pontoon barges powered by outboard motors fixed to the fore and aft hulls. If the Yapacaní was running full and swift, travelers endured a three- to four-day waiting period before crossing. Those marooned at the river's edge camped out or sought lodging at the few fishermen's shacks along the banks.

Once the river had been crossed, there was a three-kilometer stretch of trail from the western shore of the Yapacaní into Villa Busch. For those on foot, it was a tedious struggle through bog and thicket, but pedestrian travel was the surest means of getting there. Vehicles not only had to grind their way through seemingly endless traps of quagmire but also were required to navigate two or three slippery logs placed as bridges over the frequent creeks and streams along the track.

During these years, Villa Busch offered little more than the large mud-and-wattle, tin-roofed structure that housed the Corporación Boliviana de Fomento personnel who administered the colony, a few CBF outbuildings, a thatch and bamboo barracks for the soldiers stationed in the colony, and several huts inhabited by Camba fishermen and hunters. At night, a small generator gave light to the main administration building. A radio shack manned by a young Cruceñan was often the colony's sole link with the outside world.

The first CBF colonists were brought into the lowlands on trucks. Many of them were ex-miners whom the government was seeking to relocate, and most came without their families. The majority became discouraged and returned to the interior within months or even days of their arrival. In the meantime, however, radio broadcasts and word of mouth spread the news of the new agricultural colonies to the east. Many promises were made, and prospective colonists soon began to trickle into Villa Busch in search of land. These later settlers who came on their own initiative, frequently accompanied by their wives, children, and other relatives, were for the most part agriculturalists. The Corporación gave them tools, seed, and foodstuffs on a long-term loan arrangement and sent them down the road to find a parcel. The army had constructed a few houses in the colony, but most colonists arrived to find no more than wilderness right to the edge of the road. For weeks they would have to live in a palm lean-to until a better dwelling could be built.

The principal crop of the Yapacaní was, and continues to be, dry rice. Early harvests in the colony simply remained there or were laboriously hauled out, bag by bag, on the backs of men, women, children, and horses. Abandonment of parcels continued to plague colonization officials, and the settlers began using the colony only for the purpose of earning enough to acquire land closer to lowland markets.

In 1966, construction financed by USAID began on the Yapacaní bridge. The span was part of a package project that included paving the two branch roads from Montero and providing a gravel road 22 kilometers into the Yapacaní colony. As work began, interest in the Yapacaní settlement grew. It was evident that a great deal of land in the colony would soon have all-weather market access. Parcel value increased, and even sites previously ignored because of extreme iso-

lation were being claimed by highland migrants. Although no titles
to property had been given in the Yapacaní, buying and selling of
farm plots was increasing steadily. Technically, all that was sold were
the improvements to the property, but new arrivals understood, as
did the resident colonists, that the former were buying not only a
house, kitchen, pigpen, or whatever but also the land they stood on.
When a price had been agreed upon, buyer and seller would present
themselves to the CBF, or later the INC, office in Villa Busch to arrange
for a transfer of settlement rights and obligations. In essence, the
buyer received nothing more than the knowledge that his name now
replaced that of the previous colonist beside the parcel number in a
ledger. Any outstanding debts to the colonization program incurred
by the seller were transferred to the new resident. Little effort was
made to collect these debts, and they too became a matter of paper-
shuffling.

The paved highway to the limit of the Yapacaní River was opened
early in 1968, but several floods interrupted the completion of the
bridge. The primary road nevertheless meant an increase in the
number of vehicles in the area, subsequent competition for cargoes,
and lower transport fees. Although development in the colony was
still hindered by the lack of a bridge and poor internal transit networks, truckers were now paying the cost of crossing the river by
barge and braving the terrible roads in their search for cargoes of rice
and hardwoods. Villa Busch began to grow rapidly. A small outdoor
market opened in the field set aside for a town plaza where colonists
could buy goods shipped from Montero and Santa Cruz. The urban
lots that had been plotted years earlier were finally finding buyers.

When I returned to the area in 1975 after an absence of almost
seven years, I found that the colony had undergone an unexpected
metamorphosis—a comment on the impact of direct market access.
Villa Busch had become a bustling frontier town of more than 1,000
inhabitants (Solari 1975). The old Camba huts had been replaced by
highlander-owned structures of brick and cement. An office of the
civil police authority, DIC (Departmento de Investigación Criminal),
had superseded the military post for maintaining order and settling
disputes. A potable water system, evening-hour electricity, a twelve-
bed hospital run by the Methodists, and a savings and loan cooperative had also appeared. Most notable, however, was the huge covered
market, which had grown up in an area across the road from its original site.

Buying and selling activity in the colony had long since outgrown the projected plaza zone, which was now just that, the town square. A large section of Villa Busch was allocated for the new market, jointly funded by Obras Públicas and INC, and brick and tin-roofed stalls were constructed on the site. The market itself was almost invisible from the road since colonists and vendors had erected wooden kiosks on any available space in the area. On weekends, itinerant sellers from Montero and other towns along with residents from all over the colony made their way into Villa Busch to participate in the marketing festivities. Chicherías had also sprung up on the outskirts of the community, attesting to the economic prosperity of the Yapacaní.

The schools situated at seven- and ten-kilometer intervals along the main colony road had become focal points for the development of communities, and the road itself had been graded and surfaced with rock. But perhaps most important, the Yapacaní bridge now spanned the river. An 800-meter-long expanse of brilliant white concrete linked the colony to the rest of Santa Cruz, Bolivia, and the world. A trip to the departmental capital could be made in three hours instead of three days or more.

With the opening of the bridge and graveled road 22 kilometers into the colony, this section of the colony has become largely a continuation of the farming and marketing complex of the northern Santa Cruz region. Most of the land has been deforested and has passed through the progression of rice, corn, bananas, and manioc to pasture. Those colonists financially able to weather soil depletion over the years have converted much of their land to pasture and are now involved in dairying. A truck from Santa Cruz makes the trip daily to the Yapacaní to collect milk for the PIL (Productora Industrial Lechera) pasteurization plant near Warnes. Even so, according to an extension agent working in the colony, most settlers are working land much farther out since dairy operations remain small and do not alone supply adequate incomes. This same source commented that there are approximately 35 cooperatives between Villa Busch and Kilometer 27 and that most were formed to acquire wilderness land. It has also been noted that many of these coops are funded by outside sources which have an interest in acquiring large tracts of land for speculation once colonists have cleared them.

As word circulates that the road from the Yapacaní will be linked ultimately with the Chapare highway, forming part of the multination Carretera Marginal de La Selva, colonists are rushing to claim land. While some of these are new arrivals, most are old Yapacaní colonists who are members of land cooperatives. By paying a fee averaging about $120 (U.S.) a colonist can join a coop and hope for a piece of land. There are no guarantees of getting it, however, and the money is never returned. The fact that some get land and others don't has caused disgruntlement and divisiveness in many of these coops. But the hunger for virgin forest is so great among colonists that most who are able to raise the initial fee are willing to take the risk of losing it all.

Once a participant in such a coop, the prospective settler will be solicited monthly for additional funds to pay for surveys, the purchase of chain saws, rental of vehicles to carry men in and out, money for various officials, and food and other supplies. In the beginning, coop members waited until a certain parcel of land was designated for colonization. Now, with the high degree of competition for forest, coops are jumping land, claiming tracts, and then paying bribes to hold onto it. Since titles are never part of the process, money is passed around with nothing legally binding in return, jeopardizing no one but the recipient of the property. In the long run, he too will pass the land to someone else for a fee and move on. Even in the older part of the colony, the process of conferring titles moves slowly. As of 1978, fourteen years after initiation of the project, no one had yet received a clear title to his parcel.

The Yapacaní is now under public authority, and Villa Busch operates as an independent community. The town continues to expand as new neighborhoods spring up on the outskirts of what once were the operational headquarters of the colony. In 1979, the northern rural electrification project reached Villa Busch, supplying the town with power twenty-four hours a day. The market area has grown also, and prices are often competitive with those in the large Santa Cruz markets. Many vendors explained that they receive their produce such as potatoes and onions directly from Cochabamba and not through middlemen in Santa Cruz. Easy access to the colony has also made it a spot for urban people to spend Sundays. Cars loaded with middle-class Cambas and Kollas make weekend excursions to the Yapacaní River. Here they enjoy fish dinners in thatched restaurants along the river's edge, swim and boat, and then travel the three kilometers to Villa Busch to drink beer and visit the market. On a Sunday in 1978 when I visited the colony, three young men were waterskiing back and forth under the Yapacaní Bridge, a sight I had difficulty reconciling with memories of the early 1960s.

Cambas also have begun to move into Villa Busch in greater numbers. In 1975, Fr. Solari's census listed 1,151 inhabitants in the community, representing four countries beside Bolivia and all of the nation's departments with the exception of the Pando and Santa Cruz. The total absence of Cambas in Villa Busch at this time is questionable, since I know of a few families who moved into the area prior to the census. Still, Villa Busch, and to a large extent the colony as a whole, have traditionally been Kolla strongholds. Many highlanders have expressed their feeling that although Cambas have been given land in the Yapacaní, the area was opened primarily for the benefit of highland peoples. In 1980, however, I was surprised to find a new and predominantly Camba neighborhood to the south of Villa Busch. Interviews with several of the residents indicated that the growing urban aspects of the town had attracted them. While a few were renting farm parcels out in the colony from highlanders, most were engaged in day labor and the running of small neighborhood kiosks, both typical income patterns among rural Cambas.

The Yapacaní Migrants

The characteristics of the Yapacaní migrant population have been charted on several occasions by persons with varying research objectives. My 1975 study comprised in-depth interviews with colonists selected from as many varied locations within the colony as it was possible to reach. In the colonies, visits to remote sectors were often a chance affair—catching a cargo truck or agency jeep headed toward the hinterlands. Thus, whoever happened to be available became a candidate for an interview.

Four sites in addition to Villa Busch were investigated in 1975. These were Naranjal, located on a faja to the south of the primary road; El Chore, a settlement zone on the northern faja (Faja Norte); and two sectors of the faja central, El Chori at Kilometer 11 and El Palmar at Kilometer 22, the termination point of the gravel road. The only area not sampled was that beyond Kilometer 22 in the Puerto Grether–Río Ichilo region. Few vehicles frequented this stretch of trail because it was almost impassable. I had walked the 40-kilometer path to Puerto Grether in 1967 and was not eager to try it again.

Settlers in the Yapacaní colony were interviewed along with INC officials, hospital staff, and Catholic clergy working in the area. Of the thirty-one individuals residing on parcels or in Villa Busch, three were found to be Guarayo Indians from the San Ignacio region who were acting as *caseros* (caretakers) for highland landowners. Because of INC rules requiring that a parcel have a permanent resident or be forfeited, colonists who desired to work outside of the colony or on another parcel frequently left a relative behind to protect against confiscation. (The INC itself did not monitor the status of parcels in the colony, but land was in such demand that migrants seeking property would investigate any seemingly vacant plot. If the occupant did not return within a few weeks, the land was then taken over by the new arrival. After a few weeks' residence, the new colonist would make good his claim at the INC office.) It was both odd and difficult to explain why these three unrelated persons living in widely dispersed sections of the colony and all Guarayos had literally become peons of highland colonists. In each case, the Indian family had resided on the land for several years and had received some remuneration from the owner along with rights to till the soil but had had to give up part of its annual harvest to the landlord. They were, in fact, sharecropping in an area where free access to land was still possible. One of the three informants, a male, explained that he did not want to go into the wilderness to start anew since he would have to relinquish the protection of his highland patrón. It was the element of paternalism, then, that seemed to be the cohesive factor in the Guarayo-Kolla relationship. The Guarayo Indians of the eastern reaches of Santa Cruz have an almost continuous history of servitude under both religious and secular patronage. This history may explain in part the presence of Guarayos, not Cambas or Kollas, in the position of tenant-casero. Because the three Guarayos represented such a singular case, they were excluded from the remaining analysis, which reduced the sample to twenty-nine informants, all highlanders, twenty females and nine males. The relatively high percentage of females can be attributed to the fact that interviews were carried out in the home during the day when most males were in the fields. Only one male and one female of those interviewed were unmarried, and all married individuals had highland spouses. The average age of the sample population was thirty-three, well within the range of migrants interviewed in the other sites. The standard deviation for the Yapacaní informants was 11.6.

Origins of the sample population were overwhelmingly rural, only one female claiming an urban center, Sucre, as her last place of residence in the interior. The others came directly to the lowlands from a highland village. The importance of harvesting as a means of entry into Santa Cruz was underscored: over half the sample (59 percent) had worked in rice, cane, or cotton harvests prior to taking up residence in the Yapacaní. Several of those interviewed indicated that their primary purpose in coming to the lowlands had been to find any type of work and that, once in the Santa Cruz region, information about available land encouraged them to remain (table 7.1).

Other than to find work, migrants claimed a desire to obtain more and better farmland as a prime incentive for leaving the highlands. One female explained that she and her husband arrived in the Yapacaní as the result of the latter having been stationed there as a sergeant in the army unit attached to CBF during the colony's early years. When he was to be transferred, the couple decided to remain in the Yapacaní rather than move again. They owned a parcel, a restaurant, and three rental houses in Villa Busch as well has having the beer concession for the colony. A final informant, a young woman, came to the Yapacaní to visit her sister, met and married a colonist, and lives in Villa Busch.

In keeping with the rural origins of the migrant sample population including spouses, or fifty-six individuals, over half named agriculture as their means of livelihood before they moved to the lowlands (table 7.2). Six had been landless peons with no hope of obtaining property in the interior. Four were miners, three of whom had been in the first contingent of CBF recruits trucked down from the highlands. Most of those who accompanied these early colonists eventually left the Yapacaní to return to the interior or to move into more accessible regions of the department. The fourth miner was a recent arrival who explained that political difficulties had led to his self-imposed exile in the colony. A cousin in the settlement helped him obtain a parcel, which he was working.

Multiple-resource exploitation was prevalent in Yapacaní, although colonial policy discouraged the occupancy of more than one parcel or urban site at a time. Laxity in enforcing settlement rules along with inadequate record-keeping enabled Yapacaní migrants to circumvent these restrictions. Records of parcel allocation were kept in large wooden file boxes at the INC office in Villa Busch. Filing procedures were haphazard at best, but the manner in which the system had been set up had not allowed for cross-referencing the number of plots occupied by any one colonist. The parcels were filed by plot number, which was also a locational reference (by zone within the colony), and by the name of the original occupant. If occupancy changed, the forms were filed in the old folder. Thus it was important

Table 7.1. Yapacaní Migrants' Motives for Migration, 1975

Motive	Number	Percent
To obtain land	15	53.0
To find work	12	41.0
Army service	1	3.0
Visiting	1	3.0
Total	29	100.0

Table 7.2. Yapacaní Migrants' Previous Occupations
(including spouses), 1975

	Males		Females	
Occupation	Number	Percent	Number	Percent
Farming	17	61.0	17	61.0
Mining	4	14.0	0	–
Commerce	0	–	6	21.0
Army	1	4.0	0	–
Peon	6	21.0	0	–
Homemaker	0	–	5	18.0
Total	28	100.0	28	100.0

that the prospective buyer as well as the seller know the parcel number and the name of the first resident. There was no way to cross-check landholders by name except by pulling out each folder, looking for the most recent transfer, and making a list of the occupants to see how often each name appeared—a gargantuan task that has never been attempted. Thus colonists could occupy with impunity any number of parcels and urban lots that they could afford to acquire. Since administrators were concerned only with the attainment of a full complement of settlers and not with the equitable distribution of land, CBF, and later INC, ignored these infractions.

INC claimed that 1,779 families had settled in the Yapacaní colony as of 1974 (INC 1974). In other words, 1,779 parcels had been allocated. According to the church census, the actual number of families present in the colony was much lower, about 950. The discrepancy may be attributed to both the prevalence of acquiring more than one parcel of land and the seasonal absence of residents.

Five informants admitted having access to more than one parcel of land, and thirteen owned land and urban lots in Villa Busch that were often the site of a store or other business enterprise. Many of those interviewed knew of neighbors who, in addition to their

Yapacaní holdings, had land and homes in other colonies or nearby farming villages. According to Fr. Solari, a few of the Villa Busch lots were purchased for speculation by middle-class Cambas. (The fact that urban property has been purchased for speculation was verified in 1980 by chance. During a dinner conversation, a Camba colleague mentioned that his wife owned several lots in Villa Busch which had been acquired for her in the early 1960s by her father.) Most, however, were owned by colonists living on their farms in the settlement but using rental monies from houses or stores on these lots as additional sources of income. In Villa Busch, for example, 896 lots had been sold, but only 451 had owners in residence (Solari 1975).

Chain migration has played an important role in the settlement history of the Yapacaní colony, as it has in other areas of the department. Nineteen of the twenty-nine informants (66 percent) stated that they had relatives living in the colony and that the first family members to arrive were instrumental in helping their kin to obtain parcels. All of the nineteen persons claiming relatives in the settlement in addition to their nuclear family explained that, on at least one occasion, they had offered food and temporary shelter to kin arriving from the highlands. Many also assisted the new colonists in building homes and in initial land clearing.

If possible, family members or persons from the same village frequently try to find land near one another to shorten travel distance between farms and to recreate a semblance of previous communal life. Hence, many sectors of the Yapacaní are segregated by highland region, and particular localities will be well represented in a circumscribed area. For example, four of the five persons interviewed at El Palmar were from a small village in Potosí while El Chore was settled almost entirely by Cochabambinos.

In agreement with migration theory that proximity to place of origin will influence migrant site selection, it is not surprising to find that a large percentage of the colony's Kolla inhabitants come from Cochabamba, a pattern that was found in the other research areas (table 7.3). According to Fr. Solari's census, over one-third of the migrants are Cochabambinos, these having traveled the least distance to the colony. Ranked second are those from Potosí, probably the most economically depressed sector of the nation and, in a seemingly contradictive manner, the farthest from the Yapacaní. However, a glance at the map of Bolivia shows that from Potosí, even La Paz is a good distance, and in terms of the agricultural colonies the Santa Cruz region is the most accessible.

Table 7.3. Yapacaní Migrants' Origins by Region, 1975

Region	Number	Percent
Cochabamba	1,354	38.6
Potosí	949	27.0
Chuquisaca (Sucre)	379	10.0
Oruro	248	7.1
Santa Cruz	209	6.0
Beni	124	3.5
La Paz	110	3.1
Tarija	96	2.7
Argentina	20	0.6
Chile	8	0.2
Brazil	6	0.2
U.S. (missionaries)	5	0.1
Paraguay	4	0.1
Total	3,512	100.0

Source: Solari 1975.

As the figures in table 7.3 indicate, thirty-eight individuals (excluding the five U.S. missionaries) cited nations other than Bolivia as their last place of residence. It is unknown whether these were repatriated highlanders or actually Chilean, Argentine, Paraguayan, or Brazilian emigrants. Given the existence of Bolivian-Argentine migrants in other lowland localities, it is entirely possible that many of those twenty persons from Argentina were Bolivian harvesters who had entered Argentina illegally and were subsequently expelled.

As might be expected among a largely rural population such as that found in the Yapacaní colony, illiteracy rates for the sample group of migrants were high. Again, females exhibited a lower incidence of literacy skills than did males. Rates of illiteracy among the Yapacaní migrants interviewed were 56 percent for males (five out of nine) and 90 percent for females (eighteen out of twenty).

The 1980 study carried out by the Direción Departamental de Estadística (DDE) in which I participated provided up-dated migrant profiles for Villa Busch. Sixteen families were selected randomly from the 506 households surveyed by DDE in 1979. In spite of exhaustive efforts to locate them, only nine were still in Villa Busch at the time of the survey. According to neighbors who were questioned about missing cases, three returned to the highlands and the remainder as far as it was known had moved to other towns in the department. Of the four study sites investigated in 1980, Villa Busch had the highest degree of missing cases. It was also the farthest from the primate city of Santa Cruz and the most rural of the sample stratified by size of community and distance from the lowland capital.

In many instances the nine remaining informants had migration histories comparable to their 1975 counterparts. Once again, Cochabamba was named as the place of origin by over half of the informants, including the seven missing cases whose origins were listed in the 1979 survey. Five had come to find land and three to find work. One, a female, came as a visitor with her aunt, met and married her husband, and remained. Another indication of the growing urban character of Villa Busch is the higher evidence of highlanders with urban backgrounds. Three of the nine people questioned were from highland cities and had come to the Yapacaní to provide services to the community rather than to farm. In 1975 only one informant claimed an urban background. Brief conversations with people working in the Villa Busch market also revealed that they or people they knew were recent arrivals in the community and had come to continue urban occupations such as storekeeper, seamstress, truck driver, chichería owner (there are eleven chicherías in Villa Busch), bar or restaurant operator, bicycle repairman, pharmacist, baker, and numerous others. Of the seven informants who claimed relatives in the colony, five had urban-born family members who had moved to the Yapacaní only after the bridge had been completed and Villa Busch began to grow.

The exploitation of several economic niches continues as a viable economic strategy for highlanders in the Yapacaní. Out of nine informants, seven Kolla and two Camba, only the Cambas were tied to nuclear family income sources: one man worked as a day laborer while the woman remained at home, and they rented a house from a Kolla; one husband worked rented land while his wife remained at home and sold bread. Each of the Kolla informants had several operations going—farming combined with commerce, trucking, or rental properties—and in each case ownership was outright. Two of the highland informants mentioned that they planned eventually to buy land for additional income in Montero or Santa Cruz but that they would also maintain their properties in the Yapacaní. In addition to all of his other holdings, one individual had a parcel in the San Julián colony which he owned with a cousin. Like highlanders throughout the region, the Yapacaní colonist comes to the lowlands to get ahead and does so with a vengeance.

The San Julián Colony

The eastern branch of the Montero highway leads to the Río Grande, or at least to within nine kilometers of the river's western shore. On the other side, the San Julián colony begins, stretching in a northerly direction 72 kilometers along a graveled road. The colony ends at the San Julián river, but the road continues on into eastern Santa Cruz and to the villages of San Ramón, Santa Rosa de la Mina, and San Javier. All of these are Camba communities founded by the Jesuits as *reducciones* for Guarayo Indians of the area.

San Julián, like the Yapacaní to the west, has a sporadic settlement history. An initial zone near the Río Grande was set up about 1968. Fifty-hectare plots at 150-meter intervals were laid out along the unimproved road for a distance of 40 kilometers. Prior to this period, however, lowlanders from San Javier and even the more remote village of San Ignacio had settled on parts of the proposed colonial territory. Squatters' rights prevailed, and the colony had to be planned around them. Later, when San Julián was opened for official colonization, a few highlanders responded to the offer of free farmland, but the majority of residents continued to be Cambas from nearby villages. The Instituto Nacional de Colonización operating from an encampment at Kilometer 40 supplied parcel surveys and wells with hand pumps every four kilometers but little more. Soon it was evident that the colony was not progressing as planned, and funding was withdrawn.

The agricultural boom of the 1970s awakened new interest in San Julián. Financing for settlement of the area beyond Kilometer 40 was obtained from USAID ($200,000 U.S.) along with a West German loan which included technical assistance for the construction of a secondary road from the Río San Julián to the Río Grande—the length of the zone set aside for colonial development. By 1976, the road had been completed.

Unlike the first 40 kilometers of the old section of the colony which was laid out on a linear plan, the next segment of San Julián, opened in 1972, was divided into nine nucleos with forty pie-shaped parcels radiating out from each settlement nucleus. The nine nucleos occupied an area 144 kilometers square, with Nucleos 1, 2, and 3 located along the main road at Kilometers 52, 57, and 62, respectively. Nucleos 4–9 were lateral to the roadside settlement, forming a compact colonization block. All nine nucleos had wells with hand pumps.

At the time of my first visit to the colony in June 1975, the off-

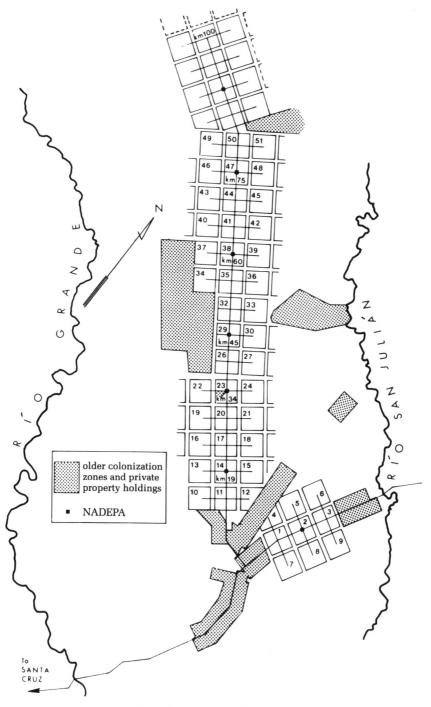

The San Julián colony

season between crops, few colonists were actually in residence. Only
Nucleos 1, 2, 7, and 8 were open for settlement; of these, 7 and 8 were
virtually empty. Nucleo 1 was composed of highlanders, many related to one another through consanguineal or affinal ties, and all
were former harvesters. Even then there was indication that this nucleo would eclipse the others by its prime location on the main road
and its focus on commerce rather than farming.

Nucleo 2 was a settlement of mixed inhabitants, the majority Cambas of Guarayo origin. In the interest of peace, INC was submitting to
pressure to segregate the colony into Camba and Kolla residential
zones, and two Camba families previously living in Nucleo 1 had
been requested to move to Nucleo 2. Part of the pressure on these
lowlanders to move was exerted by the highland colonists in Nucleo
1 who wanted the property for family members planning to move to
the colony.

Nucleo 7 was settled by a group of migrants from the Potosí area,
but none was present. Other colonists stated that a few of the Potosinos had returned to the interior to visit relatives but that most had
gone into Montero to work in the cane and cotton harvests.

Nucleo 8 was granted to a group of Bolivians who had been living
illegally in Chile and were expelled from the country en masse. The
Bolivian government, faced with the problem of relocating these repatriates, apparently saw San Julián as an available solution. Only
five of the original forty families were in residence at the time of the
1975 study, many having found a way to return to Chile. Thus Nucleos 1 and 2, situated on the main road, were the only areas in the
new San Julián colony that contained a full complement of colonists.
From the nucleated section to the San Julián River, about 12 kilometers, there were a few Guarayo families squatting on the government land.

In many respects, the San Julián colony resembled the Yapacaní of
early years. The Río Grande had to be crossed on a barge or in a ca-
noe, and like the Yapacaní River it was prone to flash flooding. The
improved road through the colony was only partially completed, and
transport costs were prohibitive. Other than by walking, the colonist's sole way in and out of San Julián was on the logging trucks that
were at work in the forests beyond the colony. The new secondary
road has lowered the cost of transport from $1.00 to 90 cents (U.S.)
per 100 pounds, but the colonists must await the completion of a
bridge spanning the Río Grande before any significant drop in cartage

fees can occur. Without funding, the Río Grande bridge is still a long way from becoming a reality.

Unlike the Yapacaní, the majority of the problems of San Julián's first nine nucleos will not be solved by the building of roads and bridges. The area is too arid for profitable rice production, and as yet the colonist has no viable substitute. (Mean annual precipitation for the Yapacaní is 1,500 millimeters, that of the San Julián area along the road approximately 800 millimeters [Cochrane 1973: 261, 358].) Much of the older section of the colony (Kilometers 1–40) already has been consolidated into large cattle ranches, and it appears that ranching will become the fate of most of the nine-nucleo area.

A revisit to Nucleo 8 in 1978 with the USAID evaluation team revealed that the settlers were not prospering. Only three of the original Chilean migrants remained, but the other thirty-seven parcels had been claimed by highlanders from Cochabamba and Potosí (many of the Potosinos relatives of colonists in Nucleo 7). We met in the center of the nucleo with about twenty-five men and women, all talkative perhaps because, in spite of our best efforts to dissuade them, they felt we could change the course of their lives. Several attempts at planting rice, the crop with the highest market value, had failed from lack of rain. Corn grew well, the colonists explained, but the price at $2.00 (U.S.) per quintal (100 pounds) minus the 80 cents (U.S.) for transport left little profit after production expenses. The settlers were also angry that the Banco Agrícola Boliviano (BAB) had not extended them any credit despite numerous costly expeditions to the office in Montero. Most admitted that they were barely subsisting on their farms and had to spend long periods in the Montero area working as day laborers to supplement their incomes. They also expressed some concern that the original nine nucleos had all but been abandoned by INC now that the new area of colonization had been opened along the Brecha Casarabe, a road cut perpendicular to the improved San Julián road at Kilometer 44.

In September 1974, INC had signed a loan agreement for the amount of $8.36 million (U.S.) to develop an area to be known again as the San Julián colonization project. Realizing that the area extending beyond the original nine nucleo settlements would continue to present climatic problems, INC cut a new trail north into wetter territory. Along this trail, called the Brecha Casarabe, a new zone would be established, to extend initially 80 kilometers into the wilderness and to consist of thirty-nine nucleos. The loan provided $5.16 million for roads, $298,000 for construction of an agricultural service center and health post, $38,000 for credit, $325,000 for wells, $1.08 million for technical assistance, research, and project administration, and $1.124 million for food provided by the World Food Program (PMA) (Nelson 1978:2). The total cost to settle 4,680 families, including roads, was estimated at $1,790 per family, substantially less than any previous effort. (The Alto Beni, Chimoré, and Yapacaní averaged $3,025 [U.S.] per colonist in settlement costs [Nelson 1978].) San Julián also differed significantly from other Bolivian colonization projects in that colonists would undergo training to prepare them for the rigors of the lowland life style. Participation in this orientation program was mandatory for the acquisition of any land parcel in the colony.

In another departure from tradition, INC contracted the orientation program to an interdenominational church organization known as the United Church Committee (CIU). This group (discussed in the chapter on Montero) came into existence in 1967 to assist with feeding, housing and eventually resettling that year's flood victims in the northern Santa Cruz region. Many were resettled in a wilderness area to be known as the Chané-Piray colony, across the river from San Julián. The CIU experimented at the time with an orientation program designed to alleviate some of the human suffering associated with relocation. In addition to providing a low-cost training/transition period for the flood victims, the orientation program also attempted to avoid the paternalistic stance so prejudicial to planned settlement in the past.

While the San Julián project along the Brecha was in the planning stages, CIU presented the Instituto Nacional de Colonización with an updated version of its flood victim program. The plan was accepted, a contract was drawn up, and an American CIU missionary with twenty years' experience in Santa Cruz was named settlement advisor. A multinational group of CIU members, CIU personnel, and other Bolivian development workers formed the core of the orientation staff. Although this group technically operated within the bureaucratic confines of INC, its multinational composition created a certain autonomy. This autonomy, no doubt, contributed to the flexibility of decision-making and to good rapport among the members, and thus to the successes enjoyed by the project.

The orientation program as implemented by the United Church Committee gave San Julián part of its unique place in settlement history and practice. The goals of the program were to help colonists adapt to a new environment, to promote community solidarity, and to stimulate the socioeconomic integration of colonists (CIU–INC 1975). To meet these objectives, CIU exposed each colonist to an intensive program of four months' duration.

The colonists arrived in groups either formed in the highlands as the result of government-sponsored propaganda campaigns or coming through the INC branch office in the nearest urban center, Montero. When they reached San Julián, colonists were met by the social promoter (*promotor social*), a trained community development worker and CIU staff member, who had been assigned to that group and would remain with it throughout the program. Two 10-by-16 meter galpones, or tin-roofed sheds, already on the site had been prepared as sleeping quarters for the colonists. A 4-by-3 palm-thatched outbuilding had also been constructed for use as a communal kitchen, and the *parque*, or food storage area, had been placed in the center of the nucleo settlement. Here food provided by the World Food Program would be stored and dispensed to colonists. The parque also served as the residence and base of operations for the social promoter. The initial settlement infrastructure was completed with a deep well, a hand pump, and two latrines.

During the first week of orientation, the promoter took the initiative. Cooking routines were set up on a rotational basis, and the two-hectare machine-cleared area in the center of the settlement was cleaned of weeds. In most instances, colonists immediately set up goal posts in this field for evening and weekend soccer games, frequently their only source of entertainment during these early years. The community garden was prepared and other basic settling-in activities took place. After about a week, the nucleo elected its first leader, whose term of office was one month. Thus, by the end of the orientation process, the group had experienced an initial learning period of decision-making with four different leaders. At the end of the orientation program, a leader was elected for one year, and five or six individuals were selected to serve on a board known as the *mesa directiva*. The function of the mesa was to deal with internal community affairs as well as regulate external relations with other nucleos, INC, or the United Church Committee. Interestingly, the leaders who were most often selected were not those individuals who may have held positions of power and authority in the highlands. There appeared to be a recognition among the colonists that here in a new environment other kinds of skills might be necessary. Hence, leaders tended to be younger men who had demonstrated both ability and interest in coping with life in the colonies.

Three major projects were completed before the orientation period ended and "settlement certificates" were issued (no actual land titles have been conferred as yet). First the nine hectares of urban area, or *radio urbano*, was cleared in addition to the initial two hectares cleared by INC machinery. This space would be used for dwellings, kitchens, latrines, and family gardens. Second, each colonist built a palm-thatched house with a latrine, and, third, 40 hectares of farmland were cleared. Land clearing was done cooperatively, although each community decided whether this was to be completed by small work groups or collectively. The actual 50-hectare parcels were not surveyed until the latter part of the program, so no individual knew exactly whose land was being cleared during the collective effort. For six weeks during this land-clearing phase, an *orientador* was made available to each nucleo. This person was usually a lowlander, but sometimes a highlander with extensive lowland farming experience. The orientator gave assistance in house building, methods of thatching, techniques of slash-and-burn horticulture, and proper use and care of tools.

Throughout the orientation period "floating" CIU staff visited each nucleo for two days every other week. They included a *mejoradora del hogar*, who assisted with organization of the communal kitchen, gave instruction in use of PMA foods, and taught general nutrition and hygiene; a nurse/paramedic who took care of health problems, made referrals to the doctor based at the INC center located at Kilometer 42 on the main road, and trained two community members from each nucleo in basic first aid procedures; and a cooperative specialist who gave instruction in consumer cooperatives and their management. During the orientation period an actual consumer coop was set up so the colonists could experience this type of activity. At the end of the orientation, it was disbanded, to be re-formed if initiated by the colonists themselves. Reinstitution of coops was only partially successful, however, due to both colonist apathy and a reluctance on the part of the entrepreneurial types to create a competitive institution to their own business interests.

Each colonist received seeds for the first year and varieties of perennial plants. Three types of rice seed were distributed: Carolina, a dry (when cooked), long grain rice that matures in ninety days, and Bluebonnett and Dorado, shorter-grained and stickier varieties. Bluebonnett and Dorado have a somewhat better market; they are frequently selected by mills because of lower breakage rates and lowland dietary preferences. In addition to rice, two types of corn seed, soybeans, common beans, peanuts, eating and cooking bananas (*guineos* and *plátanos*), citrus, pineapple, papaya, mango, sweet potatoes, and garden seeds were provided. Although several of the perennial varieties would take years to reach maturity and bear fruit, the colonist did have an initial variety of crops to draw upon for an adequate and varied diet during the first year. By the second year, colonists were marketing some of these crops with varying degrees of success.

At the end of orientation, a ceremony, or *clausura*, was held and each colonist received a settlement certificate. Although the certificate had no legal validity, it had the colonist's name and date of settlement inscribed on it. Thus, it could be used as a lever in the land-titling process to pressure the government to meet its two-year title delivery commitment. The ceremony marked the end of the initial settlement phase, and CIU withdrew from active participation although PMA food would continue for another five months.

Empirically, the orientation program appeared to assist the settler in learning to cope with a new physical environment and in developing new survival strategies. As described, the program taught basic lowland agricultural techniques, house building, crop selection, home management, leadership skills, and personal hygiene. Through previous experience, the orientation staff pared down most of the highly theoretical concepts to give the colonist only the basic information required to meet immediate needs. In the past, it was discovered that colonists' initial preoccupation with the enormity and complexity of the colonization experience tended to render almost useless any attempt to introduce a more sophisticated knowledge of agriculture, health, and home management during the early phases of settlement.

The four-month orientation program also provided a psycho-social experience that is consistent with many other kinds of rites of passage found in human society. The rite of passage as analyzed by Arnold van Gennep (1961) includes the important social dimensions of formal recognition of a change in status and personal preparation for adjustment to a particular life crisis. Although the orientation program was probably not conceived in terms of this model, it should be emphasized that the ritual importance of such a program is extremely significant in creating solidarity, group awareness, and a sense of purpose among colonists. They had survived a "trial by fire" and had met the challenge successfully. Frequently, when individuals are expected to make a dramatic alteration in life-style or pass through a particular crisis without the benefit of ritual recognition of this experience, they develop frustration, alienation, and hostility. In some of the older colonies, these psychological manifestations of stress were readily apparent among many of the settlers (see Stearman 1973, 1978). The orientation program then, in a purely ritual sense, worked to help overcome many of the emotional and social adjustment problems faced by the new colonists in San Julián.

One excellent indicator of the capacity of the orientation program to deal with problems of physical, social, and emotional adaptation to the colony was the remarkable reduction in settlement attrition rates. Although these data cover only the first year or two of settlement and are not long-term indicators, the abandonment rate of 20 percent (AID 1978) is significant compared to the average rate of 42 percent for other colonies cited by INC (1970). It also must be remembered that the highest rates of abandonment in earlier Bolivian colonization efforts occurred during the first and second years of settlement (see IDB 1971).

To date, most colonization projects, such as the Chapare, Yapacaní, Huaytú, Surutú, and spontaneous sectors of Chané-Piray, have been settled in a linear fashion along penetration roads. While this pattern allows for regularly shaped parcels and extensive frontages along the access road, colonists are spaced much like beads on a string. This lack of centralization has both immediate and long-range consequences. First, colonists are separated from one another, which creates a sense of social and spatial isolation. Traditional cooperative work groups such as the minka are difficult to initiate in those colonies where spatial separation adds to the problem of placing together people of disparate places of origin. (The minka, or minga, is a short-term cooperative work group oriented primarily toward agricultural needs such as plowing, planting, and harvesting.) Second, a linear orientation makes it almost impossible to provide services such as health care, education, and technical assistance. It is difficult to disseminate information and to initiate group activities. Third, the linear plan retards the consolidation phase where communities form and secondary services are provided. In some of the older colonies, such as the Yapacaní, community formation has suffered setbacks in several areas. Here, people have been forced to sell their land or divide the family in order to move into urbanized zones whose dis-

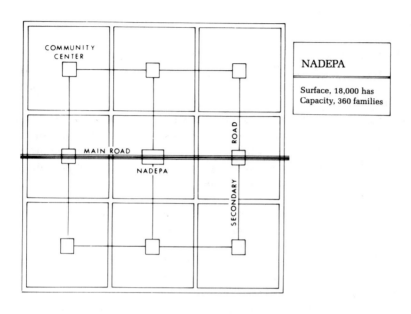

NADEPA

Surface, 18,000 has
Capacity, 360 families

COMMUNITY CENTER

MAIN ROAD

NADEPA

SECONDARY ROAD

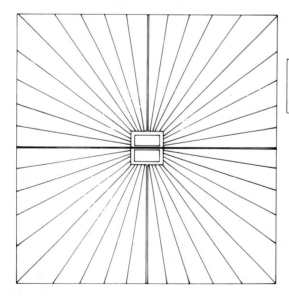

Surface, 2,000 has
Surface per lot, 50 has/family
Capacity, 40 families

Nucleo land allotments

tance from the farm parcel precluded simultaneous rural and urban life-styles.

On the other hand, the nucleated settlement pattern exemplified by the San Julián colony offers numerous advantages. The NADEPA (Nucleo Agrícola de Producción Asociada) concept forms nucleos of forty families, each with a 50-hectare parcel, into a nine-nucleo block. The central nucleo of the block is the NADEPA, where, in addition to the lots supplied for the forty resident families, space is provided for an urban lot for each of the remaining 320 colonist families in the other eight nucleos. In this manner, the system provides urban opportunity for each colonist at a maximum distance of 10 kilometers from the farmstead.

The forty-family unit, although small for a community, allows for continued solidarity and optimum communication among its members. With the NADEPA concept, these small settlements are members of a large one, which can effectively and economically supply primary services that would not be feasible at a lower level of organization.

Along the Brecha, the NADEPA system seems to work. By 1978, little more than two years after settlement, the NADEPA at Nucleo 14 had small businesses along the main road, and two rice mills (peladoras) were in competition. Colonists interviewed appeared to understand that this nucleo would eventually become the service center for that sector. The other NADEPAS had been settled for only a few months, so it was too soon to evaluate the implementation of the system. The development of the NADEPA at Nucleo 14 was spontaneous: although the settlement pattern had been predetermined, the colonists received no impetus from either CIU or INC staff to begin actual development of the center. Compared to other colonies, this natural evolution toward consolidation indicates the importance of the initial settlement pattern in the planning of agricultural colonies.

In March 1979, the major participants in the United Church Committee involved with the San Julián project formed a new group called FIDES (Fundación Interamericano Para el Desarrollo). The basic Methodist-Mennonite composition remained constant with the general assembly composed of fourteen members, half American missionaries and half Bolivians trained by American missionaries. Reasons for setting up this group appear to be twofold: it was necessary to secularize the group, at least for appearance' sake, in order to solicit funding from government agencies such as AID; and by diversifying its membership, the organization would have greater access to private funding sources as well.

The first project tackled by FIDES was a proposal for the consolidation of San Julián and its sister colony across the Río Grande, Chané-Piray. In the past, colonization programs initiated by INC or its forerunners were concerned only with the pioneering phase, which, according to Michael Nelson's settlement paradigm of three phases—pioneering, consolidation, and growth—normally lasts from five to ten years (Nelson 1973). With the inclusion of an orientation program and well-trained and coordinated technical assistants, the San Julián colony was able to move through the pioneering stage in two to three years. The old CIU team, now FIDES, was interested in seeing the colony not only through those early settlement years but into the growth phase as well. In 1978, AID sent an international multidisciplinary team into San Julián to assess the prospects for funding a first-time consolidation project. Nelson and I were both members of this seven-person team (an economist, ecologist, soils specialist, agricultural economist, management specialist, regional planner, and anthropologist). The team was favorably impressed with the progress of the colony and recommended that a consolidation program should be undertaken. After a planning study was carried out in October 1979 by a private consulting firm, the FIDES proposal was completed and submitted to AID in La Paz.

For its consolidation program, FIDES received the largest cooperative agreement grant ever given to a private volunteer organization in Latin America: $1.5 million (U.S.) to be disbursed over a period of three years (Chávez 1980). The results of this program will not be apparent for several years.

The San Julián Migrants

The San Julián colony proved to be the most difficult site in the region to get to. Even in 1978, with bus service from Montero all the way to San Ramón, getting into the colony and moving around within it called for great patience and some ingenuity. Because the Río Grande has not been bridged and continues to change course regularly, there is a 9-kilometer stretch of muddy, rutted trail from the pavement's end just east of the Okinawan settlement to the edge of the river. No matter what time of year, there are always low spots filled with mud or deep patches of loose sand. Whether in a bus or truck, getting to the river's western shore is always a great and uncertain adventure, as is crossing the river, since the huge vehicle-laden barges are towed across by a four- or five-man team pulling ropes. If the current is too strong, the pontoon may break loose and overturn and drown those on board.

Once inside the colony, there are logging trucks and other vehicles that travel the main road every few hours. They are not eager to pick up hitchhikers but perseverance usually wins out. Getting into the remote sectors of the colony, however, is more difficult, and it may take a day or two to acquire transportation. For this reason, as in the Yapacaní, colonists were selected for interviews primarily because of their availability.

As related, only three of the nine nucleos were inhabited at the time of my visit to San Julián in 1975. Nine migrant households were interviewed at this time: four in Nucleo 1, four in Nucleo 2, representing about 10 percent of the inhabitants, and one female in Nucleo 8, the settlement site allocated to the group of repatriated Bolivians from Chile. This last informant was the only person in the nucleo when I arrived. Fortunately she was interested in my work and talked openly and frankly about her experiences and those of her neighbors.

Nucleo 1.—All of the men from Nucleo 1 were in the forest clearing land for the next planting season, so all four interviews at this site were with women. Several were washing clothes by the well near the road, and two agreed to be questioned there. The remaining two informants were young women at a house several hundred meters down the main road.

The two informants at the well, from Potosí and Cochabamba, were illiterate and came from rural villages. They were related because they had married into the same family from Sucre. Both confirmed earlier reports that the nucleo consisted mostly of kin members from this highland region.

Begnigna Miranda (all names are pseudonyms), the twenty-eight-year-old Cochabambina, stated that she and her husband also had relatives in the Yapacaní colony and upon arriving in the lowlands had tried unsuccessfully to obtain land there. They came to San Julián as a second choice. Both of these migrants, as well as the two interviewed at the house, had come to the lowlands to work in the cotton harvest. All cited a general lack of opportunity as their reasons for migrating to Santa Cruz.

Both Donata Huanca, the twenty-year-old from Potosí, and one of the women at the farmhouse, Mercedes Ortega, talked animatedly about the prospect of buying a lot in Montero. Although these conversations occurred separately, many of the same phrases and expressions were used by both, leaving the impression that Montero was a frequent conversational topic in the nucleo. Both Begnigna and Donata implied that their husbands were dissatisfied with life in this particular colony because of the previous year's crop failure and were searching for better land elsewhere.

The two females at the farmhouse, Mercedes Ortega and Lucy Medina, were also related by marriage; Mercedes had married Lucy's brother. Lucy was an unmarried eighteen-year-old from Sucre. Her sister-in-law, aged twenty-three, came from Potosí and was holding her week-old first-born. Lucy explained that there were six members of her father's family as well as her own siblings present in the nucleo. She also thought that a few others might be distant relatives but was not certain. These informants retold the story of the Camba families who had been requested by INC to move out of Nucleo 1 into Nucleo 2. They were open about the concerted effort of family members directed against the presence of the lowlanders in the nucleo. The land simply was needed for other relatives, they explained.

Mercedes was the more adamant of the two in her desire to leave the colony, preferably to move to Montero. She said that she had relatives in the Yapacaní and thought that it was a much better place to live than San Julián.

Nucleo 2.—The inhabitants of Nucleo 2 were largely Camba Guarayos, many of whom had been in the region for a decade or more, as squatters on government lands. When the new colony was opened, several families moved closer to the new road, made formal petitions for parcels, and settled in Nucleo 2 to begin community life. Because I was staying with Mennonite volunteers in this nucleo and so was there during the evening hours, it was possible to interview three males who normally would not be at home during the day. Two were from San Ignacio, the third was from a small settlement near Santa Rosa. Each man had worked the forest in this area since boyhood. It was interesting that none expressed the same philosophy of settlement as that found among many of the highland colonists— to acquire and keep as much good land as possible. These rural Cambas felt that the land in wilderness areas was inalienable—there to be farmed, not owned. The men had no intention of becoming colonists. They were in San Julián because they had always worked the forest in this region and felt they had a right to be there.

The fourth informant at Nucleo 2 was a female highland migrant who was found washing clothes by the well. She had come to the lowlands with a sister to work in the cotton harvest. Both were now married, the sister living on a farm near Cuatro Ojitos. This woman, Fortunata Gutiérrez, was not certain of her age but thought she was about twenty-two. She was illiterate. Fortunata came from a mountain village in the department of Oruro where life was very hard, she said. She was more than happy to leave the highlands where she felt that she had little future, "sólo frío y hambre, no más" ("only cold and hunger, that's all"). She was confident that, together with her husband, who was a hard worker, they would make a good life in the lowlands. Fortunata finished by saying that in the highlands her husband had always worked as a peon and now he had his own land. They too had lost their rice crop the previous year.

Nucleo 8.—The only person living in Nucleo 8 when I visited the colony in 1975 was Flora Bazán, a Bolivian repatriate from Chile. She was somewhat of an anomaly in the colony. Although she had been born in a rural village in Oruro, she was taken at the age of seven by her mother to Arica, where she lived with an aunt of some means. She attended both primary and secondary schools and was about to start the university when she and her family were expelled from Chile for improper documentation. Now in her late twenties, she had decided to accompany the other Bolivian expatriates who had agreed to come to the colony. Flora said that "A lot of the people I came with were from the valley of Azapa in Arica, farming people, but now that better relations have begun between Chile and Bolivia, many got their documents and returned. I am going to try to make a go of it here, if it is possible. If not, I will just have to go somewhere else, but not the interior—there is nothing there, nothing there for anyone."

Nucleo 8 was named Nueva Azapa in honor of the Chilean valley from which many of the repatriates had been sent. When most of the original settlers left, INC attempted to remove the Chilean name and replace it with one of Bolivian origin. Since the War of the Pacific, when Bolivia lost its seacoast, Bolivia and Chile have not been on good terms. The presence of persons in the colony whose primary allegiance was to Chile and not to Bolivia was a source of aggravation to INC officials. Naming the colony after a Chilean locality served only to exacerbate the situation. Now that most of the repatriates are gone, there is little evidence of their attempt to bring their Chilean past with them.

By 1978 the increase in settlers residing in the colony gave a more

Table 7.4. San Julián Migrants' Origins by Region (heads of family), 1978

Origin	Number	Percent
Potosí	499	43.8
Chuquisaca (Sucre)	157	13.8
Cochabamba	144	12.6
Oruro	122	10.7
La Paz	114	10.0
Santa Cruz	81	7.1
Tarija	17	1.8
Beni	3	0.2
Total	1,137	100.0

Source: INC 1978

complete picture of migrant characteristics. The INC's colony survey listed 1,137 heads of family living in San Julián the greatest numbers once again coming from the economically ravaged Potosí region (table 7.4). Cochabamba and Chuquisaca, about equidistant from the Department of Santa Cruz, accounted for the next highest percentages of migrants.

In a sample of one hundred colonists selected from ten nucleos, Hess (1980) reports many of the same characteristics found among the Yapacaní settlers. Most of the sample (88 percent) had worked in seasonal wage labor as harvesters or fieldhands before coming to the colony. The need to continue this type of work to help sustain the family was evident in that 61 percent of the informants said they had sought wage labor away from the colony during 1977–78.

Hess also found that in the more recently settled areas, men greatly outnumbered women, only 46.9 percent of the households having wives present in those nucleos settled after 1976. In those areas settled between 1972 and 1976, 70.4 percent had women present. This same pattern was evident during the early settlement phases of the Yapacaní and other colonies. Ample historical evidence in our own pioneer history underscores the predominance of males during a frontier expansion. Whether male or female, nonetheless, colonists tend to be young, with little to lose by leaving their places of origin. In a subsample of the 1978 INC survey consisting of 667 individuals comprising nine nucleos, about 55 percent were between the ages of sixteen and thirty-five and 35 percent were under age sixteen. Effectively, then, almost 90 percent of the San Julián migrant sample was under age thirty-five.

Chain migration was also important in San Julián as an adaptive strategy that tended to increase numbers of migrants coming from specific areas. Of the one hundred colonists interviewed by Hess, 76 percent said that relatives had come from the highlands to visit, work, and take up land.

Finally, multiple-resource migration continues to be of significance in the highland migrants' efforts to move ahead by occupying several economic niches simultaneously. Following up on my research findings of 1975, Hess found that 20 percent of his 1978 San Julián sample was involved in some aspect of multiple-resource exploitation.

Summary

During the initial years of colonization in the Santa Cruz region, many people brought from the highlands to settle in wilderness areas eventually left the colonies. At first, most returned to the interior, as there were few opportunities available in Santa Cruz in those years. Market routes were nonexistent, and even when farm produce reached marketing centers, low prices did not make the effort worthwhile.

As the region began to develop rapidly in the 1960s, colonization areas became staging centers for many highland migrants. At the time, the colonies served much the same function as did the cane and cotton fields of later years—they provided temporary sites for beginning adaptation to lowland life. For those migrants who arrived directly from the highlands and who had little acquaintance with swidden horticulture, colonization offered an ideal learning situation. Although colonial life was and continues to be harsh and difficult, it gives many migrants needed farming expertise and at the same time provides them with a means of accumulating capital for alternative endeavors.

Today, the agricultural boom of Santa Cruz has slackened, but there remains a growing demand for arable land, including that found in agricultural settlements. More migrants are choosing to stay in the colonies, successfully adapting to life in these remote areas. The exigencies of shifting agriculture frequently require that subsequent holdings be obtained, however. Thus in such areas as the Yapacaní, it is common to find colonists moving to another parcel after they have exhausted their first- and second-growth forest. If available, new land will be acquired within the confines of the Yapacaní colony itself, but it is not uncommon for migrants to move from one colony to another in search of virgin territory. In the San Julián case, the FIDES project with its plans for consolidation that include new models for diversified land use may contribute to more stable colonial population. At present, nevertheless, most migrants in agricultural settlements have found that survival frequently means a series of step migrations to progressively better economic situations or participation in multiple-resource migration to expand income opportunities.

8

Migration and the Department of Santa Cruz: An Overview

Migrant experience in lowland Bolivia has been described in relation to a typology of settlement situations and strategies employed for successful adaptation. The Department of Santa Cruz presents an excellent opportunity for the study of migration because in many ways it is a microcosm of what is occurring on a larger scale elsewhere in Latin America. Although Santa Cruz may be considered a frontier area, it also has a large urban center in its midst. The city of Santa Cruz is not a pioneer outpost representing the fringe of civilization but rather a primate city of over 270,000 inhabitants with many of the same attractions and opportunities found in large urban centers everywhere. For this reason, the Department of Santa Cruz attracts a wide spectrum of people from both urban and rural backgrounds. When we analyze migration in such a microcosm, we see that population movement that may appear chaotic in a broader context actually represents regular and patterned forms of behavior. Movement from highlands to lowlands, from agricultural colony to village, or from town to city is part of a logical sequence of choices that depend on the migrant's accumulated experiences and goals in life.

The Highland Migrant in Santa Cruz

At the outset, migrants tend to select situations similar to their places of origins. The Kolla migrants coming directly from large highland

cities usually relocate in the city of Santa Cruz, and the rural highland migrant usually enters the lowlands in a rural setting—harvesting, fieldwork, or colonization. If a rural migrant selects an urban
residence, whether initially or after having worked in the fields, the
location most often chosen is Montero, not Santa Cruz, so in spite of
the seeming contradiction in terms, Montero remains very much a
"rural city." Precipitous growth in the last decade has failed to alter
its fundamentally rural nature. Many Camba residents of Montero insist that their town essentially is the same village it was fifty years
ago, only bigger. But it is not the same in at least one respect: the
composition of its population. Because so many highlanders have
chosen Montero over Santa Cruz, it has become the cultural center
for highland people in the lowlands. Its proximity to the northern
farmlands makes it an ideal choice for the rural Kolla looking for an
urban home.

The remaining settlement situations offer the prospective migrant a
wide choice. The adventuresome will head for the agricultural colonies, willing to trade the amenities of civilization for the promise of
huge tracts of free land. Others move into one of the smaller villages
and towns that are oriented toward either subsistence farming or
commercial agriculture. In less than a day's travel, it is possible to experience both extremes of the rural-urban migration continuum and a
full range of settlement patterns in between, and it is in this setting
that the migration process may be better understood.

Motivational Factors in Migration to and within Santa Cruz

Of the 1975 regional sample population of 154 individuals, 64 percent cited economic motives for migration (table 8.1). The study carried out by the DDE (Dirección Departamental de Estadística), a survey of 3,587 households almost equally divided between Cambas and
Kollas, supports this finding: 68.48 percent of those migrants working in the place of origin relocated because of economic incentives.
This percentage is particularly interesting because it confirms that it
is not only the jobless who seek to migrate. The economic stagnation
in the highlands in both rural and urban sectors has been a major
"push" factor for most of the Bolivians moving to the lowlands. This
situation had been worsening for many years, but not until Santa
Cruz had something to offer the migrant did population movement
into the district begin on a large scale. Alers and Applebaum saw a
similar pattern in Peru: "Motivations which are strongly economic
exercise a more influential role as pull factors than as push; that is to

Table 8.1. Motives for Migration among Employed Migrants at Time of
Leaving Place of Origin, 1979 (N = 3,587)

Motive	Percent of Total
Look for work	58.38
Have work	10.10
Family	19.11
Study	6.96
Other	2.88
Health	1.57
Total	99.00

Source: INE–DDE: 1981.

say, there is a greater propensity among migrants to feel attracted by
increased economic opportunities in a locality than to feel expelled
from the place of origin simply as a result of economic problems"
(1968:15)

When expansion of Cruceñan agriculture and growth of the petroleum industry began to increase available capital in the region, the
stage was set for internal migration. The phenomenal growth in farm
production and the labor-intensive nature of the products cultivated
created a ready market for seasonal labor. Harvesting became the
means for many to seek not only new opportunities but hope of a
better life. After working the cane fields and cotton harvest, many migrants decided to remain, finding additional markets for their labor or
purchasing small farms in the region. The agricultural boom also
contributed to the flow of capital into the lowland urban centers, and,
along with petroleum royalties, helped to finance private and public
work projects that also demanded large quantities of primarily unskilled labor. Cities such as Montero and Santa Cruz became the destinations of an urban flow from the highlands that complemented
rural migration.

A secondary stream commenced when the initial flow of migrants
into the lowlands had become steady. It was composed of people who
would find income opportunities as a result of the presence of the
migrant population itself—market vendors, storekeepers, truckers,
and, of course, chicheras.

Although economic incentives held a primary position in stated
migration motivations, many other factors were involved in the reso-
lution to migrate. Richard Wilkie noted that "the economic factor
helps condition the need to migrate, but whether the final decision to
migrate is made or not reverts in most cases to the psychological, so-

cial, spatial and environmental perceptions and attitudes within the family unit" (1968:109). Many Kolla migrants in the sample populations of both 1975 and 1979 said that they were influenced by relatives, friends, or others to make the move and, once they were in the lowlands, that decision was reinforced by similar networks of individuals. Among those who arrived as harvesters, contratados or voluntarios, peer pressure was extremely influential in the decision to migrate. Harvesters frequently arrived in groups derived from kinship ties, friendships, or local residence, and once an initial commitment had been made by one or more members to migrate, pressure was exerted on others to join them.

Although secondary to economic motives, other reasons for migrating were cited: visiting, military service, health, or running away. Runaways create an interesting situation in that they may inadvertently contribute to the migration of relatives or friends who come to the lowlands to find them. During the 1975 study, a number of parents of runaways were encountered. Some had found their offspring but had decided to remain in Santa Cruz. Others, not successful, had all decided to remain in eastern Bolivia until their children could be found. The nature of the cotton harvest, which enables children as well as adults to find employment, provides more than adequate incentive for highland youth to leave home in search of adventure and a taste of freedom from household demands. By 1980, however, the problem of runaway children appeared to be lessening, primarily because of the decline in cotton production and therefore in the need for harvesters.

Settlement Patterns

Settlement patterns of migrants in the five study sites reflected each locality's physical and social environments as well as the nature of the settlement process itself. The two major factors influencing migrants' location in a settlement were the rate and volume of migration to the area and the existing socioeconomic and physical dimensions of the site.

In Santa Cruz, Montero, and, to a certain extent, Warnes, the rate and volume of highland migration played a major role in establishing settlement patterns. When migrants arrive in large numbers over a relatively short period of time, they tend to concentrate in barrios, which then show a high degree of ethnic solidarity. The cities of Santa Cruz and Montero and the town of Warnes exhibit such specific migrant settlement zones. The pressure of large numbers of migrants moving to these cities prompted the allocation of vacant lands for the formation of migrant neighborhoods. In Santa Cruz, settlement patterns in migrant barrios have followed the spatial expansion of the city and bear a definite structural relationship to it. This process has also occurred to a certain extent in Montero, since the developmental progression of the city has been outward toward the migrant neighborhood. In Montero, lowlanders were instrumental in deciding the ultimate location of highland barrios and successfully relocated the migrant population outside of the inner core of the city.

In the village situation, as exemplified by San Carlos, migration volumes and rates have been small because of a relatively stable economic base. As a result, until recently migrants have moved into available space rather than creating separate neighborhoods. I predicted in 1975 (Stearman 1976) that if the village began to attract greater numbers of migrants, pressures would be brought to bear on the owners of larger landholdings within the three-kilometer urban radius of the community to relinquish these properties for settlement by migrants. In the late 1970s, the village began to experience an increase in Camba as well as Kolla immigration, with the result that urban lands were subdivided for sale and two new barrios developed. Still, the number of highland migrants in San Carlos remains relatively small, so Kolla migrants have found it necessary to become integrated socially, economically, and spatially into the existing village structure. Unlike their counterparts in areas of high migrant concentrations, San Carlos highlanders cannot exist apart from their Camba neighbors.

In the colonies, settlement patterns have been somewhat predetermined by a planned program of land allocation. Even so, migrants tend to chose sites near family, friends, or people from the same place of origin. In the colonies, however, highlanders are a vast majority and, unlike other sites where Cambas predominate, are not restricted to any significant degree by local residence patterns.

The existence or absence of rental housing in a locality also reflects differing rates and volumes of migration. The greatest incidence of rental housing was found in the two urban centers, Santa Cruz and Montero, where immigration rates are high. In both, migrants in need of immediate shelter created a large enough demand for housing that established highlanders eagerly took economic advantage of the situation. Thus multifamily units and inexpensive temporary shelter are prevalent in these areas. Rental complexes also exist in Villa Busch, the main settlement of the Yapacaní, which is experiencing an increase in its urban population due to the growth of marketing in the colony. In all areas that have rental housing, most of these units remain on the periphery or in the newest section of the residential district. As stabilization begins, rental housing in the barrio decreases or moves to the limits of the settlement.

Characteristics of Migrants

From research in Peru, Stillman Bradfield (1973) drew certain inferences about the nature of the individual who migrated from the countryside to an urban center. In general, the Peruvian migrants studied tended to have a higher rate of literacy and were younger than the population as a whole; they were more independent and demonstrated greater progressiveness in their thinking. As a group, the Santa Cruz sample exhibits some similarities to Bradfield's migrants but differed in other respects.

Youth seems to be a universal characteristic of migrants. Studies in many areas of the world of both urban and rural populations emphasize the tendency to migrate before age thirty (Alers and Applebaum 1968). In Santa Cruz, the mean age in the 1975 sample was 31.7, but the average length of residence in the region was five years, reducing the mean age at the time of *arrival* to 26.7. The DDE study of 1979 found the mean age of the migrant to be 26.3 years. The mean age of the Santa Cruz nonmigrant population was 16.8, much lower than that of migrants. Most migrants are young but are of working age and have fewer children than nonmigrants (see fig. 8.1).

The 1975 Santa Cruz migrant sample demonstrated a lower rate of literacy than the national average of 32.39 percent (Arze 1979), in apparent contradiction to other findings that migrants tend to have a higher rate of literacy than nonmigrants. The 1975 group of migrant informants displayed an illiteracy rate of over 68 percent. It should be noted, however, that females exhibited a much greater tendency toward illiteracy than did males, and the study sample was skewed heavily toward females—74 percent of those interviewed. A balanced sample might have shown a rate of illiteracy within or below that of the nation. On the other hand, it should be recognized that most previous migration studies have primarily involved male informants. Especially in areas where females did not have the same access to education (thereby lowering the migrant literacy rate), the

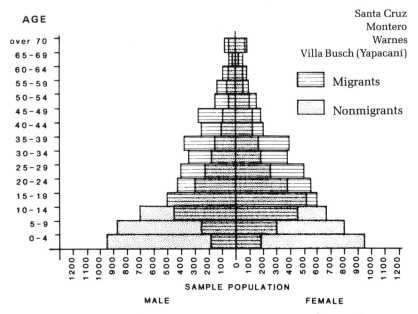

AGE

Santa Cruz
Montero
Warnes
Villa Busch (Yapacaní)

Migrants

Nonmigrants

SAMPLE POPULATION

MALE   FEMALE

Age differences between Santa Cruz migrants and nonmigrants

consistent exclusion of women from migration studies would affect the figures regarding literacy among migrants.

In attempting to compare these findings with those from 1979, several problems arise. Because over half the migrant sample consisted of lowlanders, the 12 percent illiteracy rate is far below the national average. Santa Cruz has the lowest level of illiteracy for the nation— 19.15 percent—while the highlands have 36.79 percent. Had the data been analyzed in terms of highlanders only, the illiteracy rate would have been significantly higher. Nonetheless, the results of the 1979 study, a much larger and more representative sample, support the hypothesis that migrants tend to have a higher rate of literacy than the general population.

Migrants in Santa Cruz also tend to be innovative, ambitious, and adaptable to changing situations. These qualities are best reflected in the ways in which they derive income and expand their access to available resources. The majority of highland Bolivians who move to Santa Cruz are entrepreneurial, and this characteristic is especially strong among women. Although entrepreneurship at first appeared to be linked to urbanism, it was later found that rural migrants were also highly motivated to diversify their resources by entering into commercial and other nonagricultural activities. Most interesting throughout the department was the highland women's ability to capitalize on lowland marketing opportunities. In many instances, marketplaces built by Cambas expecting to take advantage of the influx of Kollas were soon dominated by highlanders. Perhaps of all the innovations that have resulted from highland migration, the new focus on marketing has had the most far-reaching impact. Camba buying habits have changed in terms of dietary predilections, common marketing days, and preferred type of marketing facility.

Highland females generally like to sell. They will sit on street corners selling fruit, erect a small stand for merchandise, or place a table at a strategic point to offer cold drinks to passersby. Although selling is a well-established tradition among highland women, it is also perfectly suited for the lowland environment. A virtual vacuum existed in the marketing sphere in Santa Cruz prior to the arrival of highlanders. These women were able to move into an economic niche that not only suited their backgrounds and abilities but also offered them unlimited opportunity for exploitation.

Other females have found the migrant population itself a source of income. In some localities such as Santa Cruz, Warnes, and Montero, there are enough migrants to permit economic enterprises that operate as systems parallel to those of Cambas and that depend only on migrants themselves for clients. Many vendors in markets sell items in demand only by Kollas, such as the traditional pollera. The most conspicuous example, of course, is the presence of chicherías in the department; a large occupational group has migrated to Santa Cruz for the sole purpose of providing chicha to the highland populace.

Although the Department of Santa Cruz is attracting people from all of the highland regions, distance and available roads seem to affect differences in volume of migration. Cochabamba, the nearest highland city and department and the most accessible in terms of transportation networks, contributed 45 percent of the 1975 sample population (table 8.2). Other departments were presented proportionately in relation to their relative distance from Santa Cruz. The category "other" included localities such as road towns on the Santa Cruz–Cochabamba highway, and the southern department of Tarija.

This pattern remained consistent in the 1979 study. Table 8.3 confirms the prominence of the nearest highland department, Cochabamba, as a source of highland migrants to Santa Cruz. It should also

Table 8.2. Migrant Origins, 1975

Origin	Number	Percent
Cochabamba	70	45.0
Chuquisaca (Sucre)	29	19.0
Potosí	22	14.0
Oruro	15	10.0
Other	12	8.0
La Paz	6	4.0
Total	154	100.0

Table 8.3. Migrant Origins and Percentage of Total
Sample Population, 1979

Origin	Percentage
Kolla	
Cochabamba	13.53
La Paz	6.87
Potosí	6.12
Chuquisaca (Sucre)	5.32
Tarija	2.89
Oruro	2.75
Camba	
Santa Cruz	47.48
Beni	4.40
Pando	0.03
Foreign	10.61
Total	100.00

Source: INE–DDE 1981.

be noted that over 10 percent of the migrant population is foreign—Japanese, Okinawan, Chinese, German, and others.

Finally, in both surveys over half the sample population expressed satisfaction with the decision to migrate to Santa Cruz. Those migrants who wanted to return to the highlands and familiar surroundings were primarily the older ones. From an economic point of view, this attitude is hardly surprising. But many migrants, in addition to commenting on their improved economic condition, also remarked on the more agreeable climate of Santa Cruz. Several informants mentioned their dislike of the summer heat and humidity, but most found it preferable to the continual cold of the mountains. This finding is interesting in that years ago both the scientific and the lay communities agreed that highland Bolivians would be unable to adapt to the lowland environment. On the contrary, most appear to be thriving physically, as well as economically. Informants continually made such comments as "Me gusta aquí, aquí estoy bien" ("I like it here, here I am fine"), "En el interior no hay nada, frió y hambre no más" ("In the interior there is nothing, cold and hunger, that's all"), and "En el oriente hay para todos" ("In the east, there is something for everyone").

Migration Patterns

One of the immediately apparent results of studying migration on a regional scale is the emergence of a wide range of patterns or types of migration. While each of the six categories of migration outlined in chapter 1 may be considered separately for the purpose of analysis, in dealing with actual cases it is rare to encounter evidence of only one pattern. This multiplicity of migration strategies becomes an important factor in analyzing the total process of migration in a wider spatial context. Over time it is possible that a migrant might employ all six types of migration patterns in various combinations. For the purpose of discussion, however, each will be dealt with separately.

Single-phase migration.—Of the total sample populations from the 1975 and 1980 studies, less than a third reported that moving to their present location was their sole experience with migration. The majority of the single-phase migrants were residents of the city of Santa Cruz who had arrived directly from a highland city or colonists who had come from rural highland villages. The incidence of single-phase migration in Montero was much lower than that encountered in the extreme urban or extreme rural situation. In Warnes and San Carlos there were no migrants who had moved there directly from the place of origin.

Migrants from rural backgrounds who had made a single move from the place of origin were to be found only in the Yapacaní colony, which has a long settlement history. In most cases these were colonists who had been brought by CBF from the interior directly to the colony in the early 1960s. The San Julián residents, along with the more recent Yapacaní settlers, entered these colonization areas after harvest seasons in other lowland sectors or, in the case of the repatriates, after having worked in the interior.

Only in highly urbanized situations, then, was single-phase migration a significant contribution to contemporary migration processes in the lowlands. It should be emphasized, nevertheless, that, as the

case with other types of migration, single-phase may frequently represent only a particular stage in a total sequence of migrations by the
individual.

Temporary or seasonal migration.—It has been estimated by personnel of CORDECRUZ and the Federación de Campesinos that over
half of the highlanders entering the Department of Santa Cruz do so
to seek harvesting opportunities. Many use seasonal migration as a
kind of preadaptation to lowland life. There may be numerous return
trips during a span of several years, or migrants may decide to remain
after their first experience with the Santa Cruz harvests. Seasonal migration nevertheless may continue even after definitive relocation in
the lowlands has occurred. Migrants who entered Santa Cruz via the
cane or cotton fields but who subsequently have obtained private
ownership of land will on occasion continue to work the annual
harvests near Montero or Warnes. The rice harvest does not conflict
with the cane or cotton season, so many migrants working their own
small farms will return to harvesting to earn extra income, often as a
means to pay for the clearing of more land or to contract day laborers.
So seasonality may continue as a way of life for many migrants engaged in horticulture until they become economically established.

Rural migrants who have become urban dwellers also may join the
seasonal work force. In Warnes and Montero, during the peak of the
harvest season when field laborers are in demand, trucks or tractors
with flatbed trailers are driven through the migrant neighborhoods in
search of voluntarios. Those currently unemployed are hired on the
spot and taken to the fields, frequently at a better rate of pay than
those workers contracted in the highlands at the onset of the harvest.

The cane and cotton harvests also attract another type of seasonal
migrant but one not associated directly with fieldwork. The presence
of thousands of harvesters in the lowlands during the winter months
encourages many individuals engaged in service activities to make
the migration as well. Merchants and especially the chicheras will
come to the lowlands solely for the duration of the harvest, set up
shop in a rented space, and return to the highlands when it is over.

Step migration.—The progressive movement from a rural situation to one that is more urban is occurring regularly among Bolivian
migrants, as elsewhere in the world. Part of this progression may be
initiated in the highlands, to be continued once the migrant moves to
Santa Cruz. There may be temporary "regressions" when the migrant
leaves a more urban highland area, such as a secondary service cen-

ter, to work in the Santa Cruz harvests. Once the harvest has ended, this type of migrant will move back into a more urban milieu, such as Montero.

Step migration is also to be found among the colonists. After a decade or so in an agricultural settlement, a family may decide to move to a nearby village or even to Montero, where public services such as schools are available. In this and other examples of movement by stages, the "steps" may not always be in a direct progression toward increased urbanism. For example, a rural highlander may move to Warnes to participate in the harvest. From there he goes to Montero and then on to an agricultural colony. After several years of labor in the colony, part of the family may locate in a rural village such as San Carlos where a store is established. Later on, rental property in Montero may also be added to the family's holdings and permanent residence eventually established there. Viewed over time, each of these discrete migrations may be considered steps toward final settlement in a particular locality. Step migration, then, is not always a well-defined, rural-urban progression but may involve moves back and forth between rural and urban locations as new opportunities arise. These intermediate "steps" ultimately enable the migrant to achieve an urban residence.

Sequential migration.—Among many urban Kolla migrants, a series of sequential horizontal moves has come to be expected. Unstable economic conditions in the highlands make it necessary to move from city to city to avoid unemployment. For many of these individuals, the move to Santa Cruz is considered one in a sequence of similar lateral migrations.

In rural lowland areas, sequential moves are a well-established part of campesino existence, whether Camba or Kolla. When farmlands are depleted and the agriculturalist has neither the capital nor the inclination to convert to cattle ranching, the property often reverts to those with resources and incentive to put in pasture for forage animals. The swidden horticulturalist then moves to another parcel of forest which can be cut and burned for dry rice cultivation. In earlier years, there was adequate forest to permit slash-and-burn horticulture with little concern for landownership. Squatters' rights were upheld, and even the landed gentry often looked the other way when someone cut down a hectare or two for rice. Today, however, property suitable for farming is at a premium, making the practice of shifting agriculture increasingly difficult. Many farmers now must settle for second-growth forest instead of the preferred virgin forest. In the future, pressures for land can be expected to hinder significantly the mobility of the swidden horticulturalist.

Chain migration.—Perhaps the single most influential factor in the development of migration streams in Bolivia (and apparently in other areas of the world as well) has been that of chain migration. In all five study sites there was consistent affirmation of the important role of other migrants in a decision to move to the lowlands.

Chain migration operated in the city of Santa Cruz both to augment the volume and rate of migration and to determine composition of barrios. Among seasonal migrants, yearly sojourns in the lowlands had a multiplying effect, and more and more persons felt encouraged enough to leave their highland farms and villages to migrate to Santa Cruz. The agricultural colonies are filled with extended kin groups and regional residential units whose membership was recruited as a result of chain migration.

With few exceptions, individuals interviewed in 1975 and 1980 revealed that someone had supplied the additional information or impetus that resulted in migration. The rapid increase in rates and volumes of highlanders leaving the interior for lowland residence may be seen as a direct result of chain migration. As increasing numbers of migrants enter the Santa Cruz region and find employment and other opportunities, their positive feedback generates even higher rates of migration. Although the government's dream of encouraging highland people to move to the oriente is at last becoming reality, this process has occurred separately from national programs to organize and execute colonization programs. In the long run, sponsored colonization has played a relatively minor role in the resettlement process.

Multiple-resource migration.—While some of the migrants are involved in sequential, step, seasonal, or other migration patterns, another segment of the migrant population is concerned with the exploiting of multiple resources through a type of migration that permits simultaneous management of spatially and economically diverse holdings. Multiple-resource migration seems to be practiced mainly by rural migrants. Because this type of migration often involves a combination of rural and urban property acquisitions, the urban dweller does not seem to find himself in the initial position necessary for such resource expansion. An approximation to this pattern occurs in urban areas through the attainment of rental properties in a city. However, a distinction exists between property acquired specifically for the use of nonfamily and property considered an extension of the family residence, the latter case representing multiple-resource migration as it was defined earlier.

Wherever rural Kolla migrants are found, multiple-resource migration is also present. The acquisition of numerous properties in differing social and economic environments seems to be a response to the migrant's propensity for entrepreneurial endeavors as well as a result of long-standing highland traditions. The migrant family that engages in multiple-resource migration usually has been more successful and more astute in managing and accumulating resources than its counterpart that moves by step progressions or horizontally. In the latter cases, property holdings normally must be liquidated to finance the next migration. The individuals or families who engage in multiple-resource migration, on the other hand, have consolidated adequate capital to allow for the simultaneous holding of diverse properties in several localities.

This pattern of migration has proved to be extremely adaptive to the present economic structure of the Department of Santa Cruz. The small-scale farmer finds it difficult to expand his income solely through agricultural activities. Swidden horticulture is labor intensive so, unless a family has a large number of resident males, profits must give way to labor costs. Moving into other economic endeavors not only creates new sources of income; it also allows for a greater division of labor. Females, the elderly, and children who can contribute only partially to farm incomes can now be engaged in commercial or other enterprises that make them full participants in the family's economic activities.

A Migration Model

When I returned to the Santa Cruz region after an absence of almost seven years, I found many changes, including the recent arrival of an overwhelming number of Bolivian highlanders. In 1968, Kollas were encountered only in limited numbers and only in certain areas of the department. Although at the time highlanders resided in the cities of Santa Cruz and Montero, they were few and not highly visible. The majority of migrants remained in the agricultural colonies or entered the region on a seasonal basis to work in the sugarcane harvest. By 1975, highlanders were to be seen everywhere. Large barrios of mi-

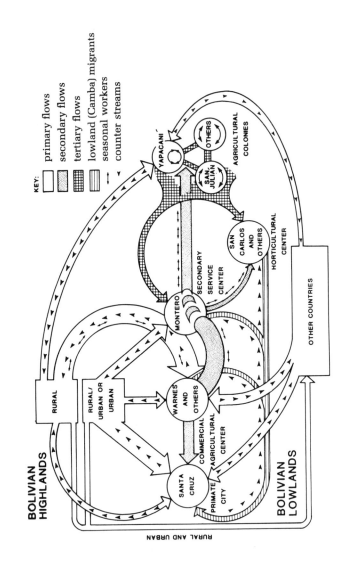

Highland-lowland migration model

KEY:
- primary flows
- secondary flows
- tertiary flows
- lowland (Camba) migrants
- seasonal workers
- counter streams

BOLIVIAN HIGHLANDS

BOLIVIAN LOWLANDS

RURAL AND URBAN

RURAL

RURAL/ URBAN OR URBAN

SANTA CRUZ
PRIMATE AGRICULTURAL CITY

WARNES AND OTHERS
COMMERCIAL AGRICULTURAL CENTER

MONTERO
SECONDARY SERVICE CENTER

SAN CARLOS AND OTHERS
HORTICULTURAL CENTER

YAPACANI

SAN JULIAN

OTHERS

AGRICULTURAL COLONIES

OTHER COUNTRIES

grants had sprung up on the outskirts of the city of Santa Cruz and Montero. Marketplaces were dominated by women wearing derby hats and polleras, and new markets had opened to meet the growing demands of a rapidly expanding population. Cotton had been introduced to the agricultural scene, and numerous small Camba towns became caught up in the flurry of commercial farming. Migrants began to settle in these communities, many of which for the first time could count highlanders among their populations. Kollas even had invaded the peasant villages scattered throughout the region. And, of course, colonization continued to be a major attraction for rural migrants.

Highlanders were in everywhere in Santa Cruz, riding on buses and trucks, swarming in the marketplaces, and settling in any available space. At first all of this activity was beyond comprehension, but as each study site was investigated, patterns began to emerge from the apparent chaos. Migration to, within, and out of the department eventually could be discerned as an orderly, systematic process that resulted in specific flows or streams of migrants. The composition of these streams was determined by such migrant characteristics as place of origin, experience or education, goals, and, finally, strategies for survival.

Primary streams.—There are three primary streams of migrants to the lowlands. The first consists of urban Kollas who are urban because they were born in a city or have made a rural-urban move in the highlands. The majority of these migrants locate in the city of Santa Cruz, where they continue an urban existence not unlike that they left behind. A small number of city dwellers from the highlands use harvesting as a means of entry, but they subsequently move either to Santa Cruz or Montero. Another segment goes directly to Montero to engage in commercial activities such as merchandising or chicha sale.

The second primary stream is composed of rural highlanders. A substantial percentage of this stream enters the lowland region as harvesters and then moves to villages or isolated farmsteads on private land or in one of the agricultural colonies. Another smaller segment comes directly from the highlands to colonies such as the Yapacaní or San Julián projects.

The third primary stream is made up of people from outside Bolivia, both foreigners and Bolivian repatriates. The movement of highland Bolivians across international borders to find seasonal or permanent work is a common occurrence. Many Bolivians enter these countries legally, but illegal migration is also prevalent. Some illegal aliens may not be caught; they may marry nationals and thereby establish legal residence, or they may acquire a set of falsified documents. If they are discovered, however, they must return to Bolivia. In recent years, countries such as Argentina and Chile have made a concerted effort to locate these illegal aliens, resulting in the expulsion of substantial numbers of Bolivian migrants. Many of those forcibly returned find living in Santa Cruz a better option than going back to the highlands. Among those coming out of Argentina, for example, are persons who have worked in the grape and vegetable harvest of Mendoza; they make the transition to cane and cotton harvesting in Santa Cruz with relative ease. Others, such as the Bolivian repatriates from Chile found the agricultural colonies where they were sent less to their liking; they have moved into lowland cities or have found a way back to Chile. The remainder of migrants from the exterior include Mennonites, Japanese, and Okinawans who are mainly agriculturalists and have settled in the hinterlands of the department. Other groups such as Lebanese, Chinese, British, and Americans may be found in the city of Santa Cruz. For the most part, migrants from other nations tend to settle in the Department of Santa Cruz in the same contexts as do other migrants. If they come from urban backgrounds, they select an urban lowland center for relocation; if rural, they may either move to the countryside or decide at that point to remain in a city.

Secondary streams.—A secondary migration stream may be defined as that occuring after the migrant makes the initial move from the place of origin. Since most urban migrants tend to remain in their urban points of destination, such as the city of Santa Cruz or Montero, secondary migration streams appear negligible among this group. The rural migrant, however, rarely moves directly from the highlands or the exterior to an immediate, long-term place of residence in the lowlands of Bolivia. The sole exception, of course, is the colonist. Most of the other rural migrants enter the lowlands through the harvests, as day laborers on farms, or pass through a brokerage center such as Montero or Warnes in hopes of finding a suitable site for relocation. From there, they eventually establish residence in some area of the department.

Tertiary streams.—After lowland residence has been established by the rural migrant, additional migration may take place, in the form of step, sequential, multiple-resource, or seasonal migration. Although returning to an earlier settlement situation is considered a "counterstream" in most migration studies (Lee 1968; Simmons et al. 1977), it sometimes may be viewed as a tertiary flow in the case of Santa Cruz migrants. For example, many rural migrants enter Montero after the harvest, live there for a while, and then depart from that locality for other settlement areas. After having lived for a number of years in a village or colony, these migrants may return to Montero not as the result of failure, which commonly accounts for migration counterstreams, but in order to continue optimizing their resources and opportunities.

Another tertiary flow exists among those migrants living in remote agricultural areas. Rather than Montero, they frequently will select a small village as a subsequent or additional settlement site. In the colonies, tertiary flows are evident among those migrants who move within and among colonial centers as a result of the need to acquire more land or land more productive than they presently hold.

Finally, many rural migrants continue to operate in the seasonal labor force. Thus a tertiary flow of migrants based on seasonality, moving from villages and colonies to zones of commercial agriculture is evident during the harvest period. These highland migrants are extremely influential in the process of chain migration in that they have direct contact with newly arrived migrants from the interior. It is the established migrant who is often instrumental in persuading the recent migrant to remain.

The Camba as migrant.—Lowlanders represent over half the population movement occurring in the Department of Santa Cruz but do not consider themselves "migrants." When Cambas are asked about migration, they will immediately begin talking about Kollas, Mennonites, or Japanese. In other words, only "outsiders" are migrants from the lowland point of view. Cambas, according to one informant, simply "move." The Camba migration stream is mainly rural-urban in nature, and it is directed toward the city of Santa Cruz in contrast to the highland rural-urban flow toward Montero. This urban movement by lowlanders has left vacancies in other areas which are being filled by new arrivals. E. G. Ravenstein described a similar situation in Great Britain: "The inhabitants of the country immediately surrounding a town of rapid growth flock into it; the gaps thus left in the rural population are filled up by migrants from more remote districts" (1885:199). In the case of Santa Cruz, these migrants "from the more remote districts" are usually highlanders.

Cambas and Kollas

Most lowlanders express certain stereotyped images of the "typical" Kolla while highlanders are just as adamant that they have accurate perceptions of the average Camba. Most Cambas maintain that highlanders are hard workers but dirty, slow-witted, and untrustworthy. Kollas often describe Cambas as lazy drunkards, unfaithful to their spouses but fun-loving and carefree. The intensity of firsthand contact is beginning to erode many of these stereotypes, but prejudices still remain strong.

The animosity of lowlanders toward highland Bolivians is a long-standing problem of national integration. Many Cruceñans insist they are "racially superior" to highlanders because of a stronger European heritage. Even so, hatred of highlanders has developed from a long history of political turmoil on a national as well as international level. The independent Cruceñan has always resisted and resented the political hegemony of the highlands. Order in the Department of Santa Cruz traditionally has been maintained by highland soldiers, exacerbating an already volatile situation. During the Chaco War, Cambas were not allowed to form their own regiments, and when the MNR came to power in 1952, once again contingents of wool-clad highland recruits were sent to Santa Cruz to help implement the reform.

Most highlanders arriving in Santa Cruz are aware that such prejudices exist but are unprepared for the level of animosity that is often demonstrated. If highlanders come to Santa Cruz with a desire to get along with Cambas, they learn quickly that the best they can hope for at present is mutual tolerance. Still, a certain degree of reverse discrimination is practiced by highlanders, and those who are gibed by Cambas may be heard to retort "Camba flojo" ("lazy Camba") or "Camba pícaro ("Camba rogue").

Although mutual acceptance by highlanders and lowlanders is a long way from realization, the situation has improved somewhat over the years. When I lived in Santa Cruz from 1964 to 1968, it was not uncommon for a village shopkeeper to refuse service to a Kolla campesino. Today, this would seldom occur. There are too many highlanders in the region to ignore them, but, even more important, lowlanders are aware that highlanders have contributed appreciably to the economic prosperity shared by all.

The migrants who come to Santa Cruz for the most part are upwardly mobile and ambitious. They are entrepreneurs who will turn most any venture into a capital gain. Lowlanders are bewildered at the rate at which the Cruceñan economy is being dominated by highlanders. The Kolla is outfarming and outselling the Camba in every corner of the region. Some lowlanders are philosophical about the apparent take-over of their territory, but for others it only leads to more bitterness.

Even now, assimilation is being resisted by both groups. Most highlanders prefer to select their spouses from other migrants or return to the interior to marry. Their children, however, are making the initial moves toward an eventual merging of these two cultures. Highland migrant children are eager to throw off the ways of their parents and adopt those of Cambas. They want to dress like lowlanders, speak only Spanish, and choose their peers from among Cambas. Many of these first-generation Cruceñans are now beginning to choose lowlanders as spouses.

Although Cambas are still the numerically dominant social group, most highlanders do not accept their cultural domination. As a result, many highland traditions not only are supported by the migrant sector but are staunchly perpetuated by it. Ralph Linton, discussing some aspects of nativistic movements, refers to this activity as "rational perpetuative nativism" whereby certain characteristics of a culture become "symbols of the society's existence as a unique entity" (1965:501). Thus traditions such as highland hair styles, the use of the pollera, and the presence of chicherías take on even greater importance in Santa Cruz than they would normally have in the highlands. Linton also mentions that retention of specific cultural elements may become a means of maintaining group solidarity. Social sanctions such as avoidance and malicious gossip often are directed toward those highland women who forsake traditional dress and thereby represent a threat to migrant cohesiveness.

Santa Cruz also presents an interesting case in acculturation: a pattern of dominance by Cambas exists, but at the same time there is an absence of the expected self-perception of inferiority by Kolla migrants. Consequently, mountain traditions persist not only because they are symbols of ethnic pride or because they have become a means to maintain migrant solidarity but because highlanders wholeheartedly believe that their way of life is superior to that of Cambas.

Because of the migrants' tenacity in perpetuating highland custom, their presence is being felt strongly among the numerically dominant lowlanders. Cambas have adopted not only new customs but a perspective on life previously unknown in Santa Cruz. The industrious

and ambitious highlander is beginning to spur the less competitive lowlander into fuller participation in the regional and national
economies.

It cannot be denied that highlanders are changing the face of Santa
Cruz, often in ways which the Camba finds distressing. Nevertheless,
few lowlanders would disagree that, since the advent of large-scale
migration of Kollas to Santa Cruz, the department has entered a new
period of economic prosperity and increased opportunity for Cambas
and Kollas alike.

References

AID (Agency for International Development)
   1978   "Project Evaluation Summary. San Julián." La Paz.
Alers, J. Oscar, and Richard P. Applebaum
   1968   "La Migración en el Peru, un Inventario de Proposiciones." Un proyecto del Instituto de Estudios Peruanos. *Estudios de Población y Desarrollo*. Vol. 1, no. 4, Série Original no. 2. Lima.
Arensberg, Conrad
   1968   *The Irish Countryman*. Garden City, N.Y.: The Natural History Press.
Arze Cuadros, Eduardo
   1979   *La Economía de Bolivia. Ordenamiento Territorial y Dominación Externa, 1492–1979*. La Paz: Los Amigos del Libro.
Beaujeu-Garnier, J.
   1966   *Geography of Population*. London: Longmans, Green and Company.
Bolivia.   Dirección Nacional de Estadística y Censos.
   1951   "Resultados Generales del Censo de Población de la República de Bolivia, levantado el día 5 de septiembre de 1950." La Paz.
Bolivia.   Ministerio de Planeamiento y Coordinación. Instituto Nacional de Estadística.
   1976   "Resultados del Censo Nacional de Población y Vivienda." La Paz.
Bonilla, Frank
   1961   "Río's Favelas." *American Universities Fieldstaff Reports*. East Coast South America Series. Vol. 8, no. 3.
Bradfield, Stillman
   1973   "Selectivity in Rural-Urban Migration: The Case of Huaylas, Peru." In *Urban Anthropology*, edited by A. Southall, pp. 35–72. New York: Oxford University Press.
Brush, Stephen B.
   1974   "Peru's Invisible Migrants: A Case Study of Inter-Andean Migration." Paper presented at the Symposium on the Community and

the Hacienda Reconsidered: The Andean Case, American Anthropological Association, Mexico City.

Caldwell, John C.
1969   *African Rural-Urban Migration. The Movement to Ghana's Towns.* New York: Columbia University Press.

Carter, William E.
1967   *Comunidades Aymaras y Reforma Agraria en Bolivia.* Instituto Indigenista Interamericano. Serie: Antropología Social 6. Mexico.

Chávez, Donna
1980   Personal communication.

CIU-INC (Comité de Iglesias Unidas–Instituto Nacional de Colonización)
1975   "Convenio del Comité de Iglesias Unidas con el Instituto Nacional de Colonización." La Paz: CIU-INC.

Clark, Ronald James
1968   "Land Reform and Peasant Market Participation on the North Highlands of Bolivia." *Land Economics* 64 (May).

Cochrane, Thomas T.
1973   *El Potencial Agrícola del Uso de la Tierra en Bolivia. Un Mapa de Sistemas de Tierras.* La Paz: Misión Británica en Agricultura Tropical, Ministerio de Agricultura.

COHA (Council on Hemispheric Affairs)
1981   "Bolivian Military Split Brings down García Meza." Vol. 1, no. 17 (June):1.

CORDECRUZ (Corporación Regional de Desarrollo Santa Cruz)
1979a   "Síntesis Socioeconómica del Departamento de Santa Cruz." Santa Cruz de la Sierra, Bolivia: CORDECRUZ.
1979b   "Diagnóstico Coyuntural. La Crisis Agropecuaria Regional y Sugerencias de una Nueva Política Económica para el Sector." Agosto. Santa Cruz, Bolivia: CORDECRUZ.

Crist, Raymond E., and Charles M. Nissly
1973   *East from the Andes.* University of Florida Social Sciences Monograph no. 50. Gainesville. University Presses of Florida.

Cusack, Patricia L.
1967   "The Evolution of Colonization in Bolivia." Unpublished paper, University of Florida, Gainesville.

Doughty, Paul
1972   "What Makes a City in Peru? A Question of Public Policy and Public Service." Working paper, 22d Annual Latin American Conference, Center for Latin American Studies, University of Florida.

Duquid, Julian
1931   *Green Hell.* New York: The Century Company.

Fawcett, Percy H.
1924   *Exploration Fawcett.* London [?]: Hutchinson.

Federación de Campesinos
1975   Personal communication.

Ferragut, Castro
1961   "Principal Characteristics of the Agricultural Colonies of Bolivia and Suggestions for a Colonization Policy." La Paz: FAO.

Finot, Enrique
1939 *Historia de la Conquista del Oriente Boliviano*. Buenos Aires: Librería "Cervantes."
1954 *Nueva Historia de Bolivia*. La Paz: Papelería y Editorial Gisbert y Cía., S.A.
Foster, George, et al.
1961 "The Dyadic Contract: A Model for the Social Structure of a Mexican Peasant Village." *American Anthropologist* 63: 1173–92.
1979 *Long Term Field Research in Social Anthropology*. New York: Academic Press.
Galleguillos, Adolfo
1970 "Análisis y Resultados Obtenidos en la Promoción y Asentamiento de Colonos." La Paz: Instituto Nacional de Colonización.
Gennep, Arnold van
1961 *Rites of Passage*. Translated by Monika B. Vizedom and Gabrielle L. Caffee. Chicago: University of Chicago Press.
Ghersi Barrera, Humberto, and Henry F. Dobyns
1963 "Migración por Etapas: El Caso del Valle del Viru." In *Migración e Integración en el Perú*, edited by Henry F. Dobyns and Mario C. Vásquez, pp. 152–59. Lima: Editorial Estudios Andinos, Monografía Andina No. 2.
Harris, Marvin
1968 *The Rise of Anthropological Theory*. New York: Thomas Y. Crowell Company.
Heath, Dwight B.
1959 "Camba. A Study of Land and Society in Eastern Bolivia." Ph.D. dissertation, Yale University.
Henkel, Ray
1971 "The Chapare of Bolivia: A Study of Tropical Agriculture in Transition." Ph.D. dissertation. University of Wisconsin.
Hess, David
1980 "Pioneering in San Julián: A Study of Adaptive Strategy Formation by Migrant Farmers in Eastern Bolivia." Ph.D. dissertation, University of Pittsburgh.
Heyduk, Daniel
1971 "Huayarpampa: Bolivian Highland Peasants and the New Social Order." Ph.D. dissertation, Cornell University.
IDB (Interamerican Development Bank)
1970 "Tenth Annual Report. 1969." Washington: IDB.
1971 "Informe Final Del Préstamo." La Paz: IDB.
INC (Instituto Nacional de Colonización)
1970 "La Colonización en Bolivia." La Paz: Departamento de Promoción de Migraciones y Servicios Sociales.
1974 "Resúmen de Colonias y Familias Asentadas en Zonas de Colonización del País a Diciembre 1974." La Paz: Instituto Nacional de Colonización.
INE–DDE (Instituto Nacional de Estadística–Dirección Departamental de Estadística)

1981 "Análisis de la Encuesta Sobre Migración Interna en Cuatro Centros Poblados del Dpto. de Santa Cruz." INE–CORDECRUZ. Santa Cruz.

INE–NN.UU. (Instituto Nacional de Estadística–Naciones Unidas)
 1980 Bolivia: Migraciones Internas Recientes según el Censo Nacional de Población y Vivienda de 1976." La Paz: INE–NN.UU.

Jackson, J.A.
 1968 *Migration*. Sociological Studies no. 2. Cambridge: Cambridge University Press.

Jisunú
 1974 Vols. 1 and 2. Septiembre y Diciembre. Santa Cruz: Academia de las Culturas Nativas del Oriente Boliviano.

Jones, David E.
 1968 *Sanapia: Comanche Medicine Woman*. Case Studies in Cultural Anthropology, George Spindler and Louise Spindler, general editors. New York: Holt, Rinehart and Winston.

Lanning, James Walter
 1971 "The Old Colony Mennonites of Bolivia: A Case Study." Master's thesis, Texas A & M University.

Lee, Everett
 1968 "A Theory of Migration." In *Migration*, edited by J. A. Jackson, pp. 282–97. Sociological Studies no. 2. Cambridge: Cambridge University Press.

Lewis, Oscar
 1965 *La Vida. A Puerto Rican Family in the Culture of Poverty—San Juan and New York*. New York: Random House.

Linton, Ralph
 1965 "Nativistic Movements." In *Reader in Comparative Religion*, edited by William A. Lessa and Evon Z. Vogt, pp. 499–506. New York: Harper and Row.

Mangin, William
 1970 *Peasants in Cities*. Boston: Houghton Mifflin Co.
 1973 "Sociological, Cultural and Political Characteristics of Some Urban Migrants in Peru." In *Urban Anthropology*, edited by A. Southall, pp. 315–50. New York and London: Oxford University Press.

Margolis, Maxine
 1973 *The Moving Frontier*. University of Florida Latin American Monograph Series, no. 11. Gainesville: University Presses of Florida.

Maxwell, Simon
 1979 "Colonos Marginalzados al Norte de Santa Cruz. Avenidas de Escape de la Crisis del Barbecho." Santa Cruz: CIAT. Documento de Trabajo no. 4.

Mintz, Sidney, and Eric Wolf
 1967 "An Analysis of Ritual Co-parenthood (Compadrazgo)." In *Peasant Society*, edited by Jack M. Potter et al., pp. 174–99. Boston: Little, Brown and Company.

Le Monde (Paris)
 1981 "Bolivia: Una Dictadura Bajo la Influencia." March 25, p. 5. Quoted and translated in *Sinópsis Boliviana*, año 3, no. 3, March.

Municipalidad de Montero
1975 *Libro de la Renta de la Ciudad de Montero*. Montero.

Murra, John (editor)
1972 "El Control Vertical de un Máximo de Pisos Ecológicos en la Economía de las Sociedades Andinas." In *Visita de la Provincia de León de Huanaco*, tomo II. Huanaco: Universidad Nacional H. Valdizán.

Nelson, Michael
1973 *The Development of Tropical Lands: Policy Issues in Latin America*. Baltimore: The Johns Hopkins University Press.
1978 "Report of Regional Development Specialist. San Julián Project." La Paz: AID.

Newsweek
1981 "Bolivia Pays at All Costs." April 6, p. 25.

d' Orbigny, Alcide
1835–47 *Voyage dans l'Amérique Meridionale*. Strasbourg: Ve. Levrault.

Orellana S., Carlos L.
1973 "Mixtec Migrants in Mexico City: A Case Study of Urbanization." *Human Organization* 32 (Fall):273–82.

Parke, Robert
1928 "Human Migration and Marginal Man." *The American Journal of Sociology* 6 (May):881–93.

Pool, D. I.
1968 "The Number and Type of Conjugal Unions as Correlates of Level of Fertility and Attitudes to Family Limitations in Ghana." Paper presented to the annual meeting of the Population Association of America, Boston.

Ravenstein, E. G.
1885 "The Laws of Migration." *Journal of the Royal Statistical Society*, 48 (June):167–227.
1889 "The Laws of Migration." *Journal of the Royal Statistical Society* 52 (June):241–301.

Reye, Ulrich
1974 "Characterísticas y Problemas del Desarrollo Económico de Santa Cruz (Macrodiagnóstico Regional)." Planificación Regional Santa Cruz. Santa Cruz: Comité de Obras Públicas. Documento de Trabajo no. 32.

Richmond, Anthony
1968 "Migration in Industrial Societies." In *Migration*, edited by J. A. Jackson, pp. 238–81. Cambridge: Cambridge University Press.

Riester, Jurgen et al.
1979 *Me Vendí, Me Compraron. Análisis Socioeconómico en Base a Testimonios de la Zafra de Caña en Santa Cruz de la Sierra*. Santa Cruz: APCOB.

Roberts, Bryan R.
1973 *Organizing Strangers: Poor Families in Guatemala*. Austin and London: University of Texas Press.

Romero Loza, José
1974 *Bolivia: Nación en Desarrollo*. La Paz: Editorial Los Amigos del Libro.

Royden, Thomas, and E. Boyd Wennergren
1973 "The Impact of Access Roads on Spontaneous Colonization." USU Series 23/73. Logan: Utah State University.
Sanabria Fernández, Hernando
1973 *Breve Historia de Santa Cruz*. Colección Ayer y Hoy. La Paz: Librería- Editorial "Juventud."
Simmons, Alan, et al.
1977 *Social Change and Internal Migration: A Review of Research Findings from Africa, Asia and Latin America*. A Report of the Migration Review Task Force. Ottawa: International Development Research Centers.
Simmons, Ozzie G.
1955 "The Criollo Outlook in the Mestizo Culture of Coastal Peru." *American Anthropologist* 57:107–17.
Solari, Tito (Fr.)
1975 Census of the Yapacáni Colony. San Carlos.
1978 Census of the Parish of San Carlos. San Carlos.
Solíz, Edmundo Franco
1974 "Estudio de Pre-factibilidad Económica del Proyecto de Enlocetado de 100.000 metros cuadrados de calles en la Localidad de Montero. . . ." La Paz.
Stearman, Allyn M.
1973 "Colonization in Eastern Bolivia: Problems and Prospects." *Human Organization* 32 (Fall):285–93.
1976 "The Highland Migrant in Lowland Bolivia: Regional Migration and the Department of Santa Cruz." Ph.D. dissertation, University of Florida.
1978 "The Highland Migrant in Lowland Bolivia: Multiple Resource Migration and the Horizontal Archipelago." *Human Organization* 37 (Summer):180–85.
Stoltman, Joseph P., and John M. Ball
1971 "Migration and the Local Economic Factor in Rural Mexico." *Human Organization* 30 (Spring):47–56.
Thompson, Stephen
1968 "Religious Conversion and Religious Zeal in an Overseas Enclave: The Case of the Japanese in Bolivia." *Anthropological Quarterly* 41 (October):201–8.
Turner, John
1970 "Barriers and Channels for Housing Development in Modernizing Countries." In *Peasants in Cities*, edited by William Mangin, pp. 1–19. Boston: Houghton Mifflin Company.
United Nations. Economic Commission for Latin America (ECLA)
1958 "Análisis y Proyecciones del Desarrollo Económico IV. El Desarrollo Económico de Bolivia." Document E/CN/12/430 y Add 1/Rev. 1. Mexico.
Urquidi, José Macedonio
1944 *Compendio de la Historia de Bolivia*. Talleres Graficos EGLH.
Ward, Barbara
1960 "Cash or Credit Crops? An Examination of Some Implications of

Peasant Commercial Production with Special Reference to the Multiplicity of Traders and Middlemen." *Economic Development and Cultural Change* 8(January):148–63.

Whiteford, Scott
    1972 "Bolivian Migrant Labor in Argentina: A Second Cybernetics Case." Paper presented at the 71st annual meeting of the American Anthropological Association, Toronto.

Whiteford, Scott, and Richard N. Adams
    1973 "Migration, Ethnicity and Adaptation: Bolivian Migrant Workers in Northwest Argentina." Symposium on Migration and Ethnicity, International Congress of Anthropological and Ethnological Sciences, Chicago.

Wilkie, Richard W.
    1968 "On the Theory of Process in Human Geography: A Case Study of Migration in Rural Argentina." Ph.D. dissertation, University of Washington.

Winsberg, Morton D.
    1968 "Jewish Agricultural Colonization in Entre Rios, Argentina: I." *American Journal of Economics* 27 (July–October): 285–95; 423–38.
    1969 "Jewish Agricultural Colonization in Entre Rios, Argentina: II." *American Journal of Economics* 28 (April): 179–91.

Zondag, Cornelius
    1968 *La Economía Boliviana—1952–1965: La Revolución y sus Consequencias.* La Paz: Editorial Los Amigos del Libro.

Glossary

Albañil—a bricklayer, mason; more generally, anyone working in the building trades.

Alcaldía—office of the mayor.

Altiplano—the high plain; a large plateau located between two ranges of the Andes mountains in Peru and Bolivia.

Amplificador—an amplifier; also describes a sound system used to play music.

Anillo—literally, ring; the concentric streets that encircle the city of Santa Cruz.

Asentados—farm labor that is settled in the lowlands but seeks seasonal employment. See *flotantes*.

Barriada—an urban slum; the term applied to the large, primarily migrant settlements on the outskirts of Lima, Peru.

Barrio—neighborhood or residential area.

Baño seco—a dry bath; gourds are filled with boiling water and placed around a person to induce sweating.

Campesino—literally, a country person; peasant.

Casero—a "house sitter"; a person hired to care for the house or property of an absent owner.

Chapapa—a platform; term applied to a rough platform used for sleeping.

Chicha—corn beer; in the highlands an alcoholic drink, in the lowlands (except among some indigenous groups) a nonalcoholic beverage.

Chichera—woman who makes and/or serves chicha.

Chichería—drinking establishment where chicha is made and served.

Cholo—a rural highland Indian who has moved to an urban area and acquired urban ways.

Chonta—palm with an edible fruit and a hard, black wood used for construction and certain tools.

Circunvalación—now the second "ring" that encircles the city of Santa Cruz; for years it was the only paved street in the city.

Cogollo—the tender shoot which grows from the center of the palm. The cogollo of the motacú palm is used for weaving mats and baskets.

Colegio—secondary school.

Compadre—literally, a coparent; the person selected to be the godparent of one's child; also the term used by the godparent when addressing the child's parent.

Compadrazgo—the establishment of fictive kin relationships, frequently through the rite of baptism.

Contratado—one who is contracted; a farm laborer in the employ of a labor contractor.

Contratista—labor contractor; individual who hires and manages labor crews and receives payment for this service.

Criollo—native to the Americas; of European parentage but born in the New World.

Cupo—literally, space; in the sugarcane industry, having a particular weight allotment at a mill.

Curandera—female folk healer.

Empleada—a domestic servant; a female employee doing nonskilled work.

Encomienda—literally, something entrusted to another; in Bolivia, an item that another purchases for you and then delivers to you.

Enfermo de los pulmones—being sick in the lungs; lung disease.

Enganchado—literally, hooked; the term used by farm labor when they take advance payment for work on a field crew.

Esposo—husband.

Faja—a belt; the term applied to trails in an agricultural colony that branch off from the main road.

Fanega—in the past, a volume measure of rice; 12 *almudes* (34 pounds per almud) made a fanega (408 pounds). Now a fanega is 185.45 kilos.

Feria—literally, fair; large, open market held on a specific day.

Finca—an agricultural establishment; in the Bolivian lowlands, used synonymously with hacienda.

Finquero—the owner of a finca or agricultural establishment.

Flotantes—farm labor that is essentially migrant; no established lowland residence. See *asentados*.

Galpón—a shed used for storage; term applied to dormitory-style housing provided to cotton-harvesting crews.

Hacienda—a large landholding typically worked by people in debt peonage. See *finca*.

Horma—a bell-shaped urn used in the past to store sugar.

Huasca—a braided leather whip.

Junta revolucionaria—the revolutionary junta or group that directed the 1952 social revolution.

Kollasuyo—the sector of the Inca Empire now pertaining to Bolivia; the term from which Kolla is derived.

Lamina—sheet of wood veneer.

Loceta—the hexagonal-shaped concrete tablet used to pave streets in the lowlands.

Loteador—individual involved in the claiming and subdividing of urban parcels for resale as building lots.

Mandada—"bossed around."

Monte—the high forest in the lowland tropics.

Marido—husband

Medio camino—halfway; a term applied to people and towns located between the highlands and lowlands; pertaining to both Camba and Kolla culture.

Minka (sometimes spelled *minga*)—a short-term, cooperative labor group.

Motacú—a large palm with heavy fronds used for roofing.

Nucleo—term applied to the settlement pattern in an agricultural colony where landholdings are clustered around a central residence area.

Orgullo personal—a sense of personal pride; "face."

Orientador—the person charged with helping highland colonists adjust to life in the San Julián agricultural colony.

Oriente—the east; in Bolivia, the lowland regions east of the Andes Mountains.

Paila—the large clay cauldron used in the production of sugar.

Paisano—a "countryman"; in Bolivia a term used to designate a highlander.

Patrón—the owner of the hacienda or finca; an individual who stands in a patron relationship to his client.

Pauhuichi—the palm-thatched, wattle-and-daub house used by the lowland Bolivian peasantry.

Peladora—rice-hulling machine.

Peón—an agricultural laborer; frequently tied to a particular land-holding through debt.

Personalismo—the desire to deal only with known people rather than with institutions and their representatives.

Pichicatero—person involved in the production of and sale of cocaine.

Pisar coca—to step on coca leaves; the leaves are crushed by foot in kerosene in the process of cocaine extraction.

Pitillo—cigarettes laced with cocaine paste.

Pollera—the wide, gathered skirt worn by highland women.

Puesto—a stall at a market.

Pulpería—small store, usually located on one room of a private home. See *venta*.

Quintal—100 pounds.

Reducción—a Catholic mission set up during the sixteenth and seventeenth centuries to settle and proselytize primarily nomadic Indians.

Safra—the three-month period when sugarcane is cut and processed.

Serrano—a person from the mountains, usually a peasant.

Shogma—an animal used to divine illness; the sick person in some manner "passes" the illness into the animal, which is then killed and examined.

Sindicato—a labor union

Siringuero—a rubber tapper.

Surazo—a "souther"; the cold wind that blows from the Antarctic during June, July, and August.

Totaí—a spiny palm known for its spherical fruit.

Trapiche—the wooden-geared press used to extract juice from sugarcane.

Unidades Domésticas—domestic units; term used to describe Andean rural settlement patterns.

Venta—a small store; synonymous with pulpería.

Voluntario—an agricultural worker who does not make use of a labor contractor to find work; a volunteer.

Yungas—the eastern slopes of the Andes, which lie in a warmer more humid region.

Zafrero—man who cuts sugarcane.

Index